"Pilate's piercing question to Jes
even more today than the day he a..
Dr. Jeff Myers answers that question. What's more, he tells us why
what we believe about truth matters so very much. Readers will be challenged, encouraged, and strengthened by his life-changing message."

Steve Green, president of Hobby Lobby

"Dr. Jeff Myers has a unique gift for communicating the universal,
unchanging Truth of the gospel. This insightful book shows the importance of biblical Truth, traces many under-appreciated ways in
which Christians throughout history have impacted the world by
living out that Truth, and gives practical advice for influencing our
neighbors with the Truth that sets us free."

Jim Daly, president of Focus on the Family

"This book is perfectly titled because *truth does change everything*. It
changes whether we live in hope, love, and faith or fear and despair.
Dr. Myers lays out what is at stake in the battle for Truth and offers
a road map for how Truth can be known and experienced. This is a
timely, insightful, and story-filled book."

Sean McDowell, PhD, author of *Chasing Love*
and *A Rebel's Manifesto*

"Dr. Jeff Myers skillfully demonstrates how Christians' manifestation of God's surpassing goodness in all facets of life and civilization
provides powerful evidence for the Truth of Christianity and the Bible,
on which our faith is based. This Truth, indeed, changes everything,
and in the best way imaginable."

Hugh Ross, astrophysicist; founder
and president of Reasons to Believe

"As an actor and filmmaker, I love good stories. And my friend Dr.
Jeff Myers's book *Truth Changes Everything* is bursting with fascinating true stories of people who loved Jesus so much they could
not help but change the world in everything from science to the arts.
No matter how tough times are, we can do the same. If your faith
and sense of purpose need a boost, I encourage you to pick up this
book right away."

Kirk Cameron, actor and filmmaker

"In this informative and simple-to-read book, Dr. Myers explains the difference between Truth and the relativistic view of 'truths.' In my view, this is at the core of our culture's current chaos. Next, he expertly shows how the Truth of Christ has benefited society in every area of life. It is a much-needed retort to the popular fallacy that the world would have less suffering and oppression without Christianity. Nothing could be further from the truth."

John L. Cooper, lead singer of Skillet, author of
Awake & Alive to Truth, host of the *Cooper Stuff* podcast

"Many people today believe that truth cannot be known and that everyone is entitled to their own 'truths.' In *Truth Changes Everything*, Jeff Myers shows how a commitment to Jesus Christ, who is the Incarnate Truth, has shaped the world in undeniable ways. Many of the advances in science, art, government, medicine, and education have roots not in secularism or humanism but in Christianity. Myers's conclusion is spot-on: Truth is a person, Truth is life, and Truth is eternal!"

Dr. Christopher Yuan, author and speaker

"Jeff Myers explains biblical objectivity in a way teens can understand. Our children swim in a sea of nihilism and risk drowning, but *Truth Changes Everything* can help hold them up until God's waves bring them to shore."

Dr. Marvin Olasky, senior fellow, Discovery Institute

"Christianity, C. S. Lewis said, could be 'of no importance' or 'of infinite importance,' but 'the one thing it cannot be is moderately important.' In a world that denies Truth exists and can be known, Jeff Myers takes us on a journey that spans hundreds of years to investigate the impact Christianity has had on the world. And the reason is clear: Christianity is true."

John Stonestreet, president of the Colson Center

"In *Truth Changes Everything*, Dr. Jeff brings a timely and deeply appreciated gift for every generation. It's much needed now in this decade."

Dr. Alveda C. King, founder of Speak for Life

"What I love about this book is that Dr. Jeff Myers doesn't just tell you that truth changes everything, he shows you through powerful stories the impact Jesus followers have made throughout history. Yes, today's culture is difficult, but when we look back to these accounts of Christians transforming the world, we see that truth doesn't need an accommodating culture to flourish. Myers does an outstanding job of calling discouraged believers to action as truth-tellers and doers. Well-researched, inspiring, and highly practical, *Truth Changes Everything* has a crucial message every Christian needs to hear."

Natasha Crain, speaker, podcaster, and author
of four books, including *Faithfully Different*

"In a world that claims it's true that there is no truth (yeah, I know, that's self-defeating), Jeff Myers shows that the way to eternal victory is to go straight through truth, and Jesus is the Truth. You'll have plenty of aha moments reading *Truth Changes Everything*. You'll also be amazed by Christianity's dramatic impact on civilization and comforted by the fact that, no matter how bad things get, Jesus is the Truth and his kingdom will triumph in the end."

Frank Turek, president of CrossExamined.org
and coauthor of *Hollywood Heroes*

"When people believe God created them to impact others and leave the world a better place, they'll be motivated, optimistic, and determined. They will be less overwhelmed even when they realize how chaotic the culture is. This can be you if you read this book! You'll want to be part of the solution to the world's brokenness, and you'll know how. Use Truth and not truths! The history of the issues and the stories of how Jesus's followers successfully made a positive difference will encourage you. You'll see yourself being part of the solution too. Get ready!"

Kathy Koch, PhD, founder of Celebrate Kids Inc.
and author of *Five to Thrive*

"In a culture that seems allergic to absolute truth, Dr. Myers cuts through the confusion with writing that is warm, winsome, and crystal clear. *Truth Changes Everything* will take you on a journey through history and demonstrate how truth doesn't just have the potential to bring change—it quite literally did change everything. While setting right some false narratives about Christianity, this book is a crushing blow to relativism."

Alisa Childers, author of *Another Gospel*
and *Live Your Truth and Other Lies*

"In a time when universal truth claims are more disputed than ever, *Truth Changes Everything* offers a compelling guide for how Christians can represent and defend their faith in a post-Christian culture. I am happy to recommend it."

Thomas S. Kidd, research professor of church history,
Midwestern Baptist Theological Seminary

"We are in a time of crisis, if not seemingly a point of no return. Times like this are meant for people of faith, for seekers of the Truth. These times try people's souls, and they are also when saints are made. People of faith changed the world in the past, and they can again. They're called to confront the spirit of the age. Jesus wants them to. In this inspiring book, Jeff Myers likewise calls them, invoking brilliant examples from the likes of Thomas Aquinas and Catherine of Siena to Abraham Kuyper and Francis Schaeffer and so many more. Myers has been equipping young people for decades with his life-changing Summit Ministries. Here, he is equipping a wider world. Myers offers not just inspiration and courage but tips and practical advice. Read this book. You and your children will benefit from it."

Paul Kengor, PhD, professor of political science,
Grove City College

"The more I speak about Jesus around the country, the more I recognize the relationship between truth and impact. Jesus and his followers changed the world because Christianity is true. *Truth Changes Everything* is a robust exploration of the nature of Truth and the impact of Jesus on nearly every aspect of human culture. It's more than simply a description of Christianity's historical impact, it's an inspiring and encouraging template for those of us who still hope to change the world as followers of Christ. If you're ready to grow in your Christian confidence so you can live boldly as a change agent, this book is for you."

J. Warner Wallace, *Dateline*-featured cold-case detective,
senior fellow at the Colson Center for Christian Worldview,
and author of *Person of Interest*

"C. S. Lewis writes, 'A man does not call a line crooked unless he has some idea of a straight line.' Our world has lost the vision of what a straight line even looks like. That's why Jeff Myers's new book, *Truth Changes Everything*, is so important. Myers reveals how high the stakes are in our struggle for truth and demonstrates through captivating stories of truth seekers throughout history how Truth with a capital T leads to flourishing, even in tumultuous times like our own."

Max McLean, founder and artistic director,
Fellowship for Performing Arts

TRUTH

CHANGES EVERYTHING

How People of Faith Can
Transform the World in Times of Crisis

DR. JEFF MYERS

BakerBooks

a division of Baker Publishing Group
Grand Rapids, Michigan

© 2022 by Summit Ministries, Inc.

Published by Baker Books
a division of Baker Publishing Group
PO Box 6287, Grand Rapids, MI 49516-6287
www.bakerbooks.com

Printed in the United States of America

Library of Congress Cataloging-in-Publication Data
Names: Myers, Jeff (Writer on leadership development), author.
Title: Truth changes everything : how people of faith can transform the world in times of crisis / Dr. Jeff Myers.
Description: Grand Rapids, MI : Baker Books, a division of Baker Publishing Group, [2022] | Series: Perspectives : a summit ministries series
Identifiers: LCCN 2022007701 | ISBN 9781540900371 (paperback) | ISBN 9781540902603 (casebound) | ISBN 9781493437719 (ebook)
Subjects: LCSH: Church and the world. | Christianity—Influence. | Change—Religious aspects—Christianity. | Truth—Religious aspects—Christianity.
Classification: LCC BR115.W6 M935 2022 | DDC 261—dc23/eng/20220224
LC record available at https://lccn.loc.gov/2022007701

Published in association with The Bindery Agency, www.TheBinderyAgency.com.

Baker Publishing Group publications use paper produced from sustainable forestry practices and post-consumer waste whenever possible.

22 23 24 25 26 27 28   7 6 5 4 3 2 1

Contents

Contents

The Point of No Return

Every moment of every day we live in a world-defining conflict. Contrary to what many think, this is not a battle between the religious and the nonreligious, Democrats and Republicans, progressives and conservatives, or blue states and red states. Rather, it is a struggle between two competing views of truth. One says that Truth (capital T) can be known objectively through reason and revelation. It is "total truth" (Nancy Pearcey), "true truth" (Francis Schaeffer), or "real truth" (Dallas Willard).[1] Truth exists always, everywhere, even when we aren't paying attention or are deceiving ourselves.[2] The other says that Truth *cannot* be so known; all we have are "truths" (lower case) that are stories we tell ourselves to make sense of our experiences. The first view says that Truth exists independently of our ability to perceive it. The second view says that truths are socially constructed. These two viewpoints, Truth versus truths, vie for first place in forming our answer to the question, "How do we find meaning in a fleeting life?"

From at least the time of the ancient Hebrews, people have believed that Truth exists and can be discovered. Now the balance has tipped in the other direction, with more than half of

Americans of all ages claiming that truths are up to an individual. This belief holds across all identifiable social and political groups. Even among churchgoing, self-identified Christians, the percentage who believe that Truth can be known has shrunk to around 50 percent.[3]

You and I live in a world where we cannot go a single day without hearing that truths are based on how we see things rather than on what exists to be seen. Truth is not "out there" to be found; it is "in here" to be narrated.

A biblical worldview, one based on the Bible and the writings of Christian thinkers throughout history, has rested firmly on the idea that Truth can be known. It says that Truth isn't constructed by our experiences and feelings, even though our deepest encounters with reality may indeed fill our senses and change our hearts. Rather, a biblical worldview says that Truth exists and that it is not merely a set of logical propositions or mathematical formulas. It is a person. It is Jesus.

Truth Changes Everything revolves around two goals. The first is to explore the difference between the Truth viewpoint and the truths viewpoint. The second is to answer the "So what?" question. Why does Truth matter? This book will take a unique approach. Some defend Truth by presenting logical arguments. Others bemoan our current age and pine for a return to a time when Truth was given more respect. Yet others poke fun at the flaws in the truths viewpoint. Instead, *Truth Changes Everything* asks the question, "What kind of world would unfold if smart, determined people lived as if Jesus really was the Truth?"

Truth Changes Everything shares the stories and breakthroughs of thinkers and doers who committed their lives to Truth as found in Jesus. It demonstrates how their faith formed a personal moral code but also a transformational worldview that changed the course of history. These world-changers simply loved Jesus and emerged as history's best philosophers, scientists, artists, and educators. This was especially so in times of great crisis when history seemed at its end.

Some of the Jesus followers you'll meet in *Truth Changes Everything* were brilliant, whimsical, and creative. Others were everyday folks who simply displayed extreme levels of resilience. More than a few were flighty, prickly, and inconsistent. These earnest yet flawed people shaped our understanding of what it means to be human, how to care for one another, how to learn and grow, how to harness science to make life better, how to form political structures that secure rights and create stable societies, how to pursue justice, and how to live meaningful lives.

If we can understand how Truth really did change everything in the past, then we can more clearly see what we lose in abandoning it and what we could gain by reclaiming it.

It is time to tell the Truth. The Bible admonishes the faithful to "tell to the coming generation the glorious deeds of the LORD . . . so that they should set their hope in God" (Ps. 78:4, 7, emphasis added). Sharing the hope that comes from Truth is my life's passion. At Summit Ministries, my team and I equip and support tens of thousands of young adults every year to embrace Truth and champion a biblical worldview. We do this through events and courses that are rich with teaching, dialogue, mentoring, and, yes, *reading*. We envision a rising generation filled with the kind of purpose that comes from basing every aspect of life on Truth.

It is a special privilege to lead Summit Ministries given its influence on my own spiritual and intellectual growth. As a young skeptic, I spent two weeks at a Summit Ministries event held at the antique Grandview Hotel, nestled in a little hippie town at the foot of Pikes Peak. There, I met Summit's first president, David Noebel, an erudite philosopher and captivating teacher.

"I hope you have a lot of answers because I have a lot of questions," I bluntly announced in our first meeting.

Noebel didn't flinch. "At Summit, we aren't afraid of questions," he replied.

Instantly, I felt at home. Life is complicated. I knew that. Satisfying answers are hard to come by. I knew that too. But finding a community filled with smart Christians willing to ponder Truth and apply it to their lives? For me, that was a game changer.

My passion for preparing young leaders with a biblical worldview took on great urgency during a recent battle with cancer. My diagnosis came as a complete shock. I'm a healthy, active person who maintains a pretty good diet and exercises regularly.

My medical team and I have acted aggressively to beat what was once a death sentence. As of this writing, we are moving in a very positive direction. I am in remission. But cancer is hard. The treatment is even harder. Pain, nausea, and fatigue make it feel like a twenty-four-hour flu for months on end. Many of my fellow patients had it worse. Some were on "salvage" chemo, fighting for a few more days of life, not for a cure. It was a horrible thing to watch.

Don't get me wrong. I feel blessed to live in an age of advanced medical technology. I'm grateful for a good insurance plan, skilled doctors, and medicine that treated my cancer and ameliorated the treatment's side effects. I cherish my loving spouse, who filled our home with hope. It meant the world to me to receive thoughts, prayers, and expressions of care from people all over the world.

But cancer was only one of the battles I fought. The other was hopelessness. Despair was a constant companion, tempting me to give up. God had given me such a rich, full life. Was it about to end?

During treatment, I could do little except read and write. The book you hold in your hands emerged out of that time of trial. What might a person write if they knew it might be the last thing they could say this side of eternity? *Truth Changes Everything* is my answer to that question.

Truth means more to me than ever before. I enter this season of life determined to fight for it. During my cancer journey, I studied the stories of many courageous heroes. Caleb from the Old Testament book of Numbers remains my favorite.

Caleb was forty years old when Moses tasked him, along with Joshua and ten other men, to spy on the land of God's promise. Numbers 13 lists all their names, but we remember only Caleb and Joshua. The ten forgotten spies surrendered to the enemy of despair without even drawing their swords.

These ten fearful spies announced that the Anakim, the people of the land, were giants living in fortified cities. This was a fact. Yet it shouldn't have mattered: God had promised that the children of Israel would inhabit the land. Even though the spies had seen God's miraculous acts many times, fear overruled their faith. God's chosen people consequently traipsed around the desert for another forty years.

Fast-forward. After forty years of wandering and five years of settling in the promised land, Caleb appeared before Joshua and said, "I am this day eighty-five years old. I am still as strong today as I was in the day that Moses sent me; my strength now is as my strength was then" (Josh. 14:10–11).

Pause for a moment before I share the rest of the story. How many octogenarians can honestly make the claim that Caleb made? How many people of *any* age maintain readiness for the battles they face?

What Caleb said next is even more astounding: "So now give me this hill country of which the LORD spoke on that day, for you heard on that day how the Anakim were there, with great fortified cities. It may be that the LORD will be with me, and I shall drive them out just as the LORD said" (Josh. 14:12).

"Give me the land where the giants still are," Caleb said, in essence. At age eighty-five. Every day for forty-five years Caleb honed his skills, telling himself, "God promised that the giants would fall, and fall they will. Even if I'm an old man when it happens."

Caleb never lost sight of God's promise. He stood in the land of giants.

The loss of Truth is a giant-sized problem in our day. Its real-life consequences are severe. Seventy-five percent of young adults say that they are unsure of their purpose in life. Nearly half are counted as having one or more types of mental illness (such as anxiety and depression). Fully half of young adults say that there is "no absolute value associated with human life."[4]

We are tempted to say, "Truth has been lost. History is at an end." Yet the testimony of Jesus followers who changed the world is one of hope. We *can* understand the times and know what course we ought to take (1 Chron. 12:32). Faith can triumph over fear.

In the past, Truth changed everything. It can do the same for us amid the unique challenges of our current age. We, too, can find Truth and share it without fear, whether around the water cooler, at the Thanksgiving table, in the laboratory, or in the halls of power.

Now is the time to take an unflinching look at what Truth is and why it is under attack. Now is the time to sit at the feet of Jesus followers who, in times of great crisis, stood for Truth. Now is the time of choosing for our own age. If ever we needed Truth, it is now.

The End of Time; the Dawn of Hope

Christmas Day 1668. The knock on the door was completely unexpected. Father Verbiest, an astronomer, missionary, and priest in the Society of Jesus, whose members are known as Jesuits, noticed the worried glances of his fellow missionaries. Exiled priests in China were never safe.

Hesitantly, Verbiest opened the door. Standing before him were four somber-looking court officials, called Mandarins. "We bear a decree from the emperor," one announced, extending a rolled parchment.

Verbiest was dumbfounded. The previous emperor, Shunzhi, had been an enthusiastic supporter of the Jesuits' work to spread the gospel while teaching astronomy. Shunzhi had called their leader "grandfather," had permitted him to build a church in Beijing, and had even occasionally attended services himself.[1]

But then, tragically, Shunzhi died of smallpox. His son, Kangxi, ascended the throne. Because Kangxi was just a boy of seven, four regents governed in his stead. These regents resented Verbiest and the other Jesuit astronomers. Who were these Westerners, trying to destroy their traditions and convert everyone to their religion? And using their "science" to sneak in their evil ways!

It all started with a dispute over a calendar. At the time, calendar-keeping was an intricate and reverent art. Tracking the movements of celestial bodies helped predict the seasons, which determined when to plant and harvest. The calendar specified what days were lucky for getting married, traveling, and designing buildings. It even dictated what to eat, and when. No one did anything without consulting the calendar.

Emperor Shunzhi had been persuaded that the missionary calendar, developed under the sponsorship of Pope Gregory XIII (1502–85), was superior to that produced by Chinese astronomers. The regents supervising the new young emperor had their doubts. How could a Christian calendar be better than the one developed over thousands of years using traditional practices?

But the regents were hiding something. The calendar they produced for the boy-emperor Kangxi was full of errors. These errors were uncovered, sparking a crisis that could have threatened the young emperor's reign. An inaccurate calendar was both a social disaster and a political nightmare. If events did not transpire as predicted, it would be a sign that the Tao, the harmony between the opposing forces of chaos and order, was disturbed. People would suspect that the emperor might be failing to maintain peace between the heavens and the earth. They would question his leadership.

Providing the emperor with an incorrect calendar was tantamount to treason. The unthinkable had now happened. Kangxi had trusted his advisors, and they had betrayed him.

Decades before, the Jesuit priest Matteo Ricci (1552–1610) had brought the Gregorian calendar with him to China as a youthful missionary, eager to share the good news of Jesus Christ. He learned Chinese so he could witness to the gospel and start a church. He also brought the latest scientific instruments and translated Euclid's *Elements of Geometry* into Chinese.

Ricci's successor, Johann Adam Schall von Bell (1591–1666), expanded Ricci's influence. So admired was he for the accuracy of his observations that the emperor appointed him to direct the Imperial Bureau of Astronomy.

But when Shunzhi unexpectedly died, the Chinese astronomer Yang Guangxian saw his opportunity to destroy the Jesuit intruders, with their ridiculous instruments and infernal Rudolphine Tablets catalog of planetary observations.

Yang published violent attacks against Christianity. He arranged to put the Jesuit astronomers on trial and have them sentenced to be cut into pieces while still alive. Before the sentence could be carried out, though, an earthquake destroyed the part of the prison where the execution was to take place. Then an extraordinary meteor was seen in the sky. And on top of that, a fire destroyed the part of the imperial palace where the sentence had been pronounced.

The superstitious regents saw these disasters as an ominous sign. They released the missionaries from prison, remanded their sentences, and decided to hide them away in exile.[2] Father Schall von Bell died en route, leaving Father Ferdinand Verbiest (1623–88) in charge. There was nothing for Verbiest to do but wait and pray for an opportunity to reach out to the young emperor.

Then came Christmas Day 1668.

"Prepare to hear the emperor's edict," commanded the senior Mandarin.

Trembling, Verbiest and his fellow priests fell to their knees. Would this be the death sentence they had dreaded for so many years?

They listened first with trepidation, then with surprise as one of the Mandarins read the emperor's command. "Father Verbiest is to inspect the 1670 calendar for errors."

Verbiest received the document and examined it carefully, boldly pointing out its mistakes.

As the Mandarins turned to leave, Verbiest received a surprising command: "You are to appear before the emperor tomorrow."

This was welcome news, of a sort. Verbiest was an accomplished astronomer, but would his expertise convince the young emperor, now fourteen, to disregard the suspicious advisors who wanted him dead?

Entering the Forbidden City, Verbiest and his colleagues were startled to find Yang Guangxian standing beside the young emperor, a smug expression on his face. Bending low toward the boy, Yang hissed:

> Your Majesty cannot use these men . . . they will try to take your empire, making many churches with the silver and blood of the poor, which are strongholds against Your Majesty; and if I had not revealed them, their perverse plans would have the effect they intended. Their law is diabolical, and as such, it professes only rebellion, as [would be expected of] those who worship a man who was crucified for rebellion on a cross (in saying which he extended his arms) and died in torment in punishment of his sin.[3]

Silence fell over the hall for several minutes. Then the young emperor spoke to Yang without bothering to turn in his direction:

> I have just asked you about mathematics, and you answer that the men from Europe are rebels. How could it be that twenty-five men who are scattered throughout China should take such a great empire? I ordered you to seek out for me men of understanding learned in mathematics for my service, given that you neither understand nor can offer anything in that regard. And you knew that Ferdinand Verbiest, a man of

such parts and learning, was in this court, and not only did you not bring him forward, but you concealed him. From this it is evident and clearly visible, that you are a bad, vile, and lowly man.[4]

Instantly disgraced, Yang saw his power unravel before his eyes.

Attempting to save face for all involved, Verbiest proposed a test. He and Yang would each complete three tests, measuring the length of a shadow cast by a sundial, the position of the sun and planets on a certain date, and the exact time of a lunar eclipse.

The emperor applauded, his courtiers following suit. "Will this satisfy you?" he asked Yang Guangxian.

"Yes, of course, Your Majesty," Yang nervously replied as the dread seriousness of his predicament fell on him.

It was an astronomy throwdown.

With the emperor looking on, Verbiest completed the tests with precision. Yang finally admitted that he had no ability to make such calculations. As a result, Yang was dismissed from office and sentenced to exile. He did not survive the trip.

Verbiest, in turn, became a trusted advisor of the young emperor Kangxi, teaching him geometry, philosophy, and music. In 1673, Kangxi appointed Verbiest to the highest level of Mandarin, a position of extraordinary influence no other European would ever attain.[5] Verbiest went on to publish twenty books in Chinese on astronomy, telescopes, and calculations of eclipses.

Kangxi reigned for sixty-one years, the longest of any Chinese emperor. Out of friendliness toward the Jesuit astronomers, he issued an Edict of Toleration, legalizing Christian missions and the practice of Christianity. This edict held sway for several decades.

Reflecting on the events of Christmas 1668, Verbiest noted in his book *Astronomia Europaea*:

> Christian Religion in China is justly represented as a most august queen who appears publicly with her arm leaning on Astronomy . . . because she was first introduced in China through Astronomy, because she was left untouched thanks to Astronomy and because after having been banished several times, she was each time called back and successfully restored to her former dignity by Astronomy.[6]

Just as Daniel had survived the lions' den and Esther had averted the genocide of the Babylonian Jews, the Jesuits had used astronomy to open the door to the gospel in a land where few had ever heard the name of Jesus.

But there is something odd about this account. What does astronomy have to do with the gospel? Aren't faith and science at war with each other, and isn't faith losing? Indeed, is not all modern knowledge improved by ridding it of the superstitious belief that Truth can be known?

As a university student, I was taught that the world was stuck in the Dark Ages until the Enlightenment, when reason replaced revelation and smart people quit believing in a personal God. The rejection of God, I was told, paved the way to a new era in science, technology, the modern managed economy, and personal—especially sexual—freedom.

This "just so" story is false. In *Truth Changes Everything*, you'll meet theologians, educators, scientists, architects, political theorists, and artists whose full embrace of Truth as revealed in Jesus set the world on a self-correcting course of flourishing.

The burning question throughout *Truth Changes Everything* is this: What difference did it make in history that smart, determined people lived as if Jesus really was the Truth? And a follow-up question: What difference would this make in our own times of crisis?

To begin answering these questions, let's look at the story of how we came to understand Truth in the first place.

Back in Time: A World of Promise

Where does the story of Truth begin?

In *Truth Changes Everything*, our narrative opens at one of history's pivotal moments, about 1,350 years after the birth of Jesus, in what is called the Late Middle Ages. It was a time of choosing unlike anything we have faced in our own day, and it happened against the backdrop of a plague that gruesomely annihilated a third to half of Europe's population.

Why begin with a plague? Partly because in our day we recognize the economic and social consequences of rapidly spreading disease. But mostly because times of suffering lay bare our true convictions. What we believe in the pain is what we really believe. This is true for civilizations as well as for individuals. Paradoxically, we often value Truth most dearly when it is slipping from our grasp. Entire historical epochs have been birthed—and buried—in such times.

The fourteenth century's pulsing energy—with its booming economy, technological innovation, and thriving trade in widely shared opinions (then in books)—might seem strangely familiar to residents of the twenty-first century. The Late Middle Ages were bright with promise. But then the Black Death changed everything. Civilization stood on the brink. Was a comeback even possible?

In the twenty-first century, we once again stand on the brink. Can Truth make a comeback? Having faced a global pandemic that killed millions and brought the world's economic system to its knees, most people today sense that our best days are behind us. Financial insecurity is skyrocketing. Crime plagues our cities. People all over the world believe that their children's lives will be worse than their own. Trust in government is near an all-time low.[7] The social fabric is tattered; we wonder if its broken threads might ever be woven back together.

Worse, disease and social breakdown may be only the tip of the iceberg. Totalitarian systems rise at a frightful pace, sponsored by aggressive nation-states armed with state-of-the-art technology. Experts call this the "world in chains" scenario. Toby Ord of Oxford University says that while our risk of extinction from natural events is less than one in two thousand, the probability of being destroyed by human-made disasters is one in six.[8] A 2017 report by experts who study threats to human existence says that "a long future under a particularly brutal global totalitarian state could arguably be worse than complete extinction."[9]

Without Truth, how will we face such challenges? If Truth does not exist, then neither does rationality. Without Truth, we have no basis for saying that human life is inherently valuable. Without Truth, what is to stop megalomaniacs from constructing their own "truths" that justify corrupt courses of action?

Without a historical perspective, our current challenges seem overwhelming. That's why we need to travel back in time to a historical pivot point in the battle over Truth. There, perhaps we will learn how the revival of belief in Truth breathed new life at the world's end, and how it could do so once again.

The End of Time

No one knows who threw the first punch, or why, but the ensuing brawl set in motion a chain of events that gripped the entire planet in terror and death.

22

The year was 1346, and the world was made new by international commerce. Trading posts such as those of the Republic of Genoa, just above Italy's boot-shaped profile, sparkled like diamonds across the Mediterranean Sea, and across the Black Sea beyond.

One of those outposts, now lost to history, was the village of Tana, nestled against the Sea of Azar in the southwest-most part of Russia. In Tana, trade goods such as cinnamon, black pepper, and furs arrived from the Asian continent. They were then loaded on ships that sailed across the Black Sea, into the Mediterranean, and from there to the rest of the world.

Into this rising hope a seemingly inconsequential fight broke out in Tana between Italian merchants and Muslim traders. The Italians gave their opponents a thrashing. A Muslim trader was killed.

Under ordinary circumstances, local officials might have held a trial to sort out the facts and punish the guilty. But the circumstances were far from ordinary. Camped outside Tana with his army was the Mongol king Jani Beg, "Khan of the Golden Horde." The khan took personal offense at the death of the Muslim trader and vowed vengeance. Sensing their fate, the Italian merchants fled, urging their ships southwest across the Sea of Azar to the fortified Genoese outpost of Caffa. Jani Beg tramped after them overland and set siege to Caffa. He would have blood.

For a year, Jani Beg vainly attempted to dislodge the Italians from their fortress. Then something unexpected and horrifying happened. Jani Beg's troops began to complain of painful swelling in their armpits, necks, and groins. The swelling quickly gave way to violent fever and bleeding. Within hours, their extremities turned black. Death was sudden and excruciating.

Surrounded by a withering army, his military campaign in tatters, Jani Beg did the unthinkable. He loaded his trebuchets

23

with the bodies of the dead and launched them into the city. The plague spread through Caffa in a matter of days. What Jani Beg could not accomplish in a year of military siege he accomplished in one day of biological warfare. The impregnable fortress of Caffa was destroyed from within.

But not everyone died. Surviving sailors fled to their ships and raced toward their home ports, hoping to leave the nightmare behind. Instead, they brought it with them. The Caffa ships docked in Constantinople, Genoa, Sicily, and even Marseilles, France. When dock workers boarded the ships, they found most of the sailors dead and the rest barely alive. In sheer terror, they burned the vessels, but it was too late. In each of those cities, a third to a half of the population died from what we now know as bubonic plague. The Black Death.

Imagine one out of every two people you know suffering the most excruciating death imaginable. Parents and grandparents and aunts and uncles and children and friends, gone forever. Where do you turn? What could possibly be true now that every hope has turned to blackness?

This is where our story begins.

The Dawning of Hope

The fourteenth-century plague that drove humanity to near extinction ought to have been the end of the world. No one would have blamed the survivors if they had turned out the lights and wrapped themselves in a cocoon of darkness to sleep away the pain.

But that is not what happened.

Instead, a mysterious change took place that ignited a renaissance of art, science, and commerce that shapes our modern world to this very day. This metamorphosis did not come about in the way we might expect. Civilization was not rescued by some new natural resource or a mighty warrior-king. Instead, the plague's survivors rediscovered an ancient biblical Truth that has lifted more people out of poverty, rescued more people from slavery, relieved the physical suffering of more people, led to greater scientific discoveries, and enlightened more souls than anything that had happened in the world from the beginning of human history to our present time.

The Truth reclaimed by artists and architects and merchants and philosophers and inventers was not new. It had been sparked a thousand years before in the dry timber of a tiny, querulous Roman outpost called Judea. Its message was simple:

The Truth can be known.
The Truth is not a series of logical postulates or a mathematical formula; it is a living, breathing person.
The Truth is Jesus.

For all of time, people had glimpsed reality as through a keyhole. Philosophers tried to widen that keyhole through endless speculation. Priests tried to widen it with bloody sacrifices. Peasants tried to widen it by faithfully reciting myths and genealogies.

Jesus came along and simply pushed the door open.
Jesus is the Truth.

At the moment when they might have turned away from God, the people of the Late Middle Ages turned toward him. They might have sensed that God was far away. Instead, they came to believe that he was right there, suffering with them. They believed in God even when their experiences told them that all hope had been lost.

The cultural significance of the belief that Jesus is the Truth is immense. Looking back at just the Late Middle Ages, we see its centrality in art, in church architecture, in the writings of sages, and in how people educated their children and built their businesses.

Jesus is the Truth.

For twenty centuries, people have fiercely debated this proposition. Some embrace it, while others deny it. A few insist that such a person as Jesus never lived.

Yet the core belief held by people of the Late Middle Ages, further nurtured a century later by the Reformation, changed how people learned and grew, valued human life, cared for one another, cultivated artistic imagination, advanced scientifically, moved toward a just society, and unleashed freedom and prosperity.

Truth changed everything. Not Truth as an abstract theory debated by scholastics but Truth as animated in the lives of smart, quirky, unstoppable Jesus followers who changed the world. In *Truth Changes Everything*, you'll read many of their stories.

In England . . . you'll meet a trust fund baby tempted to squander his life who instead sought to know Christ intimately and, in the process, discovered principles that launched a whole new branch of scientific inquiry.

In Italy . . . you'll meet a wholehearted but distracted priest who combined his passions for saving orphans and writing music into an artistic movement so enchanting that his works are still bestsellers after three hundred years.

In Spain . . . you'll meet an eccentric architect whose devotion to Christ reimagined the art of design and whose iconic work has collected one hundred thousand Trip Advisor reviews a hundred years after his death.

The men and women you'll meet in these pages loved Jesus so much that they couldn't help but change the world. Can their grit and wide-eyed amazement help us break through the grumpy, bewildered self-worship that defines our own age?

26

As we survey the rhetoric-scarred battlefield of Truth, we will see that the belief that Jesus is the Truth is in retreat. "Whatever is right for your life or works best for you is the only truth you can know," as three-fourths of millennials believe.[10]

Maybe you have found yourself wandering into this controversy over Truth versus truths. Who hasn't been at dinner with friends or family and heard someone say, "That may be true for you, but not for me"? Or "Who are you to say what is true?"

The quest for Truth faces all of us. It must begin with a clear-eyed view of the battle of ideas we now face.

Does the Truth Matter?

"You have to shed your burdens—the pain, the shame. Leave it all behind, strip it all away," said Jesus, his immaculately groomed beard perfectly framed by shoulder-length hair. "Only then you can speak your truth."[1]

Speak. Your. Truth.

Now, some might point out that this line was delivered by the messiah character in a short-running Netflix series, not by the real Jesus. But it resonates with people who want to believe "my truth is mine." What matters isn't whether my story is true or false or whether my actions are right or wrong. What matters is that I speak my truth.

This is what most people, even Jesus followers, believe about truth. The "no-judgment-allowed" mindset is growing in popularity among Christians. A study jointly conducted by Summit Ministries and the Barna Group found that self-identified Christian churchgoers under age forty-five were four times as likely as older generations to agree that "if your belief offends someone or hurts their feelings, it is wrong."[2] Just 6 percent of young adults agreed that "moral truth is absolute."[3]

Let's be clear about what this means. It does *not* mean that everyone now embraces a gauzy spirit of "live and let live."

Our age is as judgmental as any other. However, we're judging against a shifting standard. We're leaning on the *Zeitgeist*—the spirit of the age—rather than on Truth. Now, people are afraid to even talk about their convictions. Up to 75 percent of the population say they hold views they are unwilling to share, out of concern that they will be socially shamed or lose their jobs.[4]

To those who embrace Truth, this Truth versus truths controversy seems baffling. An apple doesn't become an orange just because someone labels it as such. "Reality is what it is," Truth proponents often say in exasperation. Yet even the idea of "reality" is under attack. The *New York Times* has insisted that the government appoint a "reality czar"—their term, not mine—to decide for all of us what is real.[5]

In my work with Summit Ministries, I've engaged in hundreds of conversations about Truth and the nature of reality. These conversations reveal that most people haven't thought very deeply about the subject. Many take for granted that Truth exists because that's what they learned growing up. Others reject Truth because they know unpleasant or mean people who believe in it. A few honest souls admit that they reject Truth because it conflicts with their lifestyles.

Truth is something worth having well-formed convictions about. Much is at stake. Historians Will and Ariel Durant wrote that "a great civilization is not conquered from without until it has destroyed itself within."[6] What we believe and how we act on it are more important for holding civilization together than what we buy or who we vote for.[7] If we lose the fundamental beliefs that hold us together, what is left to maintain order? Harvard sociologist Pitirim A. Sorokin phrased it bluntly: "When a society dispenses with God, with the Absolute, and rejects all the binding moral imperatives, the only binding power that remains is sheer physical force itself."[8] We've seen what physical force can do. Case study #1 is the Soviet Union, where tens of millions of citizens were terrorized and murdered by their own government. The Russian novelist Alexandr Solzhenitsyn, imprisoned for a time in a gulag for his writings, explained it simply: "Men have forgotten God; that's why all this has happened."[9]

Truth matters. It is hard to think of anything that matters more.

Why We Can't See the Truth

The biblical answer to "speak *your* truths" is to "seek *the* Truth." "Seek first the kingdom of God," Jesus said (Matt. 6:33). To seek, *zēteō* in Greek, means "to investigate something until you get to the bottom of it."

Truth is hard to find—not because it hides itself but because we're looking in the wrong place: within ourselves. It's like trying to find your way with a compass by positioning yourself so that the needle always points to you.

The apostle James, thought to be the half brother of Jesus, was so concerned about people's confusion over Truth that he apparently coined a term to describe it—the Greek word *dipsuchos*, which means "wavering between two minds." The double-minded are unstable in all their ways, James says (James 1:8).

To see Truth, we need mental clarity. But clarity itself is not enough. Clarity gets us to the starting line, not across the finish line. Of course, the Christian view is that the encounter with Truth begins with a personal relationship with Jesus Christ. But what then? "How should we then live?" asked the Christian cultural critic Francis Schaeffer.[10] If Truth is really true, we are called to a lifelong construction project in which God guides us to restore broken things on earth so that they resemble his kingdom and work the way he knows is best.

Truth, especially as it manifests in the way of Jesus, synthesizes the search to *find* Truth with the will to *live* it. Action is

31

called for, but not of the burn-it-all-down utopian sort. Rather, the way of Jesus calls for a completely upside-down way of life: Love, don't hate. Give, don't take. Create, don't destroy. Hope, don't fear. Build up, don't tear down.

The Jesus revolution changed everything—not because Jesus followers believed he was a nice man who gave strong speeches and presided over inexplicable happenings but because they encountered Jesus in a personal way and *lived* as if his teaching reflected reality as it actually exists.

Through the centuries, Jesus followers increasingly pressed his revolution forward in direct ways, such as freeing the oppressed and offering a cup of cool water to the thirsty. But as time passed, they expanded their thinking to include philosophical pondering, the exploration of the universe from its tiniest particles to its most distant stars, the development of advanced economies, and the healing of diseases.

Nothing remained untouched by the Jesus revolution. In recent decades, sociologists and economists have tried to quantify its impact. In America, so many people are helped by services offered in Jesus's name that the financial value is worth $2.67 trillion dollars per year.[11]

Around the world, the change is even more striking. Thanks in large part to efforts begun by Christian missionaries, extreme poverty has dropped by half just in the last generation, from 52 percent of the world's population to 26 percent.[12] More recent research shows that extreme poverty continues to decline. One billion more people have access to improved water supply since 1990.[13] Rates of infectious disease such as tuberculosis, polio, and malaria are at all-time lows.

Surprisingly, the Jesus revolution even set the world on an arc of liberty. After fits and starts, Jesus followers became champions of religious freedom, which included the freedom to believe nothing at all. Societies based on a biblical worldview are the friendliest places on earth, even for atheists and religious minorities.

Waking Up

Isaiah 29:10 says, "For the LORD has poured out on you an overwhelming urge to sleep" (CSB). Modern humanity isn't just confused; it is clumsy about its purpose and drowsy about its promise.

In *The Hobbit*, J. R. R. Tolkien describes a mythical race of delightful creatures who relish the comfort of home and are oblivious to the danger growing around them. How like the hobbits we are. When our tranquility is disturbed—by war or pandemic or economic instability—we only want to get back to normal. But normal is gone. There is not even a "new" normal. There is only a quest, on the other side of which is transformation.

Jesus called this transformation "life to the full" (see John 10:10). And even the sleepiest of us can find it if we dare. As Tolkien put it, "There is a seed of courage hidden (often deeply it is true) in the heart of the fattest and most timid hobbit waiting for some final and desperate danger to make it grow."[14]

The Jesus followers who changed history embraced this quest. They buoyantly chased the conviction that Jesus *is* Truth. Living out this conviction unleashed centuries of creativity and passion. It could do so again, even if most people reject the very idea of Truth. History isn't about what most people do. It is about the courageous, creative few. As Bill Brown from the Colson Center puts it, "One person sincerely committed to a cause is more valuable to that cause than a thousand who are merely interested."[15]

Before we explore how Jesus followers changed the world, though, we must first understand the truths viewpoint. We'll examine it now and then look more closely at the Truth viewpoint in the next chapter.

The "truths" (Lower Case) Viewpoint Says That Truth Cannot Be Objectively Known

"Speaking your truth is the most powerful tool we all have," said billionaire TV star and entrepreneur Oprah Winfrey in a speech at the Golden Globes.[16] Kudos to Oprah for using her hugely influential platform to inspire courage in those who find themselves ignored in the face of pain and mistreatment. We need to hear these stories.

But the way Oprah phrased it, "speaking your truth," implies something that undercuts the valuable point she was making. There is a world of difference between speaking *your* truths by *telling* your story and speaking *the* Truth and *illustrating* it with your story.

The truths viewpoint says that we must give up the search for Truth that is always true for everyone, everywhere, all the time. "All we can know is how each of us sees things," it says.

But how does this help us when we are facing genuine disagreement? A friend and I once witnessed a crime. Afterward, a police detective showed us a lineup of suspects. I pointed to one of them, quite sure he was the culprit. Later, after the detective left, my friend gave me an incredulous look. "Why on earth did you point to that guy? He was the wrong one!"

I was stunned. I *thought* I had picked the right one. My friend thought I had picked wrongly. She may have been correct because I was only half paying attention when the crime occurred. Possibly the guilty man went free as a result. What was I to say? "Well, *my* truth is that that was the guy"? Of course not. That would be absurd.

There is no escaping the Truth versus truths conflict. What we believe about whether Truth exists runs in the background of everything we say and do. It affects our beliefs about God, gender, race, politics, and everything else.

34

The battle over Truth flares up when we least expect it. We're sprawled across the sofa, scrolling through social media, when suddenly hordes of snarky comments appear on the horizon under full sail.

Conflicting stories cannot be true and untrue at the same time and in the same manner. We cannot have unrestricted access to abortion and restrictions on abortion at the same time. We cannot have a 30 percent tax rate and a 75 percent tax rate on the same people at the same time. We cannot have fracking and no fracking at the same time, in the same place. PETA, People for the Ethical Treatment of Animals, is not the same as PETA, People Eating Tasty Animals. There is a meaningful difference between these viewpoints, and we know it.

Before I became president of Summit Ministries, I served as a professor and entrepreneur focusing on helping people improve their communication skills. Here's what I've concluded about communication amid disagreements: What it's about is never what it's about. On the surface, you may be arguing about a hot topic such as abortion, but below the surface is always a hidden pain, a demand for respect, or a feeling of guilt.

Every disagreement we have, every tough topic, comes down to whether it is even possible for us to know Truth or whether truths are things we make up for ourselves.

Where the "truths" Viewpoint Comes From

The truths viewpoint is not new. Here are four ways philosophers have sought to justify it throughout history.

Sophism: Truth Is Whatever Helps You Win

In ancient Greece, a public speaker named Gorgias made a living by teaching people how to make their case in court. He didn't care what they wanted to say or why; he got paid to help them win. Gorgias explained his strategy in a book called *On Nature or the Non-Existent*. While the original text has been lost, we have enough fragments to know Gorgias's core argument:

- Nothing exists.
- Even if something exists, nothing can be known about it.
- Even if something can be known about it, knowledge about it can't be communicated to others.
- Even if it can be communicated, it cannot be understood.

To Gorgias, the search for Truth was pointless. We should seek to win, not to be right. Historians call Gorgias and like-minded teachers "sophists." *Sophia* is the Greek word for "wisdom." Today, sophism carries a negative connotation; it is the root word for *sophistry*, by which we mean a tricky, manipulative argument.

The nineteenth-century German philosopher Friedrich Nietzsche (1844–1900) tried to rehabilitate sophism. He considered it superior to other views about knowledge and communication. According to Nietzsche, "Every advance in epistemological and moral knowledge has reinstated the Sophists."[17]

Deflationism: Truth Is Just Window Dressing

Today, few philosophers will come right out and say, "Truth doesn't exist." Rather, some shrug off the search for Truth using what is called the "deflationary" view of truth. Saying "It is true that the sun rose today" is the same thing as saying "The sun rose today." Adding the word *true* to the statement does not add value. Therefore, discussions about Truth are meaningless.[18] The deflationary view has come under severe criticism.

Christian philosophers oppose it, but so do atheists and agnostics. They point out that the difference between the two statements above says something about how words (and sentences) work, but it isn't helpful in figuring out whether the sun rose.

Pluralism: Truth Is in the Eye of the Beholder

Other philosophers hold to a "pluralist" view of truth. They try to split the difference by arguing that some things can be objectively known, while others cannot. "At sea level, water boils at 212 degrees Fahrenheit" describes a physical phenomenon that we can consistently observe. But it is different to say things like, "That painting is beautiful" or "Ronald Reagan was a great president." In these statements, truth is in the eye of the beholder. What we call "truth" is relative to our personal or cultural situations, say advocates of pluralism.

Pluralism recognizes that we each have preferences. We are shaped by our experiences. But taken to an extreme, pluralism implies that we humans cannot make meaningful distinctions between truth and falsehood, or between good and evil. Can we really say that all paintings are equally beautiful? Is it really the case that no one can know the difference between a bad president and a good one? Or what about moral issues? Is there really no difference between saying "It is good to care for abandoned puppies" and "It is good to torture abandoned puppies"? In its moderate form, pluralism calls for a gentle approach to human differences. In its extreme form, it makes moral decision-making impossible.

Pragmatism: Truth Is Whatever Works

Complicating the matter is a view called "pragmatism." In the last hundred years or so, pragmatists such as C. S. Pierce, William James, John Dewey, and more recently Richard Rorty have said that we cannot know Truth objectively. We can only know what *works*. James wrote, "Truth *happens* to an idea. It *becomes* true, is *made* true by events."[19] Instead of trying to get people to see reality, we *make* truth by interpreting past events and the phenomena of the physical world in a way that makes our future course seem obvious.[20]

One flaw in pragmatism is that it opens the door to propaganda. If truth is "made true by events," then what is to stop crafty people with lots of money or influence from manipulating public perceptions to advance their viewpoint and squelch others'?

Pragmatists will say that this is an unfair criticism. "People still have an obligation to give reasons for what they believe," they say. "Beliefs must be meaningful, responsible, and capable of being tested." Yet in denying that ultimate truth may be objectively known, pragmatists essentially turn the world over to skilled arguers rather than truth-seekers.[21]

These Four Views Eventually Fail

These four views all express the idea that reality cannot be known through our attempts to find truth. They are not entirely without merit. The sophists were correct that viewpoints ought to be argued for. Deflationism rightly points out that people often flippantly use the word *truth*. Pluralism helps distinguish between facts and opinions. Pragmatism helps us live together despite our differences.

Theoretically, it should be possible to come to an agreement about most things without having to fight about whether Truth exists. In America, for instance, we drive on the right side of the road. The decision to drive on the right or the left is not a moral one. Other nations do it differently. The point is that we all *agree* on how to do it. It is a rule, or a norm, not a reflection of some eternal Truth about roads and driving.

But when it comes to the difficult moral decisions every society must make, these views fall short. What about sex trafficking or the subjugation of women or the confiscation of private property by the government? If these are just societal norms, does that mean that other societies might have different rules and we must be okay with that?

Some people believe so. I once conversed with a professor who told me, "Our society has no right to judge other societies." Her statement was clearly a judgment, but I let that point go. Instead, I described the practice of *suttee*, an ancient Indian tradition of ending a man's funeral by burning his body on the funeral pyre and then throwing his widow *alive* into the flames.

"Is that okay?" I asked.

"I can't say without first understanding their culture," she murmured half-heartedly.

I pressed, "Would it be okay if it was *your daughter* being thrown onto the flames?"

She admitted that it would not.

"But *why* not?"

The professor turned and walked away, leaving the question hanging in the air between us.

To be fair, even atheists such as the philosopher Simon Blackburn insist that such violations of human rights are not okay, "anywhere or any time."[22] When pressed for his reasoning, though, Blackburn takes refuge in statements of consensus, such as the United Nations Universal Declaration of Human Rights (1948). But how do we know that such statements represent reality, and not merely the opinions of leaders who are strong enough to get their way? When asked how people from different countries espousing different beliefs came to agree on a list of human rights, the Catholic philosopher Jacques Maritain famously quipped, "Yes, we agree about the rights, but on condition that no one asks us why."[23]

The truths viewpoint is summed up nicely by the frustrated detective character in Umberto Eco's *The Name of the Rose*: "There was no plot . . . and I discovered it by mistake."[24]

The Truth viewpoint doesn't settle for such explanations. It insists that there is a better way, and that we can find it. Is it a plausible viewpoint for today's world? Let's examine it and see.

Can Truth Be Known, and How Would We Know It?

Imagine that we are together in a room. I look out the window and say, "It is raining outside." Would it be reasonable for you to reply, "It may be raining outside for *you* but not for *me*"? If we both understand what rain is, we can look together to see if my claim lines up with the way things are.

The Truth viewpoint says that while not everything is as obvious as whether it is raining or not raining, Truth exists and can be known. Reality is stable and open to understanding because it makes itself accessible through knowledge. We can know about it. We can learn about it. We can base our thinking and actions on it. This applies to physical phenomena, such as the human circulatory system, but also to categories of meaning, such as justice and liberty.

Those who believe Truth can be known do not claim to know *all* of what is true. Rather, they argue that what we *can* know may be *truly* known. We navigate reality as a driver navigates a city using a map. No map describes the city's every detail. If it did, the map would be as big as the city itself. The question is not whether the map's detail is exhaustive but whether it accurately represents the contours of the city as it really is. Is Fourth Street really the next street to the east of Fifth Street or not? Either it is, or it isn't.

Reasons to Believe Truth Can Be Known

It is hard to summarize all the thinking that has gone on behind the Truth and the truths viewpoints. It would literally take volumes to detail the arguments for one side or the other. Anything I say risks oversimplification, but here are some points that Truth advocates often use to make their case.

Truth Rises

Truth seems to rise to the surface, even when people deny its existence. To say "The Truth cannot be known" is to claim to know something true. Similarly, when someone says, "You can't know what is true for me," they are claiming to know what is true for *you* as well as for them.

Claims about reality and morality, say Truth advocates, must be defended. You don't need to be a philosopher to practice this in conversation. If someone says, "X is wrong," ask, "What is your understanding of right and wrong based on?" Further, you can ask, "Is that true, and how do you know?" and "I understand why you would claim to know what is true for you, but why are you also claiming to know what is true for me?"

Things and Ideas Have Essences

The truths viewpoint says that we don't see things as they actually are—we only see what we interpret of their presumed existence. If I say "A Ferrari F12 Berlinetta is a cool sports car," I'm not making a statement about an automobile but a statement about my personal idea of coolness and sportiness. This

42

is how advocates of the truths viewpoint frame the issue. We can't see what exists. We just see what we see.[1]

The philosopher Edmund Husserl (1859–1938) offered a devastating critique of this view. He points out that thoughts and ideas have "essences," certain qualities that make them what they are. Thoughts and ideas are *about* things, and they are *intended* to be about things.[2] Let's say a coworker makes a comment like, "No religious belief can be known to be true." Of course, this is a belief about religion that your coworker assumes to be true, but let's step beyond that obvious contradiction for a moment. Husserl would point out that the ideas your coworker is talking about—existence, religion, belief, knowledge, and truth—have essences. They mean things to your coworker and to those to whom the comment is addressed. Each word can be consistently defined. Each conveys certain meanings and not others.

This may seem like so much philosophical gobbledygook, but the idea of essences points to the existence of Truth. Important ideas such as justice and liberty can be known to be meaningful. Without meaningful ideas, social interaction is pointless. We cannot expect to be taken seriously when we point out injustice if the idea of justice has no essence.

Words Are Meaningful

Those who advocate truths over Truth say "the truth cannot be known" and yet insist that this is a true statement. Philosophers call this kind of statement "self-referentially absurd." But some theorists such as Ludwig Wittgenstein (1889–1951) argued that this apparent contradiction is just a trick of language. Our words ring true because we use them artfully, not because they refer to real things, such theorists claim.[3]

Yet this is unsatisfying as soon as we apply it even to the words in that statement itself. If words do not refer to real things, why would we treat the words themselves as meaningful?

Granted, words are not the same as the things or ideas to which they refer. A chair (physical object) is not the same thing as the word *chair* (an element of speech). But we use words to *intentionally* talk *about* things or ideas. Imagine that I enter a Paris furniture store, point to a chair, and ask, "What is that?" The clerk would reply, "*Une chaise.*" Though the clerk and I are using different words, we are *intentionally* talking *about* an object that both of our minds perceive as a chair, distinct from other objects we might find in a furniture store. We talk as if our words are meaningful because they represent certain things and not others.

Advocates of the truths viewpoint ignore this basic premise. They *say* that words are not tied to reality while sneakily using words to *create* perceptions they then treat as real. This can lead to deadly word games. Every act of cruelty and violence against people begins with word games.[4] In Rwanda, Hutu leaders demonized Tutsis as "cockroaches" before calling for their extermination. Hundreds of thousands died. Nazis called Jews "vermin" to justify the Holocaust. Today, pro-abortion advocates refer to unborn babies as "products of conception" to minimize their value as human persons. "When words lose their meaning people lose their lives," warned my late friend Professor Michael Bauman.[5]

We Can Make Rational Arguments

The link between our mental lives and reality may be established through reason. Rationalism sets the boundaries of thought. I can use reason to test the relationship between a mathematical proof and reality. I can use reason to test the relationship between a scientific theory and reality. I can also use reason to make wise personal decisions about reality. If I am standing on top of a tall building without a railing, I watch my footing very carefully because reasoning from the law of gravity tells me that if I fall, I will go down, not up, no matter how beautifully I tell my personal story of "upness." Tumbling off the building without the aid of a safety device or parachute won't violate the law of gravity; it will prove it. Reason connects me to reality. It allows me to approximate truth. This helps me make good decisions.

People often wonder about the relationship between faith and reason. The atheist philosopher Simon Blackburn agrees that the "true for you but not for me" kind of relativism is unhelpful, but he goes further to state that religious claims, such as belief in God, are also unhelpful. To his way of thinking, religious claims cause us to stop short of deep intellectual inquiry. He is not completely wrong. If a student wrote on an exam, "I don't know how the chemical reaction of combustion occurs. I guess God does it," his teacher would consider that to be a poor answer. But this does not mean that no true answer to the question exists. Similarly, God's acts are not beyond knowing or describing. Faith is not outside the bounds of reasoned inquiry. People might disagree with us, but even when they do, they assume that their words and ours are intelligible. There is no escaping reason.

There Is a Knowable Difference between Facts and Opinions

A fact is something that is known to be true. An opinion is an interpretation of facts. Many people confuse the two, especially when they speak out on social media: "Restrictions against abortion do violence to women," or "Rich people are evil." Such statements present opinions as facts.

To the truths viewpoint, this is no big deal because no real differences exist between facts and opinions anyway. We cannot know what is factual—all we have are our stories of what is true for us. *lazy?!*

But we *can* know the difference between facts and opinions! We can use the scientific method to observe, measure, and repeat experiments about the natural world. For historical events, we can examine newspaper accounts, listen to the testimonies of witnesses, or perhaps look at pictures or watch film footage. In public policy, we can examine the financial and social costs versus the likely benefits of proposed laws. In philosophy, we can define our terms and give reasons for why our arguments are sound. Someone might disagree with our conclusions, but their disagreement only makes sense if we are sure that we are talking about the same thing.

Some simple examples make this obvious. It would be silly for a person to say, "Well, maybe in your culture a water molecule is made up of two atoms of hydrogen and one atom of oxygen, but in my culture, it is different," or "Perhaps it is true for *you* that Martin Luther King Jr. was shot on April 4, 1968, but how dare you impose that belief on me?"

In addition to scientific and historical facts, moral facts also exist. "It is wrong to murder" and "It is wrong to cheat on a test" are not mere opinions, as those who hold to the truths viewpoint would argue.[6] Moral facts can be objectively known and remain true independent of our willingness to obey them. Evidence may be produced to demonstrate that they are true. Philosopher Richard H. Beis has collected an extensive list of moral absolutes that are universally demonstrated in every culture that anthropologists have studied. These include prohibition of murder or maiming without justification; prohibition of lying, at least in certain areas such as oaths; the right to own property such as land, clothing, and tools; preference of common good over individual good; and sexual restrictions.[7]

The novelist Flannery O'Connor said, "Truth does not change by our ability to stomach it emotionally."[8] That we can know the difference between facts and opinions demonstrates the role of evidence in drawing reasonable conclusions about reality. It is important to keep the difference in mind when we speak. We may also ask others, "What evidence demonstrates that your claim is factual?"

The Capital-T Truth Viewpoint in History

You don't have to be a Christian to hold that reality exists and may be known. Most philosophers find discussions about Truth meaningful, even though they may not be Christians.[9]

Much thinking about Truth was shaped by pre-Christian Greek philosophy. To the Greeks, reality is made up of ideas—perfect forms of the things we see on earth. Plato (428/427–348/347 BC), for example, theorized that the abstract world of ideas contains "forms" on which things in the observable world are based. There is a "form" of a tree on which the trees we see are modeled. This ideal tree produces an "essence" that allows us humans to quickly categorize the trees we see. Similarly, justice is a form on which our human idea of justice is modeled. Good categories make for good living.

Aristotle (384–322 BC) spent most of his time organizing his observations into categories. It makes sense that he did this. In this world, we notice many distinctions: light/dark, cold/hot, male/female, good/evil. That these sometimes overlap does not make the distinctions meaningless, because we have ways of knowing the difference. The categories "male" and "female" are biologically based. We can see the differences not only by observing them but also by drawing blood and looking through a microscope to see what happens as each person's cells divide and whether the chromosomes are XX (female) or XY (male). This isn't the only distinction. Scientists say there are sixty-five hundred genetic differences between males and females.[10] If a female says, "But I don't *feel* like a female," it is because she is focused not on the underlying reality but on her self-perception.

Categories work well when we are describing the physical world. For instance, we can categorize different kinds of rocks. If I pick up a rock and say, "This kind of rock is igneous," you might reply, "No, it is sedimentary." To resolve our disagreement, we could consult a geology textbook to see which of our two statements best corresponds to reality. If I'm thinking about building my house on one kind of rock foundation or another, it pays to know the difference.

What about things outside the physical world, such as God? Greek philosophers expressed varying viewpoints, just as people do today. But most were fairly committed to the idea that "god" was more a force, like light and sound, than a personal, capital-G God. Even a personal God would have to obey the Truth of the universe. Truth is so true that even a willful God couldn't change it. That's what most Greeks believed.

The Greeks also held that a well-trained mind that is not deceiving itself will be able to see what is obvious. The Greeks called this obviousness *logos*. It's a great word that means "word" or, more accurately, "the verbal expression of a thought." Truth exists and we can express it truly, though not exhaustively.

But in the hands of biblical writers, the word *logos* came to mean so much more.

What Does It Mean to Say That Jesus Is the Truth?

Many of history's greatest minds embraced a belief in God, despite what we hear from skeptics such as Professor Richard Dawkins and talk show host Bill Maher. Plato, Aristotle, St. Augustine, St. Thomas Aquinas, William of Ockham, René Descartes, Baruch Spinoza, Gottfried von Leibniz, John Locke, George Berkeley, Immanuel Kant, and Georg W. F. Hegel were all theists, in one form or another. Even David Hume, whom atheists embrace as one of their own, declared, "The whole frame of nature bespeaks an intelligent author; and no rational enquirer can, after serious reflection, suspend his belief a moment with regard to the primary principles of genuine Theism and Religion."[11]

The Bible moves beyond an abstract idea of God. From its first pages, the Bible proclaims that at the heart of reality is a God who knows and cares. God is personal. This claim, made throughout the Bible, is found as early as the second chapter of Genesis, where Creator-God (Elohim) and Relator-God (YHWH) are revealed to be one and the same (YHWH Elohim, or the Lord God). This makes sense philosophically. Ultimate reality is either matter or mind. Did matter give rise to mind, or did mind give rise to matter? We can observe that matter doesn't make choices. Also, matter decomposes. This implies that at one point it was composed. Minds, however, are personal. They make choices. They contemplate. They act. The Bible reveals that the ultimate, personal Mind behind everything is God. We can be knowers because there is a Knower in whose image we are created.[12]

The Gospel accounts go even further. One of Jesus's disciples, John, spent most of his long life reflecting on his three incredible years by Jesus's side. In his Gospel, John opens with the passage, "In the beginning was the Word, and the Word was with God, and the Word was God" (1:1 NIV). The word *Word* here is *Logos*. It is the same word Greek philosophers used to describe the obviousness of reality. John wants his readers to understand that the *Logos* is more than a concept. It is the person of Jesus. John says, "And the Word became flesh and dwelt among us, and we have seen his glory, glory as of the only Son from the Father, full of grace and truth" (v. 14).

Not only can God be known, but he has also personally appeared in his creation. God took on a body. He became incarnate. As we will see, the incarnation of God through Jesus changed everything. Jesus followers were convinced that Jesus was God in the flesh. It came up over and over again as they carried out their world-changing work. Heedless of their personal safety, reputation, or economic security, they willingly gave their lives in the pursuit of what they believed. They did not struggle to gain an evolutionary advantage; they struggled to give that advantage to others, even at great cost.

What the Bible Says about Jesus Being the Truth

Today's battle over Truth versus truths isn't far removed from the way Jesus's first followers experienced it. Jesus's disciples were Jews who had grown up in a Greek-ified culture (scholars use the term *Hellenized*, which comes from a word that means "to speak Greek"). Jews and Greeks approached reality differently. The Greeks, following Plato, insisted that the power of reason frees us from the cave of shadows so we can stumble out into reality's sunlight. Jews, on the other hand, believed they could know what is real because God had revealed it in the Holy Scriptures.

Early Christians, based on the gospel, taught that God was not only "out there" but also here with us. It wasn't an entirely new belief. The ancient Hebrew name for God that expresses his personal relationship with his people is YHWH, from the Hebrew verb "to be," or "to breathe." God's nature is as present with us as the act of breathing. Truth continues to be something you find, but it is also something that finds *you*. It is personal, live, conscious, and expressive. We may reach out for God, but when we find him, we realize that he was the one reaching out to us.

By reporting that *Jesus* is the Truth, though, Jesus's disciples transformed the debate about reality itself.

In his Gospel, John doubles down—and triples down—on the conviction that Truth has made itself known in the person of Jesus. In his writings, John offers many reasons for believing that Jesus really is the answer the world is looking for. He even draws from ancient prophecies such as this one from Isaiah, written eight centuries before Jesus:

> The people who walked in darkness
>   have seen a great light;
> those who dwelt in a land of deep darkness,
>   on them has light shone. (Isa. 9:2)

In many printings of the Bible, the words of Jesus are displayed in red letters. Much of John's Gospel is printed in red, meaning that John is directly quoting Jesus's words. Jesus said that the Spirit of God will guide his disciples into all Truth. He prayed that his disciples would be sanctified in the Truth. When on trial before Pilate, Jesus said that his purpose in the world was to bear witness to the Truth. Many believed the disciples' testimony. Others rejected it. Yet to those who believed, John said, God gave the right to become his children (John 1:12).

This is a profound claim. The ancient philosophers longed for a meaningful life. They believed they could discover life's purpose by finding the answers to three questions: "What is good?" "What is true?" and "What is beautiful?" Educated people of Jesus's day would have been familiar with Greek philosophy. I wonder if Jesus may have been addressing their mindset when he proclaimed, "I am the way, and the truth, and the life" (John 14:6). "I am," he seems to be saying, "the answer to the philosophers' quest."

51

What Difference Does It Make to Say That Jesus Is the Truth?

For more than two millennia, the followers of Jesus have relished the personal comfort they receive from their belief in him. But in the centuries following Jesus's earthly sojourn, his followers increasingly believed something more: "Jesus is the Truth" is a statement about reality itself. It opens a world of wonder. It restores hope. It unleashes good in the world.

Even those who reject the claim that Jesus is the Truth can understand what a transformative belief it is.

To Christians, the claim that Jesus is the Truth is *euangélion* (good news). It isn't just good because it assures us of eternal life. It is good because it gives us direction when we feel foolish or aimless or stressed, or when we are tired or insecure. It is the answer to everything, from how to bring good into a marriage to how to navigate global conflict.

How is this good news *good*? Picture a world in which all reality is apparent to everyone. There is no brain fog. Each one of us knows what the good life is and pursues it with childlike glee. We think with crystal clarity, acing every exam, seeing through every scheme, and missing not a single great opportunity. And we create. Wow, do we ever create: art, music, architecture, inventions, medical advancements.

In such a world, we would all have so many great ideas that there would be no reason to envy anyone else's gifts. Fear would rule no longer. People would live with open hands rather than closed fists. We would have everything to live for and many things worth dying for.

Yet even in John's day, the idea that one man could bring enlightenment to the whole world defied imagination. Many rolled their eyes. The answer to all our problems was born of a virgin and rose from the dead? Come on, man.

Even strong believers sometimes wobble in the wake of such astounding claims. Poets have tried to make sense of it. One songwriting team framed it with gentle honesty: "this is such a strange way to save the world."[13]

But save the world it has. The Jesus revolution offered both a way to find truth and a reason to live for it here and now, and not merely in some future state.

Why "Jesus Is the Truth" Is Revolutionary

How might the world's story have turned out differently had the Romans not been so cruel? Egged on by Jesus's enemies, Roman soldiers killed him on a criminal's cross. Crucifixion was a "fire and forget" kind of torture: just nail them up there and let them torment themselves to death. Efficient. Humiliating. Maximally painful. One hundred percent deadly. Every victim became a writhing, groaning teachable moment: "Don't forget your place, peasants."

And yet Jesus rose above it. Literally. In what historian Gary Habermas calls the most verifiable fact of ancient history, Jesus appeared to his disciples fully alive three days after his death.[14] They couldn't stop talking about it. Many of them eventually had to be killed, so noisy were they.

Amazingly, Jesus followers did not hold a grudge about this. Their guy didn't see himself as a victim, and neither would they. Jesus had told them that he was giving up his own life, out of love. "Greater love has no one than this, that someone lay down his life for his friends," Jesus had said (John 15:13).

Some revolutionaries call their followers to vengeance. Jesus was a more dangerous sort of revolutionary. He called his followers not to defeat their enemies militarily but to win them over through love. Instead of ignoring your opponents or trying to shut them up, you hang out with them. In time, Christians believe, many more will become raving fans.

The Church Needs to Understand Its Own Beliefs

What we believe about God, the world, and ourselves subtly affects the ten to twenty thousand decisions we make every day.[15] Granted, most decisions are innocuous: Should I disregard my doctor's advice and supersize my lunch order? But over time, decisions metastasize into habits. If those decisions are bad ones, they will compromise our mental immune system, confusing us about reality and prodding us to believe wrong things, make wrong decisions, and treat others wrongly.

The Bible, Christians say, is God's revelation about how to make decisions based on "the way"—how life works best. It contains rules, but following the rules is not the point. Drivers don't get behind the wheel just to see how many traffic laws they can obey. They drive to go places. A soccer player who says, "Coach, I didn't help our team win, but you must admit that I followed every rule to a T" should not be surprised if the coach is dissatisfied with this sort of play. Following soccer's "Laws of the Game" is not the goal of the game; meaningful victory is. Similarly, the Bible's rules exist to guide us, as a train is guided by its tracks, toward a world of flourishing, order, and blessing.

Most pastors and Christian teachers believe Truth can be known—and known in the person of Jesus. But they still seem largely unaware of how often their congregations filter their experiences through the truths viewpoint. Pollster George Barna has demonstrated that only 19 percent of churchgoing, born-again Christians hold a biblical worldview. Nineteen percent. The other eighty-one percent either are not aware of or disagree with core Christian doctrines about God, Jesus, the

Bible, sin, redemption, and ethical living—all matters of what is true about reality.

Having a biblical worldview means to be on board with Jesus's revolutionary transformation project. History is in the making. And history is not merely a sequence of chronological happenings. History is going somewhere, and it is going there for a reason.

What critics try to write off as mass delusion has, in fact, bent the arc of history. Over and over again, in many different cultures and times, believers have experienced transformation and have begun to live in an entirely different way. The descriptions of such conversion are coherent and consistent. It is impossible that people coordinated them across nations and time periods just to get the story straight.[16] As Cambridge philosopher C. D. Broad suggests, we ought to treat these experiences as truthful unless we have positive evidence that they are not.[17]

The conversion of many people to Christianity doesn't *prove* that Christianity is true. It does, however, *illustrate* its Truth. Jesus said, "If I am not doing my Father's works, don't believe me. But if I am doing them and you don't believe me, believe the works" (John 10:37–38 CSB). The way of Jesus is not true because it works; it works because it is true.

The world-changing actions of history's Jesus followers are what this book is about. How should we begin to tell their stories? Let's start with what is most basic: how the belief that Jesus is the Truth changed forever our understanding of the value of human life.

How Jesus Followers Have Changed How We Value Human Life

The Late Middle Ages were a time of ignorance, superstition, and poverty. Drab hovels lined stinking streets. Life was barely worth living.

Or so we are told.

Suffering was indeed widespread in the Late Middle Ages, but to Christian thinkers and activists, suffering did not define their age. Rather, they were guided by the belief that humans possess souls and bear God's image. Life in their world gathered its meaning from the eternal. The typical twenty-first-century person seeks self-understanding by gazing in a mirror. Typical fourteenth-century people discovered it by looking up. They anticipated salvation, for Jesus had said in Luke 21:28, "So when all these things begin to happen, stand and look up, for your salvation is near!" (NLT).

When people in the Late Middle Ages gazed at the heavens, they didn't see a cold vacuum. Beauty, they believed, fills us with wonder and turns our hearts to God. Nowhere was this sense of wonder more evident than in Siena, a prosperous city in the Tuscan region of Italy. Tourists and worshipers visiting the Siena cathedral sense the Sienese love of beauty as they pass through the cathedral's ornately carved facade and take in the columns of alternating bands of dark and light marble and the breathtakingly painted ceiling depicting the sun, moon, and stars in their courses. In the Middle Ages, people could gaze at the cathedral's enormous altarpiece, the Maestà—Italian for "majesty"—painted by Duccio di Buoninsegna, and offer prayers at each one of the Maestà's dozens of panels depicting the life of Christ.

Catherine of Siena was the city's most famous resident. Born at the height of the Black Plague's devastation in 1347, Catherine was the twenty-third of twenty-five children. Only half of her siblings lived to adulthood. At least three died in the plague. Catherine lived only to age thirty-three. Yet her extraordinary life is still celebrated around the world every April 29, St. Catherine's feast day.[1]

Catherine experienced mystical visions from God beginning at seven years of age. When Catherine was fifteen, her sister Bonaventura died. Catherine's parents wanted to arrange a marriage between Catherine and her sister's widower, but Catherine shocked the family by telling them that she was already committed. She was the bride of Christ.

Because of Jesus, Catherine taught, every human life is valuable. We are souls connecting heaven and earth, not merely bodies occupying space. Our lives have meaning through Christ, and our souls may be purified in him. Christ's perfection—not our performance—gives our lives great significance.

Through nearly four hundred letters compiled by Catherine's mentor, Raymond of Capua, we know a great deal about the visions Catherine received. One was based on John 15:5, where Jesus says, "I am the vine; you are the branches. Whoever abides in me and I in him, he it is that bears much fruit, for apart from me you can do nothing." Speaking from God's perspective, Catherine said:

> Indeed I am the gardener, for all that exists comes from Me. With power and strength beyond imagining I govern the whole world: Not a thing is made or kept in order without Me. I am the gardener, then, who planted the vine of My only-begotten Son in the earth of your humanity so that you, the branches, could be joined to the vine and bear fruit.[2]

To Catherine, Christ's incarnation was a present reality, not merely a historical event. This conviction infused her with tremendous boldness in confronting church corruption and ministering to the destitute.

As we saw earlier, the Black Death was one of the greatest times of suffering in human history. Remember that across Europe a third to half of the people died from the excruciating disease. Terrified commoners dug mass graves until there was literally no place else to bury the dead. Life seemed to have little meaning beyond an inevitable and painful death. Anyone who could afford to, fled.

But Catherine did not flee. From her mentor we know that when the plague returned to Siena in the 1370s, Catherine ran toward its victims rather than away from them. She comforted them and prayed with them for salvation. Doubtless you've heard such stories before. But have you ever stopped to wonder why Catherine did this? Did she have a death wish?

Here's an excerpt from one of Catherine's letters, imagining God's message about those who were suffering: "The value is not in the suffering but in the soul's desire. Likewise, neither desire nor any other virtue has value or life except through My only-begotten Son, Christ crucified, since the soul has drawn love from Him and in virtue follows His footsteps."[3]

Follow Catherine's train of thought: We have souls. Our souls desire God. This desire has value because of Jesus. So why run toward suffering rather than away from it? Because in suffering we draw near to God, as he has drawn near to us through Jesus. If you want to be with Jesus, you sit with the suffering. That's where Jesus is.

What Makes Human Life Valuable?

Today, we instinctively sense that every person has value, at least in theory. Life is special, but why? What is the source of its value? Indeed, what does it even mean to be a human person?

The truths viewpoint insists that what we call truth is "in here," not "out there." If you want to know where you fit in the grand scheme of things, you don't examine your place in the world. You examine your own feelings. This is a predominant way of thinking in America. Ninety-one percent of Americans agree with the statement "The best way to find yourself is by looking within yourself."[4]

History's Jesus followers would have been appalled by this self-centeredness. Even Aristotle, a pagan, said that we can know our value only by knowing our *telos*, our ultimate purpose, which he said is to live virtuously and to think well. But if the truths viewpoint is correct, Aristotle was wrong. There is no ultimate point. As the renowned scientist Edward O. Wilson bluntly phrased it, humanity has no purpose "beyond the imperatives created by its genetic history."[5] We fight to reproduce and to postpone dying for as long as possible. These natural impulses are all that exist.

Naturalistic belief is at the core of the worldview promoted in higher education today. For an investment of hundreds of thousands of dollars, students learn that there is no ultimate point in life. Yet many honest scholars admit that this way of thinking raises more questions than it answers. The secular psychologist Rollo May acknowledged, "Today we know a great deal about bodily chemistry and the control of physical diseases; but we know very little about why people hate, why they cannot love, why they suffer anxiety and guilt, and why they destroy each other."[6]

A biblical worldview does not share this uncertainty. A biblical view holds that human life is sacred. Humans are made in the image of God (Gen. 1:26–27). Human value is established before birth (Ps. 139:13–16). Taking human life is wrong (Exod. 20:13). The Bible seems to teach that while human sin is a curse, humanity itself is a blessing. Humans are of a different order, not just different by degree, than nonhuman animals. We have a higher purpose, concluded the Christian philosopher Dallas Willard, which is "to love and serve others, and to be loved and served by others."[7] Our *telos* is tethered to God's *telos*. The truths viewpoint says that our lives are valuable only to the extent that we tell our stories in a convincing way. Human life is cheap for those who lack the ability to do so; they are a burden, not a blessing. This perspective was captured powerfully in the movie *Avengers: Infinity War*, in which a demigod named Thanos gains power and destroys half of all life in the universe. When his kidnapped "daughter" Gamora confronts him, he scoffs.

Thanos: "You were going to bed hungry, scrounging for scraps. Your planet was on the brink of collapse. I'm the one who stopped that. You know what's happened since then? The children born have known nothing but full bellies and clear skies. It's a paradise."

Gamora: "Because you murdered half the planet."

Thanos: "A small price to pay for salvation."[8]

Thanos believes the universe is finite. It cannot support everyone. Some must go. What Gamora sees as an act of utter horror—killing half of all life—Thanos sees as a necessary act of will.

But many people ask, "Isn't it true that having so many humans on the planet leads to misery?" Population expert and respected economist Julian L. Simon flatly contradicts this common belief: "There is no evidence to prove that a large population creates poverty and underdevelopment."[9] True, some poor countries are crowded. But some of the most crowded places on the planet—cities like Hong Kong and Singapore—are also the most prosperous.

Is it possible that the biblical belief that humans are a blessing holds true, even in a world with a growing population? In 2018, economist Paul Romer won the Nobel Prize for pointing out that people are the solution to, not the cause of, poverty. Given the opportunity to be creative, humans take earth's finite resources and rearrange them in a way that benefits everyone.[10] To put it another way, it's a population bloom, not a population bomb.[11]

Certainly, an unacceptably high percentage of the world's population lives in dangerous, inhumane conditions. But what is the solution? According to economist Barry Asmus and theologian Wayne Grudem in their book *The Poverty of Nations*, what best reduces poverty is not the redistribution of scarce resources but the removal of barriers to economic success.[12] Growing evidence shows that as wealth has increased, the world's population has experienced several decades of large improvements in safe drinking water, a growing food supply, lower infant mortality, higher life expectancy, shrinking of child labor, and even expanded college enrollment.[13] Pollution is also decreasing, as increasing wealth provides the time, energy, and money needed to clean the environment.[14]

Where did these innovations begin? By recognizing the image of God in all people.

That humans have an ultimate purpose is a hard sell to those who think the point of life is mainly to avoid death. Even Jesus's disciples struggled with this. After his friend Lazarus died, Jesus instructed his followers to open Lazarus's tomb. "Lord, by this time there will be an odor," said Lazarus's ever-practical sister Martha. "Jesus said to her, 'Did I not tell you that if you believed you would see the glory of God?'" (John 11:39–40). Those gathered around couldn't see past the nature of physical death. Death was the ultimate limit to existence, in their experience. Jesus raised their eyes to God's limitless power. We need this larger perspective because, as N. T. Wright says, "Death itself tells lies about God and about Jesus."[15]

In the Late Middle Ages, even as people faced seemingly unbearable suffering, they had something we lack in facing our own trials: a core belief that the eternal gives meaning to the temporal. What did they understand that we do not? The answer for them, as for Catherine of Siena, was found in the nature of the soul.

The Nature of the Soul

The existence and nature of the soul are central to the writings of Thomas Aquinas (1225–74). Aquinas was a priest whose magisterial work *Summa Theologica* weaves together faith and reason and is still regarded as one of the greatest philosophical works of all time.

While other medieval scholars gave up hope that faith and reason could be reconciled, Aquinas taught that the two fit together perfectly. To Aquinas, says the scholar Chris R. Armstrong, "faith completes reason and reason upholds faith."[16]

At the core of Aquinas's teaching on the soul is the *imago Dei*, the image of God. Aquinas concluded, quoting Augustine, that "man's excellence consists in the fact that God made him to His own image by giving him an intellectual soul, which raises him above the beasts of the field."[17] Humans possess the image of God. We imitate God's intellectual nature and have been given a natural inclination to know and love him, even if we do so imperfectly. God's joy has been put in our hearts (Ps. 4:7).

Aquinas's thought influences us to this day. We exist, and we know that we exist. We know that we are individuals. We change a great deal throughout life but recognize that the core of who we are—our substance—is continuous. We do not become less of a person if we lose an arm or a leg.[18] Also, humans act intentionally. We have mental states that are more than merely physical. This "us-ness," to Aquinas, is evidence that we have souls.

Aquinas begins his case for the soul with the work of the Christian martyr Boethius (480–524) and with Aristotle (384–322 BC). It may strike us as odd that a Christian thinker would rely on the teaching of a pre-Christian Greek philosopher, but Aquinas didn't see it as a problem. Pagan thinkers weren't wrong; they just didn't have all the pertinent information. Oxford theologian Michael Ward summarizes the medieval approach this way: "If paganism could be shown to have something in common with Christianity, 'so much the better for paganism,' not 'so much the worse for Christianity.'"[19]

Here I need to mention a controversy that some who support abortion have created by misinterpreting Aquinas's teaching on the soul. Based on the best information available to him at the time, Aquinas guessed that the soul comes into the unborn child when it begins to move in the womb, which Aquinas thought was about forty days for boys and eighty to ninety days for girls. Before that, some abortion advocates say, the esteemed Aquinas would not have regarded abortion as the killing of a human person.[20]

The Catholic Church and most Christians reject the conclusion that Aquinas would not have seen abortion as the killing of a human soul. Because of the science of embryology, we also now know something that Aquinas did not: fetal development is one continuous process. As Robert P. George and Christopher Tollefsen note, "There is widespread agreement among embryologists both that a new human individual comes into existence when there is a single, unified, and self-integrated biological system, and this happens no later than syngamy [the lining up of the twenty-three pairs of chromosomes]."[21]

Elective abortion cuts against the view that, as Dr. Seuss memorably phrased it in *Horton Hears a Who*, "a person's a person, no matter how small."[22] Even among abortion's most sophisticated defenders, it is relatively uncontroversial to say that human life begins at conception.[23] The philosopher Peter Singer, an advocate of abortion and even infanticide, admits, "There is no doubt that from the first moments of its existence an embryo conceived from the human sperm and egg is a human being; and the same is true of the most profoundly and irreparably intellectually disabled human being."[24]

People may support abortion on demand for a variety of reasons, but according to Aquinas's teachings and the beliefs of most Christians since that time, human beings are "ensouled" from the moment of conception.

By the late 1800s, the study of the soul had been deemed so important that it led to an entirely new academic field, psychology (based on two Greek words, *psyche*, or "soul," and *ology*, "the study of").

But if, as secular psychologists believe, the world is made up of matter and nothing more, then where is the room for thinking about immaterial souls? Almost immediately in the developing field of psychology, scholars began deleting references to the "soul" and replacing them with the "self." Our problem as humans is that we don't know and care for our "selves" as much as we should. We should measure our humanity based not on the existence of the soul, as Aquinas and others thought, but on how our selves interact in the situations in which we find ourselves. The late Harvard professor Joseph Fletcher called this "situation ethics."[25]

While Aquinas taught, based on the Bible, that the soul comes from God, secular psychologists insist that the "self" comes mainly from our evolutionary nature. If there is any distinction between us and our primate ancestors, they insist, it is because we use human language to connect with one another.

Some Buddhists, such as the spiritual leader of Tibet, the Dalai Lama, agree with secular psychologists that the idea of the immaterial soul is outdated. He goes so far as to say that belief in the soul is dangerous. It is "the source of all our misery."[26]

What difference does it make that history's Jesus followers believed in the soul? The answer is instructive and even surprising.

How Jesus Followers Shaped Our Understanding of Human Value

The Difference between Humans and Animals

In the biblical creation account, just after God creates humans—both male and female—in his image, God blesses his human creation and instructs them to rule the birds of the air, the fish of the sea, and the animals on the ground (Gen. 1:28).

To a secular worldview, this is absurd. Everything came into existence through natural processes, it claims. We bear the image of no god. We are not in charge. We are nothing more than meat machines, as artificial intelligence pioneer Marvin Minsky memorably described humans.[27] We differ from animals only in that we are more adept at developing complex societies.

Not all secular thinkers are on board with the naturalistic view that humans differ from nonhuman animals only by degree. Noam Chomsky, an MIT cognitive scientist, concluded that our genetic similarities with nonhuman primates are not enough to help us fully understand human value. Many years ago, the Columbia University psychologist Herbert S. Terrace set out to prove Chomsky wrong. His hope lay in a male chimpanzee whimsically named Nim Chimpsky. Terrace hoped to show that Nim's sign language vocabulary of 127 words provided the missing link between humans and their nonhuman ancestors. But as Terrace prepared to publish his findings, he replayed videos of Nim in slow motion and realized that most of Nim's signs were prompted by his teachers. Nim wasn't trying to talk with his handlers; he was trying to get a reward by imitating them.[28] Nim could use words but didn't have much to say.

In sharing his mistaken assumptions about Nim, Terrace acknowledged that humans differ from nonhuman animals in *kind*, not just *degree*. Only humans use phonetic speech in a richly symbolic fashion to exercise free will. Only humans use language to sequence their thought.[29] Only humans use language to understand and connect with one another.[30] As philosopher J. P. Moreland puts it, animals have desires, but not the desire to have desires. They don't appear to think about their thinking, Moreland says, nor are they aware of their awareness.[31]

The unbridgeable difference between humans and nonhuman animals does not, of itself, prove the Bible's creation account. It does, however, call into question a central tenet of a secular worldview, that everything about humanity can be explained through naturalistic processes of evolution.

Against the naturalistic worldview, a biblical perspective maintains that what makes us valuable as humans rests in the personal nature of God, not in the self. God's reality was such a fact of life to ancient Hebrews that the term used in the Bible as the personal name of God—YHWH, often transliterated as Jehovah—is translated as "I am." In ancient Hebrew, one literally could not say "I am" because that was God's name. Making oneself the center of reality was a linguistic impossibility, according to Jewish thought; our existence is contingent on God's existence.[32]

Rights for All

From its very first pages, the Bible insists that the human is a living soul (*nephesh* in Hebrew; Gen. 2:7). A person's deepest value resides in the soul, even if, as with an unborn child or a profoundly disabled individual, a person's animating spirit is less than fully actualized.[33]

The biblical case for the soul unfolds in the law of Moses. When the children of Israel came out of slavery in Egypt, the surrounding world was a horrifying place. Baby killing was common. Humans were sacrificed to the gods. Slavery was accepted as a social good. The devaluing of women and children was culturally acceptable.

The teachings of the first five books of the Bible, what Jewish people call the Torah, put in motion a process to set the world right. Mosaic law was a breakthrough for how societies should treat people and wisely govern themselves. It was intended as a self-correcting system that would tip the balance in favor of greater justice over time. The prophet Amos put it beautifully: "But let justice roll down like waters, and righteousness like an ever-flowing stream" (Amos 5:24). Amos envisions justice as an endless supply of water from which everyone may be refreshed.

Jonathan Burnside, professor of biblical law at the University of Bristol, England, admits that much of Mosaic law seems like a mishmash of regulations about personal hygiene, diet, proper worship, and sexual ethics. Yet as a legal scholar, Burnside finds that the Torah offers profoundly helpful insights into justice by addressing care of the earth, property, welfare, criminal law, marriage and divorce, and sex.[34]

Take Exodus 21:33–34 as an example: "When a man opens a pit, or when a man digs a pit and does not cover it, and an ox or a donkey falls into it, the owner of the pit shall make restoration. He shall give money to its owner, and the dead beast shall be his." If you're a Bible reader, perhaps you've come across verses like this and wondered, *Why does God care about the digging of pits and oxen and donkeys?* But consider the profound legal principle at stake. If you, through negligence, do something to harm your neighbor's interests, you must set things right. This is "love your neighbor" applied to everyday life. In fact, a whole body of law, what we call "tort law," is based on it.

The idea that every person is valuable as an image bearer of God is central to our understanding of law. Often called the inherent-rights view, this soul-based perspective says that we have rights by virtue of being persons. We don't have to earn them. No human can give them, and no government should be able to take them away without the due process of law. America's founders summarized these rights as "life, liberty, and property." The founders were convinced that government did not *grant* these rights but merely *secured* them.

The inherent-rights view is often thought to be an Enlightenment invention from the 1700s, but the Yale ethicist Nicholas Wolterstorff says that it goes back to the Mosaic law, which put "love your neighbor" into action. Merely having an orderly society is not enough. "Hitler's Germany was extraordinarily orderly; the trains ran on time. It was a profoundly wrong order, however," Wolterstorff observes.[35]

Jürgen Habermas is Europe's most prominent public intellectual, and an atheist. Yet he insists that the very ideas of equality, freedom, human rights, and democracy are "the direct legacy of the Judaic ethic of justice and the Christian ethic of love. . . . To this day, there is no alternative to it."[36]

What Habermas claims is not only for Western nations such as those in Europe and North America. After extensive study, the political scientist Robert D. Woodberry found that "conversionary Protestants" (i.e., missionaries) were "a crucial catalyst initiating the development and spread of religious liberty, mass education, mass printing, newspapers, voluntary organizations, and colonial reforms, thereby creating the conditions that made stable democracy more likely."[37]

Care for the Body

Gary B. Ferngren is a professor of history at Oregon State University who specializes in the relationship between science, ancient medicine, and religion. Ferngren argues that the concept of *imago Dei* is what led to the very idea that human bodies, souls included, have dignity. "It was to save the body that Christ took on flesh in the Incarnation," he writes. "Not only the soul, which in traditional pagan thought was eternal, but the composite of body and soul, which constituted man, was to be resurrected."[38]

The idea that human bodies as well as souls have value undergirded the development of medical charity, as we will see in the next chapter. In the time of Christianity's early development, nonbelievers thought that suffering should be alleviated only for the deserving. "Christianity, however, insisted that the love of God required the spontaneous manifestation of personal charity toward one's brothers: one could not claim to love God without loving his brother," says Ferngren.[39]

Christian thinking about the value of the body traces back to an early church father named Basil (330–79). Known by the moniker "Basil the Great" for his good works, Basil was raised in a wealthy and prestigious Christian family. In his forties, he founded his own monastery at Caesarea where both men and women offered help to sick people and a safe refuge for travelers. It came to be known as the Basileias, and it is often credited with being the earliest version of what we now know as the hospital.

Basil himself was interested in medicine and encouraged the men and women who served in the Basileias to study the diseases they encountered so they could treat them better in the future. Basil described their mission in a letter to the governor, writing, "We establish hospices for strangers, both those who are visiting on a journey and those who are in need of some care because of illness."[40]

Basil saw medical science as a gift from God, not something to be feared or rejected. He believed that all healing, whether miraculous or otherwise, comes from God. He once wrote, "God sometimes cures us . . . without visible means when he judges this mode of treatment beneficial to our souls; and again He wills that we use material remedies for our ills . . . to provide an example for the proper care of the soul."[41]

Preserving Human Value, Even in War

The intentional killing of human beings has been part of the human experience since one of Adam and Eve's sons, Cain, killed his brother Abel. When God asked Cain, "Where is your brother Abel?" Cain shot back, "Am I my brother's keeper?" God replied, "What have you done? Listen! Your brother's blood cries out to me from the ground" (Gen. 4:9–10 NIV). Dennis Prager points out that the Hebrew text says "bloods," not "blood." The Talmud interpreted "bloods" as referring not just to Abel's blood but to the blood of all his potential descendants who would never be born.[42] The killing of a person destroys not only that person but also the potential of that person's offspring.

71

Today's debate, though, is whether all human lives are worth living.[43] Communist and Nazi leaders in the twentieth century believed they could end the lives of others based on their ancestry, physical infirmities, or insufficiently "pure" thinking. Shockingly, many American scholars at the time of Hitler's rise agreed philosophically with the Nazis' eugenics program. Prominent foundations such as the Rockefeller Foundation and the Carnegie Foundation funded eugenics research. Of course, once they saw how the Nazis had used their research to justify exterminating large groups of people, they were horrified. But it was too late. Ideas have consequences. Abortion, euthanasia, and selected procreation (terminating pregnancies based on the sex of the child or its likelihood of physical disabilities) are among them.

Aquinas, based on his understanding of the soul, inevitably encountered the question of human killing. War was an ever-present reality in the Late Middle Ages. Mongol conquests, the wars between Scotland and England, the Hundred Years' War between France and England (which actually lasted 116 years), and the conquest of Eurasia by the Timurid Empire killed millions, perhaps tens of millions.

Sadly, humanity's story is one of nearly constant warfare. Historians Will and Ariel Durant reveal that in the three and a half thousand years of recorded history, only 268 years saw no war.[44]

But is war ever justified, given the inherent value of human life? Aquinas said it depended on several specific factors, which we will examine in more detail in a later chapter:

- War must be declared by a legitimate authority. The ruler "does not bear the sword in vain" (Rom. 13:4). Only sovereign nations may declare war; individuals must not.
- War must have a just cause—to right a wrong, to punish those who refuse to right wrongs they have brought about, or to restore what has been unjustly seized.

- War must have a right intent, which is to advance good or oppose evil. A desire to inflict harm or a cruel thirst for vengeance cannot justify war.[45]

Aquinas's thinking established a "just war" tradition that civilized nations follow and continue to refine to this day.[46] It was a Christian invention, based on a biblical belief in the inherent value of human life. Military historian Kelly DeVries points out that the just war tradition has affected everything about war, including the development of armor, fortifications to limit civilian casualties, and deployment of military surgeons to tend to wounded warriors.[47]

What Should We Do Now?

If humans indeed have souls, what difference should it make to how we live? Here are three actions we can take based on the biblical understanding of the soul:

1. *Act as if every human possesses inherent value.* Core to the Bible's teaching is that God reveals himself to us. Theologian P. J. Leithart puts it this way: "Every time you see a human being, every time you see *anything*, you're encountering a revelation of God."[48] The Jesus followers we met in this chapter responded to God's mercy by being merciful. They responded to his love by being loving. "We love because he first loved us," wrote the apostle John (1 John 4:19). Further, as Jesus taught in the parable of the good Samaritan, this love is not limited to family or tribe or class. Jesus taught his followers to love their enemies, expecting nothing in return (Luke 6:27–38).

2. *Live as if every human being has purpose.* The philosopher Richard Swinburne notes that all mammals seem

to have sensations, thoughts, desires, and even beliefs. But humans additionally have purposes, things that we intentionally, consciously do.[49] We don't just live in the world; we make the world. Our work matters, not just for our survival but for the thriving of those around us. It is part of our calling as human beings.

3. *Promote the kind of community that recognizes the* imago Dei. Everyone—even nonbelievers—benefits from recognizing the value of each soul. The nineteenth-century poet James Russell Lowell put it this way:

> I challenge any skeptic to find a ten-square-mile spot on this planet where they can live their lives in peace and safety and decency, where womanhood is honored, where infancy and old age are revered, where they can educate their children, where the Gospel of Jesus Christ has not gone first to prepare the way. If they find such a place, then I would encourage them to emigrate thither and there proclaim their unbelief.[50]

A biblical view of human value promotes cultivation of the soul, care for the body, and a tradition of rights, even under the unbearable reality of war. Thomas Aquinas and Catherine of Siena are examples of Jesus followers who cultivated this understanding. Aquinas led by thinking. Catherine led by doing. Both occupy a vital place in history. They illustrate how the biblical teaching on the soul makes life worth living for all of us.

In later chapters, we'll expand on what the *imago Dei* might look like in community by exploring politics and justice. In the next chapter, we'll dive into the way influential individuals committed to Jesus as the Truth have made an enduring contribution to the care of those who are ailing.

How Jesus Followers
Have Changed How
We Care for One Another

Carrie was at the end of her rope. Her first husband having died of alcoholism, she berated elected officials for failing to promote public sobriety. In her book, she records her prayer: "Oh Lord . . . they are going to break the mothers' hearts, they are going to send the boys to drunkards' graves and a drunkard's hell. I have exhausted my means, Oh Lord, you have plenty of ways . . . please show me something to do."[1]

Carrie's actions are now the stuff of legend. She picked up a hatchet and marched into bars, singing and praying while smashing barrels of liquor. These "hatchetations," as she called them, earned her more than thirty arrests, the fines for which she paid through the sale of souvenir hatchets. Excess proceeds went to form a home for women and children plagued by alcoholic husbands, a forerunner of today's women's shelters.

Few people today think well of the antics of Carrie Nation (1846–1911). People in her own time thought poorly of them as well. Saloons across the nation brandished posters saying, "All nations welcome, except Carrie." Her efforts led to a national ban on alcohol sales, which is widely considered to have been a disaster during the thirteen years that it was in the Constitution.

But at the time, America was seriously drunk. In the 1800s, the average American drank five gallons of liquor every year, mostly whiskey and rum. Assuming that some people didn't drink at all, and that women and children drank less than men, this means the typical man in America was likely drinking enough to be drunk *every single day*. Historian Ronald D. Utt notes that more alcohol was drunk in the 1800s, even by children, than ever before or since. It was slowly killing the country. In the 1800s, for those who survived to age ten, life expectancy had dropped from fifty-seven to forty-eight years.[2]

Concerned wives and mothers could do very little to address the drunkenness. For the first century after America's founding, married women didn't have the right to own property. They couldn't vote. If their husbands were irresponsible, women could do little to improve their situation and protect their children. Carrie's extreme actions, as well as the efforts of those who agitated for women's right to vote, must be seen in this light. They believed that their families and ultimately America itself would fail unless at least some of the people at the polls were sober.

Public health and medicine are a significant legacy of Jesus followers who embraced Truth. In this chapter, we'll look at how the biblical principles they advocated led to advances in charity, modern medicine, the valuing of people, and societal and mental well-being.

Why Be Good?

"Why be good?" is a question that makes or breaks civilizations. In my days as a professor, I asked the question of many students. Their answers were revealing and often funny: "Because God says," "Because I want to stay out of jail," or "Because my mom would kick my butt across the state line if I did something stupid." Most students responded simply, "Because life will go better that way."

Staying out of trouble and wanting to have a good life are not bad motivations, but they are rooted mostly in self-interest. I do what *I* think is good because it will go better for *me*. It's a common way to approach life for those who believe in truths rather than Truth.

The German philosopher Friedrich Nietzsche (1844–1900) was the king of self-interest. "The best is lacking when self-interest begins to be lacking," he said.[3] But what about those who, because of poverty or sickness or addiction, can't or won't secure their own self-interest? Nietzsche pled with doctors to "demand that degenerate life be ruthlessly pushed down and thrown aside—the right to procreate, for instance, the right to be born, the right to live."[4]

Opposite of Nietzsche's rantings is the way of Jesus. Love, don't hate. Give, don't take. Create, don't destroy. Hope, don't fear. Build up, don't tear down. "The way of Jesus Christ was to give witness to the truth," said theologian Rocco Buttiglione, "not through the blood of the offenders or the sinners, but through his own."[5]

Throughout the centuries, Jesus followers transformed our understanding not only of what it means to be a human person but also of how we ought to care for one another. They saw self-sacrifice as a joyous response to God's expression of his mercy, a way to organize things on earth to look the way they look in God's kingdom. Jesus said, "Let your light shine before others, so that they may see your good works and give glory to your Father who is in heaven" (Matt. 5:16).

This "You first, not me first" kind of life has been a profound gift to the world. Let's look at how it has advanced acts of compassion.

How Jesus Followers Advanced Charity

At the birth of Christianity, the powerful Roman Empire demonstrated little caring for everyday people. History professor Gary B. Ferngren remarks, "In a world of gods not renowned for their compassion, Roman culture simply did not encourage a felt responsibility to assist the destitute, sick, or dying. Individuals were expected to care for their own health in any way they could."[6] Women, children, and slaves were viewed as lower in value than property-owning males. Female infants or infants with defects were abandoned and left to die.

In fact, a common view in the Roman Empire was that mercy and pity were defects of character. Rational people were encouraged to "curb the impulse" to be charitable and leave cries for help unanswered, says the historian Rodney Stark.[7] The satirist Lucian mocked Christians for their self-sacrifice, calling them "deluded creatures" who were easily taken advantage of.[8] Julian the Apostate complained, "These impious Galileans [i.e., Christians] feed not only their own poor, but ours as well, while no one in need looks to temples."[9]

Why would early Christians risk societal shaming and their own well-being to care for others? Because they were convinced that Jesus had commanded them to love their neighbors (Mark 12:31) and care for the sick (Matt. 25:34–40). If Jesus told them to do it, then he would watch over them in the process. If they died, Jesus would take care of them in the life to come (John 14:1–3). Not fearing death, they were free to live.

When a plague hit the north African city of Carthage in AD 251, the Roman governing authorities did nothing to stop the spread, treat the sick, or bury the dead. Instead, they offered sacrifices to their gods. Persecution broke out against Christians, who were blamed for the crisis. The bishop of Carthage, Cyprian (c. 200–258), encouraged Christians to love their enemies and extend help to those who persecuted them. Ferngren writes, "He urged the rich to donate funds and the poor to volunteer their service for relief efforts, making no distinction between believers and pagans. Under Cyprian's direction, Christians buried the dead left in the streets and cared for the sick and dying. For five years he stood in the breach, organizing relief efforts, until he was forced into exile."[10]

The Christian charitable impulse accelerated in the wake of the Black Death in the Late Middle Ages. Historian Yaron Ayalon says that Europeans, based on a biblical worldview, responded to the Black Death by working to contain and prevent the spread of the disease, developing public sanitation, and helping the poor. History does not show a similar thing happening in the Middle East, where Islam was the dominant worldview. Why not? Muslims also believe in God. Muslims are commanded to give to charity. Muslims understand, as Christians do, that disobeying God can place us under his judgment. So why the radical departure between Christian and Islamic societies?

Ayalon says that the difference is probably due to the church. For Christians, the church encompassed every area of life from birth to death, had its own political system and courts, and developed an efficient system for collecting charitable gifts and distributing them to those in need.[11] When secular political systems found themselves in disarray, the church stepped up until they could regain their footing.

In the last chapter, we talked about the soul. This chapter is about the body. In Christian theology, both are important. Humans have ensouled bodies. How a society honors both body and soul is a sure sign of its nobility. This respect for the body grounded works of charity, but it also led to the development of care for physical ailments.

How Jesus Followers Advanced the Study of Medicine

The author Wendell Berry writes, "The grace that is the health of creatures can only be held in common. In healing the scattered members come together. In health the flesh is graced, the holy enters the world."[12]

While Christians have a long history of caring for the sick, going back to the time of Jesus and the early centuries after Christ through Cyprian and Basil the Great, the development of modern medicine largely arose out of the Christian response to the Black Death.[13]

As we will see shortly, much of what passed for medical science prior to the Black Death relied on medical writings from shortly after the time of Jesus's ministry. Today, we can't imagine relying on thousand-year-old medical advice, but until the Late Middle Ages, people largely believed that their troubles were caused by external forces over which they had no control. The belief in fate made innovation nearly impossible, even for well-educated people. For example, the medical faculty at the University of Paris was asked by the King of France what caused the plague. Ayalon says that they blamed "a triple conjunction of Saturn, Jupiter, and Mars in the fortieth degree of Aquarius, which had occurred on March 20, 1345."[14]

Yet while many passively blamed fate, religious organizations began cultivating a more practical response, mainly by forming hospitals to care for the sick. Church leaders developed both the theology and the practice of medical care, while parishioners funded the work. Adam Davis, a historian of medieval Europe, writes:

> This new concern with the plight of the sick and poor shows up consistently in the testaments (wills) of the period. Among thirteenth-century testaments in Flanders, 85 percent included

charitable bequests to aid lepers, hospitals, widows, and the ransoming of captives. Forty-four percent included a bequest to at least one hospital. Similarly, in east-central France, two-thirds of all wills from c. 1300 included distributions of coin and/or food to the poor.[15]

Why did Christians care so much about serving the poor and sick? Quite simply, charitable acts were a way to imitate Jesus. At other times in history, Christians venerated those who devoted their lives to contemplation. In the Late Middle Ages, many more saints were canonized who had devoted themselves to hospital work.[16]

Medical care was largely accomplished through monasteries of the Catholic Church, but as the Reformation grew in influence, dissenting groups such as the Moravian Brethren and Pietists at Halle responded in a similar way. Today, hospitals founded by Catholics, Methodists, Baptists, and other Christian denominations continue the tradition of medical care. In America, about one in five people who are hospitalized receive care in institutions founded by Christians.[17]

Such caring often came at an extraordinary cost. During the Black Death between 1348 and 1351, the mortality rate among the clergy was far higher than that of the general population because they risked their lives to care for the sick.

Christians influenced the government's response to the Black Death as well. They encouraged sanitation and held public funerals to honor the dead. The idea of the quarantine—the practice of isolating the sick for forty days—also had a spiritual origin, based on the forty-day tradition of Lenten fasting. The number forty is highly significant in the Bible. Noah is said to have endured forty days and forty nights of rain while sheltered in the ark. The children of Israel wandered in the wilderness for forty years. Moses and Elijah fasted for forty days. Jesus endured forty days of fasting and temptation in the wilderness.

Not only did Christian caregivers help overcome a fatalistic attitude about suffering, they also overcame a persistent misunderstanding of the human body. For much of history, people had turned for medical advice to the works of Aelius Galenus, better known as Galen (129–?), a second-century doctor whose prolific writings—more than twenty thousand pages of his writings survive—guided medical thinking for more than a thousand years.

Galen taught that the cause of disease was an imbalance in four bodily fluids: blood, phlegm, black bile, and yellow bile. This idea exerted tremendous influence in medicine up until the 1800s and persists today in personality tests of the four temperaments—sanguine, phlegmatic, melancholic, and choleric.

The Flemish Christian doctor Andreas Vesalius (1514–64) carefully studied Galen's works. He admired them. But the more he studied the human body, the more he sensed that things did not add up. Vesalius decided to dissect dead bodies to create detailed drawings of nerves, veins, and muscles.

The English Christian doctor William Harvey (1578–1657) carried on Vesalius's work. Drawing on Leviticus 17:11, where Moses says, "The life of the flesh is in the blood," Harvey cultivated the study of human anatomy. Harvey wrote, "The examination of the bodies of animals has always been my delight; and I have thought that we might thence not only obtain an insight into the lighter mysteries of Nature, but there perceive a kind of image or reflex of the omnipotent Creator himself."[18]

Shortly before his death, Harvey told a young chemist named Robert Boyle, whom we will meet in the chapter on science, that "so Provident a Cause as Nature had not so Plac'd so many Valves without design."[19]

Despite the Christian convictions of men such as Vesalius and Harvey, a persistent myth has arisen that on the whole Christianity thwarted, rather than advanced, medical research. The Khan Academy page on dissection states, "Even though the Catholic Church prohibited dissection, artists and scientists performed dissection to better understand the body."[20]

The idea that Christianity hampered the development of modern medicine seems to have arisen through the work of a nineteenth-century historian named Andrew J. White, who framed the Middle Ages as the enlightening triumph of science over against the darkening superstition of religion. White asserted that decrees issued by Pope Alexander III in the 1100s and Pope Boniface VIII in the 1300s banned the study of human anatomy through dissection of corpses, setting back medical progress by centuries.[21]

But is it true? Many leading scholars have their doubts. According to University of Delaware history professor Lawrence G. Duggan, the statement by Pope Alexander III that "the church abhors blood"—and thus the study of the body is taboo—is a "literary ghost," "not to be found either in the text of the Council of Tours, 1163 AD (to which they all attribute it) or in any other Church Council."[22]

Perhaps the most extensive study of the issue was conducted by James J. Walsh (1865–1942), a priest and scholar with earned doctoral degrees in medicine, philosophy, and science. Walsh maintained that the supposed war between science and religion was based on a falsehood. Boniface VIII's *De Sepulturis* decree, which purportedly banned human dissection, was rather a statement giving direction for the preparing of corpses for burial. According to Walsh, it "has absolutely no reference to the cutting up of the human body for teaching purposes."[23]

The historical record bears out Walsh's conclusions.[24] But Walsh went further. Walsh found abundant evidence that leaders of the church, rather than discouraging the development of medicine, were "just as liberal and judicious patrons of science as they were of art and education in all forms."[25]

Many of those advancing medicine were women. When many university-trained doctors fled the Black Death in the 1300s, societies of women formed hospitals under the guidance of the Catholic Church. These women risked their lives to bring healing to others. One historian wrote of the sisters of the Hotel-Dieu hospital in Paris that "the sisters endured with cheerfulness and without repugnance the stench, the filth and the infections of the sick, so insupportable to others that no other form of penitence could be compared to this species of martyrdom."[26]

Kate Campbell Hurd-Mead, an obstetrician and women's rights activist, says that women legally practiced medicine throughout the fourteenth century all across Europe.[27] Harvard professor Katharine Park notes, "Anything having to do with medicine, health care, the human body—women are at the center. We're going to have to rewrite a whole lot of pieces of history of early medicine."[28]

When you google "women's rights" today, images come up of marchers carrying signs and often wearing *Handmaid's Tale* uniforms or pink beanies shaped like vaginas. This caricature obscures the contributions made for women's rights by women who persisted in advancing medical care, often because of their faith.

Sadly, there are many recorded instances of historic trials in which women practicing medicine, especially of a homemade or naturalistic variety, were accused of witchcraft. William Harvey, the English doctor who advanced our understanding of human anatomy, was one who helped defend women against these charges. In a 1634 trial of four women accused of witchcraft, Harvey brought scientific evidence to bear to show that the charges of witchcraft were false and secured their release.[29]

How Jesus Followers Advanced Societal and Mental Well-Being

The biblical ideal for society is captured in the Hebrew word *shalom*, which is used over two hundred times in the Bible. It is variously translated as "peace," "welfare," "security," "contentment," "sound health," "prosperity," and "friendship." To wish a person shalom is to wish that person's restoration to a state of wholeness in relationship with God, others, and creation.[30]

The loss of shalom is a tragedy, as many secular studies have now shown. Harvard professor Robert Putnam, for example, demonstrates that the erosion of what he calls "social capital" leads to a loss of wisdom, companionship, and the passing of inspirational values to the younger generation.[31]

Dire consequences follow the erosion of social capital. Nearly one in ten Americans ages twelve or older has a substance use disorder involving alcohol or illicit drugs.[32] The problem worsens in times of great loneliness, such as occurred during 2020's COVID-19 lockdowns.[33] Not only is substance abuse on the rise, but so are mental health concerns such as anxiety, depression, and thoughts of suicide.[34]

Addiction also has spiritual implications as people try to escape the pain of their lives. Addiction specialist William L. White says that "addiction becomes one's religion, drugs become one's God, and rituals of use become one's rites of worship."[35] In a study of the faith of twentysomethings, sociologist Jeremy Uecker found that although young people can (and do) return to faith from just about every circumstance, drug and alcohol addiction is one behavior that more often leads to a lifetime of diminished religiosity.[36]

For much of the twentieth century, the secular rejection of the soul led to harsh addiction treaments, such as electric shock therapy, accelerated drug use (Sigmund Freud famously advocated the use of cocaine to fight alcoholism), and behaviorist tactics such as mind control, social shaming, and incarceration. These strategies failed to treat people with dignity and bring about lasting change. In recent years, secular therapists have abandoned these approaches and embraced something more like a biblical approach, though generations of families have meanwhile experienced long-term harm.

The biblical approach to addiction and mental health begins with the assumption that every person has dignity as an image bearer of God. It approaches addiction with humility, not contempt. We are "wounded healers," as the modern-day Christian mystic Henri J. M. Nouwen put it.[37] Just as Jesus sympathizes with us in our weakness, we can sympathize with those who suffer (Heb. 4:15). This is even true—perhaps especially so—when those wounds are partly self-inflicted.

The tradition of treating addiction as a disease goes back at least as far as the American founder and medical doctor Benjamin Rush (1746–1813)—a committed Christian. In the early 1900s, the church-based Emmanuel Clinic led to the founding of Alcoholics Anonymous, which has helped tens of millions of people overcome addiction to alcohol and other drugs.[38] Brian J. Grim from the Pew Research Center and Melissa E. Grim from the Religious Freedom and Business Foundation found that 73 percent of addiction treatment programs in America have a spirituality-based element. They are largely run by volunteers from 130,000 religious congregations.[39]

The Impact of Christian Caring

Christian caring has literally changed the world. In America, more than seventy million people are helped by services offered in Jesus's name. As I mentioned in chapter 3, in economic terms, the financial value is worth $2.67 trillion per year.[40]

Around the world, the change is even more striking. Many secularists condemn missionaries for imposing their values on others. But, like other aspects of history, the true story is much more nuanced. Medical care has always been a significant part of missionary endeavors—again, often led by women. The Methodist missionary Gertrude Howe (1847–1928), for example, arranged for Chinese women to receive medical training in the United States. Of these, doctors such as Kang Chiang (known as Ida Kahn, 1873–1931) and Shi Meiyu (known as Mary Stone, 1873–1954) not only cared for the sick but also fought for women's rights in China.[41]

Today, health-care initiatives spearheaded by Christians have had an astounding result. While governments give aid to secure loyal allies, religious groups give aid out of compassion. The following eye-opening statistics come from the Philanthropy Roundtable:

- US voluntary giving to the overseas poor now totals $44 billion annually (the US government distributes $33 billion).
- Religious Americans adopt children at two and a half times the overall national rate.
- Local church congregations provide most of the day-to-day help that resettles refugees and asylum seekers arriving in the US.
- The bulk of volunteers mentoring prisoners and their families are Christians.[42]

The world faces many serious problems, but we can be thankful for the fruit of these efforts. I mentioned some of these statistics in chapter 3, but the evidence is worth reviewing here. According to researcher Scott Todd, extreme poverty has dropped by half just in the last generation, from 52 percent of the world's population to 26 percent.[43] One billion more people have access to improved water supplies since 1990.[44] Infectious disease rates are at all-time lows. Many of the efforts securing these advances are now carried on by secular governments and nongovernmental organizations. If you trace their histories, though, you'll see biblical influence and reasoning at every step.

What Should We Do Now?

Even if we are not medical professionals, there are many lessons we can learn from the stories and evidence presented in this chapter. We should do the following:

1. *Cultivate an attitude of gratitude rather than of self-interest.* Messiah University professor Michael Zigarelli says that gratitude is a "parent virtue"—from which other character qualities spring.[45] A multitude of studies show that grateful people are happier and more well-adjusted. Gratefulness is even related to physical health and hope for the future.[46]

2. *Pay it forward.* Good works are contagious. James Fowler from the University of California at San Diego and Nicholas Christakis from Harvard tested the "pay it forward" model of charity and found that it led to a domino effect of kindness and cooperation. Once you've experienced it, Fowler says, "You don't go back to being your 'old selfish self.'"[47] The secret to such generosity is not a sense of self-fulfillment but an ability to put oneself in the place of the recipient and have a spirit of gratitude for the ability to give.

3. *Embrace mutual brokenness.* True caring arises not out of pity for "those people" but by recognizing that we are all afflicted with spiritual poverty.[48] As the psalmist wrote, "The sacrifices of God are a broken spirit; a broken and contrite heart, O God, you will not despise" (Ps. 51:17). Early Christians established a tradition of fasting to save money to give to the destitute.[49] Isaiah 58:6 says, "Is not this the fast that I choose: to loose the bonds of wickedness, to undo the straps of the yoke, to let the oppressed go free, and to break every yoke?"

4. *Celebrate healing.* The Puritan author Richard Baxter (1615–91) said, "In this country and time, I must confess that I have known as many physicians to be Christians, as, proportionately, in any other profession, except preachers of the gospel."[50] Many people who despise pastors will listen to a physician, he said. Training to be a healer is a godly calling.

Jesus *is* the Truth. This is what Jesus followers who led the development of medical science from the time of Basil believed, and it changed forever how we care for one another. This same principle changed the world in other ways as well. In the next chapter, we'll look at some of the innovations in the field of education—how we learn and grow.

How Jesus Followers Have Changed How We Learn and Grow

The teacher's success was modest, at best. His "college" consisted of one building where just 478 students studied during his twenty-six-year career. One biographer of the teacher said, "Neither was he an intellectual giant or a particularly consistent thinker."[1]

Yet the teacher kindled in his students a deep excitement about liberty, which he believed was best pursued by one "who is most sincere and active in promoting true and undefiled religion."[2] True religion, he believed, would overcome many disadvantages: "We see that a man truly pious, has often esteem, influence and success, though his parts may be much inferior to others, who are more capable, but less conscientious."[3]

The teacher's passion impressed his students. One of them, who later took his place as head of his school, said that the teacher had *presence* in greater quantity than anyone he had ever met except George Washington.[4]

The teacher's name was John Witherspoon (1723–94). The school he led, now called Princeton University, is often rated as America's top institution of higher education. Witherspoon's building, Nassau Hall, has been beautifully restored and houses Princeton University's administrative offices.

But it is not Princeton University's fame that secures Witherspoon's influence. It is his students. Of the 478 young men he taught, 114 became ministers, 49 became US representatives, 28 became US senators, 26 became state judges, 17 became members of their state constitutional conventions, 14 became delegates to the state conventions that ratified the Constitution, 12 became members of the Continental Congress, 8 became US district judges, 5 became delegates to the Constitutional Convention, 3 became US Supreme Court justices, 3 became attorneys general, 2 became foreign ministers, and 1 became vice president. Witherspoon's most famous student was James Madison, who became the father of the Constitution and president of the United States.[5]

Witherspoon was a flawed man. His reputation has recently been tarnished by the revelation that he owned two slaves and supported a policy of gradualism rather than immediate abolition of slavery in the colonies (though he personally taught African American students and welcomed them into his congregation, a move that was highly controversial at the time). Yet there is perhaps no other educator who had a greater personal influence on America's founding. His students made America a land of freedom, even for people who scorn the biblical worldview for which he stood.

Our word *education* comes from the Latin word *educare*—the root word being *duce*, meaning "to lead into." Good educators lead students out of ignorance and toward Truth. By doing this, they offer hope for the future.

Yet today, education is under attack. Often its attackers are educators themselves, who forsake Truth for a politicized form of indoctrination. This happens in the way students are taught history, social studies, and sex education, as documented by the liberal cultural writer Helen Pluckrose and mathematician (and atheist) James Lindsay in their book *Cynical Theories*.[6] It also extends to science and math. In 1972, the postmodernist anthropologist Melville Herskovits wrote, "Even the facts of the physical world are discerned through the enculturative screen, so that the perception of time, distance, weight, size, and other 'realities' is mediated by the conventions of any group."[7]

Read that quotation again. Even "the facts of the physical world"? "Doesn't two plus two equal four, no matter how you feel about it?" you might ask. While that particular mathematical formula is not being questioned, to my knowledge, curricula such as that provided by the Oregon Department of Education's "Pathway to Math Equity Micro-Course" does politicize mathematics by encouraging teachers to spot "the ways that math is used to uphold capitalist, imperialist, and racist views."[8] According to such educators, there is too great a focus on "getting the 'right' answer."

Certainly, I hope the next generation will be wise, just, kind, and cooperative. But when children are encouraged to view historical, scientific, and mathematical facts as cultural artifacts that may be embraced or disregarded without consequence, we have crossed a line. Facts matter because reality matters. If you are going to fly an airplane from New York to London, you ought to carry enough fuel for a thirty-five-hundred-mile journey—even if you wish it were half that distance or grew up believing that the continents touch. A good education teaches us to deal with things as they are, even as we imagine how our lives might be changed for the better.

Christians who believed that the Truth was found in Jesus changed the world of education, transforming how we learn and grow. Again, they did not believe they knew the Truth *exhaustively*. But they did believe they could know it *truly*. As a result, they changed history and offered us clues as to how we might reclaim educational excellence in our own time.

The Biblical Foundation for Education

The Bible elevates learning as a primary value. We learn about the past to become wise in the present and equipped for the future. Moses wrote, "Remember the days of old; consider the generations long past. Ask your father and he will tell you, your elders, and they will explain to you" (Deut. 32:7 NIV). The late Rabbi Jonathan Sacks wrote, "[Moses] knew that if you plan for a year, plant rice. If you plan for a decade, plant a tree. If you plan for posterity, educate a child."[9]

The Old Testament vision for education comes full circle in the New Testament. "Jesus is the Truth" is a claim involving both the mind and the soul. It involves both memory and action. St. Augustine thought that the point of education was to "gather our whole soul somehow to that which we attain by the mind."[10] Jesus said, "If you abide in my word, you are truly my disciples, and you will *know* the truth, and the truth will set you free" (John 8:31–32, emphasis added). The Greek word for "truth" here is *alétheia*, which means "reality." We know reality through Jesus. This sets us free to live a different kind of life.

Learning is more than just gathering facts. True learners grow in their ability to dialogue, reason, and point others to the Truth. Learning is a way of loving our neighbor.

Any good education will inform students about virtues such as justice and moderation. A biblical education goes beyond this to root knowledge in faith, hope, and charity, which G. K. Chesterton calls "unreasonable" virtues, because they are of divine origin. We don't arrive at them by merely submitting to biological imperatives such as survival and reproduction. Chesterton says, "Charity means pardoning what is unpardonable, or it is no virtue at all. Hope means hoping when things are hopeless, or it is no virtue at all. And faith means believing the incredible, or it is no virtue at all."[11]

What we think of as education today flowered in the Late Middle Ages. It accelerated in the wake of the Black Death through the cry of *Ad Fontes* ("back to the fountain") as educators refocused on Christ's presence and suffering. Historian Tom Holland, a longtime skeptic who finds himself increasingly drawn to Christianity, beautifully explains how and why:

> It is the audacity of it—the audacity of finding in a twisted and defeated corpse the glory of the creator of the universe—that serves to explain, more surely than anything else, the sheer strangeness of Christianity, and of the civilization to which it gave birth. Today, the power of this strangeness remains as alive as it has ever been. It is manifest in the great surge of conversions that has swept Africa and Asia over the past century; in the conviction of millions upon millions that the breath of the Spirit, like a living fire, still blows upon the world; and, in Europe and North America, in the assumptions of many more millions who would never think to describe themselves as Christian. All are heirs to the same revolution: a revolution that has, at its molten heart, the image of a god dead on a cross.[12]

God

"God with us" changed everything, and it continues to do so today, even for those who deny Jesus ever existed.

Yet dangers still face us. Colossians 2:8 warns, "See to it that no one takes you captive by philosophy and empty deceit." We must be alert to erroneous views.[13] In a world of counterfeits, a fully formed education offers wisdom to discern what is genuine.

Humans Are Designed to Learn and Grow

From birth, humans are hardwired to learn and grow. Researchers have shown that babies vocalize to mimic human speech.[14] They imitate the "turn-taking" of conversation. They react to the quality of feelings expressed in the voice and can discern emotions and match them to facial expressions. Most infants desire communication so strongly that they are more interested in the sound of adult voices than in any other sound, including instrumental music.[15]

Long before formal schooling begins, children learn and grow through their parents' influence. Mothers naturally adjust their speech in a way that facilitates an infant's language growth.[16] This "motherese" involves shorter sentences, more common nouns, a high pitch with exaggerated vocal contours, and long pauses between sentences.[17] Fathers tend to communicate with children differently than mothers, but their role is no less important. Research shows that communication with fathers helps bridge children to the outside world.[18]

When children are old enough, parents turn their attention to schooling. Remember, though, that *schooling* and *education* are different things. Schooling helps us gain credentials so we can get a job. Education, on the other hand, helps us gain wisdom to see the meaning in all we do. It promotes what psychologist Mihaly Csikszentmihalyi calls "flow," a sense of well-being and competence in our activities. According to Csikszentmihalyi, the greatest flow comes when we are working hard at things we find fascinating. The lowest sense of flow is when we are at leisure, doing things like watching television.[19] We aren't meant to be passive observers. We are meant to be lifelong learners. Studies of older adults show that those who keep learning experience a greater sense of well-being, autonomy, and fulfillment.[20]

People can get a good education regardless of their religious beliefs, but a biblical worldview promotes lifelong learning for all its adherents—something we see even in the way places of worship are designed.

Christian Architecture and Learning

Jesus followers, focused on the incarnation, built a form of worship that used liturgy, music, prayers, and even architectural features to promote learning.

As far back as fifteen hundred years ago, it was common practice to build churches in the shape of a cross when viewed from the air. Of course, no one at the time could see them from there. Rather, congregants were *in* the cross, with the service being led from where Jesus's head would have been on the original cross. This placed the congregants where Jesus's body would have been hanging, as a reminder that we are "the body of Christ and individually members of it" (1 Cor. 12:27). Congregants entered and exited at the foot of the cross, enacting Isaiah's prophecy, "How beautiful upon the mountains are the feet of him who brings good news, who publishes peace, who brings good news of happiness, who publishes salvation, who says to Zion, 'Your God reigns'" (Isa. 52:7).

Even the geographical positioning of church buildings— facing east—reminds us that the rising sun ought to turn our attention to the risen Son. Many architectural breakthroughs came from efforts to raise the ceiling as high as possible so that the eyes of the congregants would be drawn upward. As Pope Benedict XVI explained, "The upward thrust was intended as an invitation to prayer and at the same time was itself a prayer."[21] Everything about the church helped worshipers learn about God through Christ.

Orthodox churches are built somewhat differently but still incorporate deep symbolism. As far back as the 400s, Orthodox churches featured a dome with Christ Pantocrator (Christ the Almighty) at the top, with angels below, and in descending order the prophets, apostles, and saints. Worshipers stand during the service in the company of this mighty host, reenacting the gospel of Christ, "in whom are hidden all the treasures of wisdom and knowledge" (Col. 2:3).

In the Late Middle Ages, after the Black Death, church architecture shifted, taking on a more personal significance through a perpendicular style (with walls going straight up rather than arching inward). Some speculate that this was to save money or because so many engineers and artisans had died that no one remembered how to build the old way. But there is another possible explanation: light. The perpendicular style allowed larger windows, bringing in God's light, while previous windows were smaller and more decorative. In places such as King's College Chapel, Cambridge, these enormous windows are embellished with gorgeous stained glass, telling the story of Jesus, interspersed with Old Testament stories that foreshadowed aspects of Christ's ministry.

The powerful effect of this light speaks to the drama of teaching and learning. In cathedrals previously lit by candles, light fell mostly on the altar and the priest. With the perpendicular style, the congregation itself was bathed in light. The stained glass told the gospel story *to* congregants, but it also shined the light of the gospel *on* them, illuminating the assembled as they prepared to share Jesus's light, as he had instructed in Matthew 5:16: "Even so let your light shine before men; that they may see your good works, and glorify your Father who is in heaven" (ASV).

All of this was intentional, weaving together theology, geometry, astronomy, and physics. Robert Grosseteste, an early scientist, identified light as not only the first act of creation but also *how* God created. God is the Father of light. Christ is the first radiance of that light. This light is received not through priests but directly through Scripture. That's the doctrine of *sola Scriptura*, a Latin phrase implying that Scripture, not priests or the church hierarchy, is Truth's primary source. It was a cornerstone of Martin Luther's Reformation. By the way they shed light on the congregation, architects were, in a way, designing the Reformation a hundred years before Luther wrote about it.[22]

A biblical worldview generates structures and forms that promote learning. Yet the story of the biblical worldview goes even deeper, to the very tools of learning themselves.

How Jesus Followers Advanced Literacy

Humans differ from nonhuman animals in their ability to use speech. Using just a few sounds—forty-four of them in English ("ah," "oo," "ch," "th," etc.)—we can produce an infinite number of sentences.[23] This book is full of never-before-used sentences. So are your everyday conversations. Even though a language may include hundreds of thousands of words, mastery of just a thousand of them enables us to convey fine distinctions and shades of meaning that connect us to others, express clear thoughts, and improve our circumstances.[24]

Thought flowers in speech. That's why it is important to have a good vocabulary. As communication scholar Frank E. X. Dance puts it, "A picture is worth a thousand words only as long as there is available the thousand words with which to interpret the picture."[25]

In the Late Middle Ages, scholars expanded the reach of education by translating texts from Latin—the academic and theological language of Europe at that time—into the common languages of the day. Having the Bible and ancient sources in the common language helped people connect personally with their faith. It also grew them intellectually.

In England, John Wycliffe (ca. 1330–84) led this movement toward education for everyday people. An Oxford professor who risked persecution to translate the Bible into English, Wycliffe said, "The laity ought to understand the faith, and as the doctrines of our faith are in the Scriptures, believers should have the Scriptures in a language they fully understand."[26] Moses heard God's Word in his own language, Wycliffe reasoned. So did Jesus's disciples. Everyone ought to have that opportunity.

In the process, Wycliffe literally standardized the English language itself, much as Luther's writings later did for the German language. More than eleven hundred English words are recorded for the first time in the Wycliffe Bible, words such as *treasure, mystery, glory, horror, female, sex, childbearing, affliction, first fruits, grasp, problem, zealous, crime, conscious, communication,* and *persuasion.* Wycliffe even introduced the word *wordy.*[27]

Still today, much of the work of literacy revolves around the Bible and its teachings. Baylor University distinguished professor David Lyle Jeffrey notes that "literary culture in Europe, much of Africa and the Americas is inseparable from the culturally transformative power of Christianity."[28] Scholars have translated the Bible, or parts of it, into 3,415 languages. Most of these languages had never been written down until translators developed them to introduce the Bible. As a result, 5.7 billion people have access to the Bible in their native language.[29]

Literacy changed the world, but that was only a start. What good is knowledge if we don't use it to develop wisdom? The poet T. S. Eliot wrote the following in the introduction to a pageant play called *The Rock:*

> Where is the Life we have lost in living?
> Where is the wisdom we have lost in knowledge?
> Where is the knowledge we have lost in information?
> The cycles of Heaven in twenty centuries
> Bring us farther from GOD and nearer to the Dust.[30]

Dorothy L. Sayers, a friend of C. S. Lewis, gave a lecture called "The Lost Tools of Learning" at Oxford University in 1947. She said, "Although we often succeed in teaching our pupils 'subjects,' we fail lamentably on the whole in teaching them how to think: they learn everything, except the art of learning."[31]

Sayers recommended that educators return to the trivium, a classical method of instruction used in ancient Greece and revived in the Late Middle Ages. The trivium focuses on grammar (use of words), dialectic (logic), and rhetoric (graceful expression). Sayers's thoughts have been a driving force in the revival of classical education. Hundreds of schools and colleges, including public charter schools and homeschool courses, now use classical education with promising academic results.

How Jesus Followers Advanced Virtue in Education

When one of my graduate school professors advocated the truths viewpoint, I challenged him.

"According to this view, how do you justify giving grades?" I asked.

"What do you mean?"

"Well, if you give me an F, you are judging me for not conforming to a standard that I cannot know to exist. If you give me an A, you are judging me by patronizing me."

My question irritated him, something I later came to regret when he "rewarded" me with an extremely complicated question in my comprehensive exams, one that took nearly a week to answer.

The point I was making is that if Truth cannot be known, education is impossible. We must have a knowable standard by which we assess our ignorance and awaken the dormant powers of our minds. Without Truth, we can *school* people, but we cannot *educate* them.

Based on their Christian convictions, education pioneers in the Late Middle Ages formed dozens of universities, such as the University of Paris (1150) and Oxford University (1167). After the outbreak of the plague, they doubled down on the need for education and formed even more institutions to teach theology, philosophy, and science.[32]

Many today have been led to believe that the medieval world was hopelessly ignorant and cruel. As an example, consider this tongue-in-cheek exchange in Charles Dickens's novel *Dombey and Son*:

"Those darling byegone times, Mr. Carker," said Cleopatra, "with their delicious fortresses, and their dear old dungeons, and their delightful places of torture, and their romantic vengeances, and their picturesque assaults and sieges, and everything that makes life truly charming! How dreadfully we have degenerated!"

"Yes, we have fallen off deplorably," said Mr. Carker.[33]

Despite what we have been told, medieval education was both broad-minded and practical. C. S. Lewis said that medieval schoolboys learned "farriery, forestry, archery, hawking, sowing, ditching, thatching, brewing, baking, weaving, and practical astronomy." According to Lewis, "This concrete knowledge, mixed with their law, rhetoric, theology, and mythology, bred an outlook very different from our own."[34] Scholars call this approach to education the "medieval synthesis." Educators emphasized organizing, categorizing, and synthesizing past thinking.

It is impossible to overstate the impact the medieval synthesis has had on the world of education. In his book *Person of Interest*, J. Warner Wallace notes that the top fifteen universities in the world were all started by Christians, many with the express purpose of advancing the Christian religion. Christians have founded ten times as many universities as all other major religions combined.[35] One literally cannot explain the advance of education apart from its Christian roots and inspiration.

By the late 1880s, Christians had been so successful in forming educational institutions that 80 percent of the colleges in the United States were church related. Hundreds of these institutions still exist, training millions of students a year.

Christians also took care to expand educational opportunities for the less fortunate. At the outbreak of the Civil War, the Freedman's Aid Society started colleges for freed slaves. Many of these, such as Howard University, Berea College, and Fisk University, continue thriving to this day as what are often referred to as Historically Black Colleges and Universities (HBCU).

Gladys West (1930–) is one scholar who changed the world based on the training she received at a historically Black university. Her pioneering work in mathematics led to the development of the global positioning satellite system. A strong Christian, West says, "I don't ever remember a time where Jesus and His Church were not a part of my life."[36] She views mathematics as a language God has given to develop the mind and improve the world.

A biblical worldview directly confronts the truths viewpoint. It says that we *can* learn. We *ought* to learn. Learning together is better. Learning about lots of things and not just our narrow viewpoint is best. A good education involves asking hard questions and not just accepting what our professors say. And all of this is nested in a code of morality that comes from God himself.

Even Horace Mann (1796–1859), the founder of modern public education and one who did not consider himself to be an orthodox Christian, admitted in the early 1800s, "Our system earnestly inculcates all Christian morals; it founds its morals on the basis of religion; it welcomes the religion of the Bible."[37] The alternative is unthinkable, he believed, noting that "the whole frame and constitution of the human soul show, that if man be not a religious being, he is among the most deformed and monstrous of all possible existences."[38]

What Should We Do Now?

Christians ought to lead the world in educational innovation today, as they have done in the past. It is through academic engagement that we learn the shape and tempo of a world beyond our senses—a world of information, inspiration, and connection between God and people, between people, and between people and the physical world they inhabit. This immaterial, supernatural world provides a rich storehouse of transforming knowledge for those who will discipline themselves to access it.

So what should we do now? I recommend doing the following:

1. *Recommit to the search for Truth.* Seeing ourselves as the center of reality is the problem, not the solution. Scholars Richard Paul and Linda Elder put it this way: "People are by nature highly egocentric, highly sociocentric, and wantonly self-interested. Their goal is not truth but advantage. . . . Blind faith, fear, prejudice, and

self-interest are primary organizers of much human thinking."[39] We should humble ourselves, swallow our fear of not knowing the right answer, ask questions, and grow.

2. *See God in every subject.* "The world globes itself in a drop of dew," said Ralph Waldo Emerson. "God reappears with all his parts in every moss and cobweb."[40] Everything displays the glory of God. Every academic subject is relevant to him. Through algebra and calculus and geometry, we use the language of mathematics to account for the space and time dimensions God has given us in creation. Because of the Word, we find ourselves motivated to study words to sense their rhythm and to shape ideas. Through the study of history, we mark the unfolding of God's purposes. Music and the arts reveal the beauty of creation. The study of justice opens our hearts to virtue. Athletics prepare us to engage our spirits and our bodies to face the future with grace and courage. Truth grounds all areas of education.

3. *See Scripture knowledge as central to education.* It was common practice until the twentieth century to teach the Bible in schools. This changed through the influence of education theorist John Dewey (1859–1952), who saw Christianity as opposed to democracy.[41] Dewey wished for supernatural belief to be swept into the dustbin of history by the broom of the scientific method and saw himself as the one doing the sweeping. But times have changed. The possibility of a secular consensus about the meaning of life has collapsed just as fast as the education system's effectiveness. What do we have to lose by refamiliarizing ourselves with Scripture? As University of Chicago professor emeritus Leon

Kass says, "In these confused and dangerous times, with most Western nations struggling to articulate why they should exist at all, and with the human future in the balance, we can ill afford to neglect any possible sources of wisdom about human affairs."[42]

4. *Cultivate our souls through learning and growth*. The great need of our time is not to cherish our "selves" but to cultivate our souls. The truths viewpoint says that there is no chance of finding Truth, leading many to wonder why they should even seek it. Christians ought to lead the way in the search for Truth through speaking, writing, thinking, risking, experimenting, and playing. The search for Truth doesn't narrow our range of options; it expands it. It opens closed minds, releasing mental and spiritual energy into the world.

It is time for *Ad Fontes*. It is time to go back to the fountain. What Sayers called "the lost tools of learning" are available to us still, if we are willing to renew the search for Truth and bring the change our society so desperately needs.

Some may think that I am lifting up a biblical approach to education to turn back the clock and erase progress. But as we will see in the way Christians developed modern science, this is not the whole story. Not even close.

How Jesus Followers Have Changed the World of Science

Science takes things apart to see how they work. Religion puts things together to see what they mean," said the late Rabbi Jonathan Sacks.[1] Science and faith are often pitted against each other as rivals, as if science is based in rational fact and faith is something wholly "other." The work of early scientists who operated from a biblical worldview shows that science versus faith is a false dichotomy. As we will see, these scientific pioneers recognized a harmony between natural and spiritual exploration, one that changed the face of science.

Early scientists believed so deeply in this harmony that they often used a musical metaphor to describe their exploration. Perhaps you've heard the old hymn "This Is My Father's World," which includes this line: "All nature sings, and round me rings the *music of the spheres*."[2] Today, we might find the phrasing to be old-fashioned, but it powerfully expresses the way creation bursts with song, inviting us to join its chorus. A singing creation is a central theme in the development of science, one that highlights the difference between the Truth viewpoint and the truths viewpoint in science.

Three thousand years ago, King David wrote that the heavens *declare* the glory of God and *proclaim* his handiwork (Ps. 19:1). The universe lyrically assures us that we are not nakedly insignificant but rather clothed in God's glory. One well-known book illustration from the early 1300s pictures David gazing into the heavens, where Jesus—the Good Shepherd who in earthly form will descend from David's line—blesses his kingship.[3] The universe is not cold or distant. Rather, it is, in the words of C. S. Lewis, "a world lighted, warmed, and resonant with music."[4]

Sir Thomas Browne (1605–82), an English polymath who wrote on science, medicine, and religion, said, "For there is a musick where ever there is a harmony, order or proportion: and thus far we may maintain the music of the Sphears; for those well-ordered motions, and regular paces, though they give no sound unto the ear, yet to the understanding they strike a note most full of harmony."[5] Browne's description of musical harmony resonates with the Genesis account of creation. In Genesis 1:2, God "hovered" over an earth that was without form and void. The Hebrew word for "hovered" is *merakhfet* (pronounced something like muh-rah-khuh-fet, with a throat-clearing "kh" sound). This word occurs only in the Genesis account. Its root word, *rachaph* (raw-khaf), means "to brood," or "to move," or "to shake." Worship leader Dan McCollam pictures it as the vibrating of an instrument's strings. God vibrated—sang—over chaos, bringing it into order.[6]

In *The Magician's Nephew*, C. S. Lewis also describes creation as God's song as the young Digory Kirke and his companions witness the birth of Narnia:

> In the darkness something was happening at last. A voice had begun to sing. It was very far away and Digory found it hard to decide from what direction it was coming. Sometimes it

seemed to come from all directions at once. Sometimes he almost thought it was coming out of the earth beneath them. Its lower notes were deep enough to be the voice of the earth herself. There were no words. There was hardly even a tune. But it was beyond comparison, the most beautiful noise he had ever heard.[7]

That God sang the universe into existence is especially intriguing given the advent of "string theory" in physics. String theory says that the universe is made up of tiny vibrating strands of energy. It is a controversial theory with many detractors. Yet physicist Steven Weinberg (1933–2021) said, "Many of us are betting the most valuable thing we have, our time, that this theory is so beautiful that it will survive in the final underlying laws of physics."[8]

Music. Beauty. These do not seem like scientific concepts. But for medieval scientists operating from a biblical worldview, music and beauty gave them the "why" for the "what" of the science they were developing. Medieval works in theology, philosophy, and science—rooted firmly in the belief that Jesus is the Truth—expressed a conviction that the universe was filled with beauty. Exploring it, from its tiniest particles to its most distant stars, was, as Johannes Kepler (1571–1630) put it, to think God's thoughts after him.[9] Might the recovery of this musical metaphor cast the battle over science versus religion in a new light?

The Battle over Truth in Science

In the conflict over Truth, science ought to be a unifying force. Even those who deny that reality is knowable still occasionally spout slogans such as "Science is real!" when they find its conclusions acceptable to their worldview.

But even though the scientific method is a great way of developing knowledge, we err if we think that it is the only path to knowing reality. Science is never pure, insists Harvard history of science professor Steven Shapin in his book by that title, and it is produced—as his subtitle memorably phrases it—by *People with Bodies, Situated in Time, Space, Culture, and Society, and Struggling for Credibility and Authority.*

Scientific discovery is a human enterprise, and thus fallible. In 2011, researchers at Bayer looked at sixty-seven recent drug discovery projects and found that 75 percent could not be replicated in their in-house laboratories. Only 11 percent of preclinical cancer research reports studied by reviewers could be validated.[10]

The fragility of science does not mean we ought to ignore scientific studies. Rather, we ought to understand what science is and does, what its underlying assumptions are, and how to keep it from falling victim to the truths viewpoint. In this we may be guided by the fascinating stories of believers who gave us the gift of science in the first place.

The story of science is the story of religious devotion combined with a conscious reliance on principles that proceed naturally from a biblical worldview. Its rise began in the Late Middle Ages as people took their faith beyond the church doors and began exploring the world they heard described therein. Belief in God, not the rejection of him, set the tempo for the symphony of wonder they enjoyed.

Let's look at why Jesus followers committed to a biblical worldview have invented, transformed, and sustained science, and then why, historically, such exploration still fits more comfortably with a biblical view of the world than with its secular counterparts.

Science as One of God's Two Books

The word *science* comes from the Latin word *scientia*, or "knowledge." The National Academy of Sciences defines *science* as "the use of evidence to construct testable explanation and prediction of natural phenomena, as well as the knowledge generated through this process."[11] Observation, measurement, and repetition are commonsense rules of thumb that guide the scientific method.

Medieval theologian Hugh of St. Victor (1096–1141) said, "The whole of the sensible world is like a kind of book written by the finger of God."[12] In addition to the Bible, medieval scientists thought that God had given us a second book, the book of nature. The two are consistent with each other.

This "two books" analogy still guides many Christians in the sciences. James Tour, a leading nano-engineer, says, "I build molecules for a living. I can't begin to tell you how difficult that job is. I stand in awe of God because of what he has done through his creation. Only a rookie who knows nothing about science would say science takes away from faith. If you really study science, it will bring you closer to God."[13]

Francis Collins, former director of the National Institutes of Health and the scientist who headed up the Human Genome Project, a project arguably bigger and more complex than the Apollo program, which sent human beings to the moon, says, "Science is not threatened by God; it is enhanced. God is most certainly not threatened by science; He made it all possible."[14]

It is nearly impossible to overstate the historical impact of people who thought highly of God's creativity in nature. Christians holding to a biblical worldview have led the way in the practice of scientific thought in such fields as botany, microbiology, physiology, chemistry, taxonomy, paleontology, genetics, surgery, and dozens of others (see the endnote for a link to hundreds of such pioneers).[15]

Oxford mathematician John Lennox has claimed that over 65 percent of Nobel Prize laureates identified Christianity as their religious preference (another 20 percent were Jewish, which is striking because Jewish people account for only 0.02 percent of the world's population).[16] According to historian and sociologist Rodney Stark, of the fifty-two active scientists who made the most significant contributions during the Scientific Revolution, only one was an atheist.[17] Modern science did not rise in rebellion against God; it rose to applaud him.

Consider this short list of scientists for whom the Christian faith was central to their work:

Robert Grosseteste (1175–1253). Beginning in the twelfth century, scientists who believed in a divine Creator began systematizing their knowledge about the world. At Oxford University, Robert Grosseteste developed methods for observing and experimenting with nature. One of his students was Roger Bacon (1220–92), the famous thinker who further laid the foundation for the Scientific Revolution. Amusingly, the name Grosseteste comes from the German word *gross*, which means "large," and *teste*, which is related to the French word for "head." So yes, there literally was a Professor Fathead!

Nicolaus Copernicus (1473–1543) was a Christian who got into astronomy because he studied the Bible carefully and wanted to reliably determine the date of Easter. On the relationship of science to his faith, Copernicus said, "To know the mighty works of God, to comprehend His wisdom and majesty and power; to appreciate, in degree, the wonderful workings of His laws, surely all this must be a pleasing and acceptable mode of worship to the Most High."[18]

Sir Isaac Newton (1643–1727), unorthodox in many ways, saw himself as a Christian and wrote more about theology than he did about physics. Many think of Newton, one of the greatest figures in the history of science, as the culminating figure of the Scientific Revolution. He wrote in his great work *Principia Mathematica*, "This most beautiful system of the sun, planets and comets could only proceed from the counsel and domination of an intelligent and powerful Being." This

Being, Newton went on to specify, is not just the "soul of the world" but "Lord over all."[19]

Maria Sibylla Merian (1647–1717), the German-born naturalist, studied insects and beautifully illustrated them, making a significant contribution to entomology. Her book *Metamorphosis* became a model for scientific illustration. To Merian, the study of insects was a spiritual pursuit. As an example, she viewed the metamorphosis of caterpillars to butterflies as a picture of human salvation. Perhaps this sheds light on what the apostle Paul says in Romans 12:2: "Do not be conformed to this world, but be transformed by the renewal of your mind." The word *transformed* is the Greek word *metamorphoó*, from which we get our English word *metamorphosis*.

Leonhard Euler (1707–83) was a physicist and mathematician who wrote not only about science but also about the inspiration of Scripture and the importance of Christianity. He taught his children the Bible and had vigorous debates with atheists. Euler's discoveries were so numerous that physicists and mathematicians today joke that to avoid naming everything after Euler, they are forced to name discoveries and theorems after the first person to rediscover them *after* Euler. The Swiss mathematician Nicolas Fuss eulogized Euler by saying, "He was entirely imbued with respect for religion and his piety was sincere and his devotion was full of fervor."[20]

Mary Anning (1799–1849) was a Protestant dissenter (her family had separated from the Catholic Church). At a young age, she became obsessed with hunting for dinosaur fossils. One of her remarkable discoveries, the uncovering of a fossil of a marine reptile called Ichthyosaurus, took place when she was twelve. At age twenty-four, she discovered the first complete fossil of Plesiosaurus. It was such an unexpected find that even the founder of paleontology, George Cuvier (1769–1832), initially thought it was a hoax (he quickly changed his mind once he carefully studied Anning's research). At age twenty-seven, Anning made a third groundbreaking discovery of a jumble of bones with a long tail and wings. It was the first Pterodactyl discovered outside of Germany. Despite her incredible work, Anning received little credit for her finds. Sadly, she died from breast cancer at age forty-seven and nearly disappeared from the pages of scientific history. Yet more than 150 years after her death, a panel of experts gathered by the Royal Society listed Anning as one of the ten most influential women in British science history.[21]

James Clerk Maxwell (1831–79), considered the third most important physicist in history next to Newton and Einstein, was another devout Christian who believed in the authority of the Bible and in miracles and saw science as a religious calling. He began his research with a prayer: "Almighty God, Who hast created man in Thine own image, and made him a living soul that he might seek after Thee, and have dominion over Thy creatures, teach us to study the works of Thy hands, that we may subdue the earth to our use, and strengthen the reason for Thy service."[22]

Clearly, for these pioneers, science and faith were not at odds. But what does this have to do with us today? Surely, we stand on the shoulders of giants, but being there, aren't we able to set our faith aside and pursue pure science?

How a Biblical Worldview Advances Science

Assumptions determine conclusions. Christianity was important to the founders of science not just because they happened to be Christians but because they embraced a biblical worldview and a biblical attitude toward science. Let's look at each.

A Biblical Worldview of Science

As I've already mentioned, many today see science as unrelated to faith. Only half of scientists surveyed in 2009 by the

Pew Research Center believed in God or a higher power, as compared to 95 percent of the American public.[23] How did we move from faith being central to scientific discovery to the sense that it is irrelevant? Harvard professor Steven Shapin lays the blame at the feet of the Enlightenment, which promoted the belief that rationalism could cure humanity's fall into sin and restore virtue.[24] As faith in rationalism began to replace faith in God, science became a nontheistic form of worship. To quote Jonathan Sacks, "In the beginning people believed in many gods. Monotheism came and reduced them to one. Science came and reduced them to none."[25]

Yet the principles on which science operates are consistent with a biblical understanding of the world. We might even say that they are based on it. In their book *The Soul of Science*, Nancy Pearcey and Charles Thaxton list seven such principles:

1. Nature is valuable enough to study (as opposed to ancient Greek thought, which said that the mind, not the physical world, was most important).

2. Nature is good, but not god (as opposed to animistic religions that left nature alone because it was the exclusive abode of the gods).

3. Nature is orderly (as opposed to religions that taught that the world was unpredictable because it was ruled by a pantheon of unruly and unpredictable gods).

4. Nature's laws can be precisely stated and understood (as opposed to ancient religions that taught that creation was too mysterious to be consistently known).

5. Humans can discover nature's order (as opposed to the ancient Eastern belief that nature was not the product of a rational mind and therefore not subject to rational thinking).

6. Detailed observation is possible and important (as opposed to Aristotle's thinking that if an object's purpose was understood, detailed observation of it was unnecessary).

7. The universe is rationally intelligible because God is rationally intelligent (as opposed to philosophies that trusted limited human intelligence as the only kind that really exists).[26]

All seven of these principles find their place in the Bible's description of God and the world. As the University of Texas–Austin philosopher Robert C. Koons plainly states, "Without the faith in the rational intelligibility of the world and the divine vocation of human beings to master it, modern science would never have been possible, and, even today, the continued rationality of the enterprise of science depends on convictions that can be reasonably grounded only in theistic metaphysics."[27]

In addition to a biblical worldview, Christians also advanced science through a uniquely Christian attitude toward their work.

A Christian Attitude toward Science

If he were born today, Robert Boyle (1627–91) might be considered a "trust fund baby." Boyle's father, the Earl of Cork, often called "the first colonial millionaire," possessed a fortune so vast that he would likely be a billionaire if he were alive today. The novelist Daniel Defoe said of Boyle's family that it was "the most [ennobl'd] branches of any in England and Ireland."[28]

Boyle was born at Lismore Castle, a forty-two-thousand-acre Irish estate featuring an enormous home originally built by King John in 1187. Boyle's father acquired the property from Sir Walter Raleigh (the castle still exists and may be rented for a modest $100,000 per week).

Many young men in Boyle's position lived for leisure—socializing, hunting, and traveling abroad. In his funeral sermon for Boyle, his friend Gilbert Burnet noted that Boyle neglected all display of "pomp in clothes, lodging and equipage."[29] Instead, he invested his life intensely to science. Today, Boyle is regarded as the founder of modern chemistry.

Among Boyle's breakthroughs is "Boyle's Law," which describes the relationship between the pressure and the volume of a gas. He rejected the classical Aristotelian teaching of four elements (earth, air, fire, and water) and instead sketched out his thoughts on what later became atomic theory, that all matter is made up of corpuscles (atoms) that are constantly in motion, and that every phenomenon is the result of the collision of these particles.

In addition to his scientific writings, Boyle authored a book called *The Christian Virtuoso*, in which he described what it would take for a Christian to be an outstanding scientist (his term was "experimental philosopher"). His criteria included being without material ambition, focused on truth, humble, honorable, and devout.[30]

Here are five aspects of Boyle's attitude toward science that proceeded from his biblical worldview.

■ *A sense of awe.* Ian G. Barbour, reviewing the writings of early scientists, showed that "the sense of the grandeur and wisdom of God was evidently a very positive experience for many of them and not just an abstract intellectual formula or a concession to cultural respectability."[31]

This was true for Boyle. The universe is an artifact we may explore as creatures who have been designed for this purpose. He wrote, "But withal, I declare, that to embrace Christianity, I do not think I need to recede from the value and kindness I have for Experimental Philosophy." Excellence in experimental philosophy "affords a Man of a well-dispos'd mind, toward the being a good Christian."[32]

As Boyle saw it, God designed us to discover. In *The Christian Virtuoso*, he wrote that God has furnished us with the means to pursue knowledge. Using our reason is an act of worship and obedience to God.[33]

Boyle was especially intrigued with the human eye, perfectly designed to receive light and create a lively representation of the objects of sight.[34] But having an eye is of no use if one will not see. Most people pursue only truths that satisfy their appetites, Boyle thought. They should, instead, pursue the kind of knowledge that goes beyond gratifying passions or interests. They should "be much more dispos'd to value Divine Truths, which are of a much higher and nobler Order, and of an Inestimable and Eternal Advantage."[35]

Humility. Boyle believed that good scientists understand the limits of scientific research; they are humble about the claims they make. Science ought to be a humble enterprise; it has much to be humble about. The physicist Richard Feynman (1918–88) admitted in his book *Six Easy Pieces: Essentials of Physics Explained by Its Most Brilliant Teacher* that despite great scientific progress, we simply don't know a lot of things about our universe. We know energy exists, but we do not know what it is. We do not know all the basic laws of physics. We do not know where the laws of physics come from. We do not know how the universe got started. We do not know the fundamental laws of particles. We cannot explain the nuclear or electrical forces that explain gravitation. We do not know the machinery behind quantum behavior.[36]

In the hands of a humble person, a lack of knowledge is what fuels scientific curiosity. James Clerk Maxwell, the highly regarded physicist we met earlier, says, "Thoroughly conscious ignorance is the prelude to every real advance in science."[37] The fallibility of human observation makes sense from a biblical worldview, which says that humility is the antidote to arrogance and error.[38]

● *Open-handedness.* In addition to his breakthroughs in chemistry, Boyle innovated in science by writing out his theories and conclusions, supported by detailed explanations and drawings, and submitting these writings to other scientists for peer review. This is a common practice today, but the Harvard history of science professor Steven Shapin quoted earlier argues that it originated with Boyle.[39]

Francis Bacon (1561–1626) was another who believed that open-handedness helped counteract self-deception and false persuasion. Bacon's theology, rooted in the biblical idea that humans are subject to sin, was the basis of the careful, studious approach to discovery that he pioneered. A conscious awareness of human sinfulness helped counteract the "idols" that could corrupt science.[40]

● *Rigor.* "Rigor" comes from an old-fashioned word meaning "stiff." Scientific work is said to be rigorous when it is conducted with exceptional attention to detail. Many nonscientists underestimate the extraordinary amount of hard work that goes into a successful scientific endeavor. Boyle elevated scientific rigor—as opposed to rhetoric—in the way he studied his subject matter and carefully documented everything he observed. In fact, he rigorously documented everything he read as well, from studies of nature to Scripture.

In science, a persuasive argument is one in which the scientist lays out working assumptions in careful detail, explains the hypotheses that will guide the research, and makes predictions about what the results will show if the hypotheses are correct. Then, somewhat counterintuitively, the scientist sets about trying to prove these hypotheses wrong, rather than right. If the hypotheses survive this process, they are tentatively accepted and published in a way so that others can independently test them.

Rigor is important because from the tiniest discrepancies, big breakthroughs often emerge. Johannes Kepler discovered elliptical planetary orbits because his calculations *almost* worked out, but with an error of eight minutes—less than one-twentieth of 1 percent. Instead of calling it good enough, Kepler went back to the drawing board. "Because they could not have been ignored, these eight minutes alone will have led the way to the reformation of all astronomy," he said.[41]

Consistent with a biblical worldview is the idea that the world is designed. But research that submits this principle to the scientific process of careful examination is rare. This ought to be remedied. Design enthusiasts ought to lay out their assumptions, test them, try to disprove them, and then gradually build a framework for understanding the universe's fine-tuning that would prove helpful in future research. There are no shortcuts to this.

An example of how this research might be done is a 2020 paper published in the *Journal of Theoretical Biology* by the Norwegian scientist Steinar Thorvaldsen and the Swedish mathematician Ola Hossjer. These researchers developed theoretical models based on fine-tuning that can be used to understand functional proteins, protein complexes, and cellular networks.[42]

* *Beneficence.* A biblical worldview contributes to scientific inquiry by insisting that knowledge ought to lead to a practical benefit for God's image bearers and the world in which they live.

Hildegard of Bingen (1098–1179) was so influential that she is only the fourth woman in history to be named a doctor (teacher) of the Catholic Church. Because the body, mind, and soul are inextricably connected, Hildegard believed, health and holiness go hand in hand. She was onto something. As professor of church history Glenn Myers notes, "The words 'health' and 'holiness' come from the same root, meaning 'to make whole.'"[43]

Hildegard wrote two texts relating to physical health: *Physica* (*Natural Things*), which includes hundreds of natural remedies for human ailments, and *Causae et Curae* (*Causes and Cures*), about the origins and treatments of diseases.

Though some of Hildegard's remedies might seem antiquated, many are relevant to recent medical research, including her discussion of aromatherapy and the connection between the gut, mind, and mood. In her writings, she considered many facets of the human person as possible causes of disease and recommended creative remedies—for example, music—for maladies such as depression.

While practicality is not the hallmark of what makes for good science, the insistence that scientific breakthroughs help humanity is certainly a hallmark of what makes science good. I've long admired George Washington Carver (c. 1864–1943) for insisting that science be used to practically benefit people. An agricultural scientist, Carver studied peanuts (for which he found three hundred food and industrial uses), sweet potatoes, and soybeans. His innovations in fertilization and crop rotation have contributed greatly to meeting the world's food needs. Biographer Linda O. McMurry says that Carver, a man of deep faith, served "magnificently as an interpreter and humanizer" of science.[44]

Boyle, in his scientific research, sought to use his learning to relieve human suffering. Ted Davis, professor of the history of science at Messiah University, writes, "Boyle deeply felt that physicians had a religious duty to be more forthcoming with effective remedies—and to provide them even to those who could not afford to pay. It was a lifelong theme, running through many of his writings, which came to a climax near the end of his life, when he published a collection of medical recipes for this very purpose."[45]

What Should We Do Now?

In other chapters of this book, I offer specific steps Christians can take to reclaim the legacy of history's Truth-tellers. As I look back over this chapter, I realize that the action steps that emerge from the Jesus followers we studied are already covered by the discussion of a biblical worldview and of a Christian attitude toward science.

Let me simply emphasize this key point in closing: Jesus followers changed the world of science. They loved Jesus so much that they couldn't help but explore deeply, work hard, and humbly advance scientific inquiry. Christians today can thrive in science, as they have for centuries. They can seek truth and pursue advances that bring knowledge and healing to all the nations of the world.

The music of the spheres still rings today, displaying the harmony between the natural world and the life of faith. We see this in the art of science, but we also see it in the science of art. That is the topic to which we will next turn our attention.

How Jesus Followers
Have Changed
the World of the Arts

Everyone called him Prete Rosso ("Red Priest") because of his flame-red hair curling out in all directions. Antonio Vivaldi (1678–1741) was a strange one—forever humming and jotting down musical ideas as he absently performed his priestly duties. Once, inspiration struck him in the middle of leading Mass. Vivaldi dashed away from the altar to scribble some notes, returning several minutes later as if nothing had happened. The other priests were not amused, but the head of the diocese took pity, commenting dryly that "being a musician, Vivaldi could not be in his right mind."[1]

Clearly, Vivaldi needed to write music full-time, but how could this happen? It simply was not a priestly thing to do. The answer came in a delightful convergence of passion and ministry: Vivaldi became a composer for orphans.

In eighteenth-century Venice, orphans were everywhere. Many children found themselves unwanted because of being born through prostitution or because of physical defects. Babies were discretely dropped off at an orphanage through a special drawer in the wall designed for that purpose. The Ospedale della Pietà was one such orphanage. At the Pietà, thousands of children received food, clothing, and education. Boys were trained in a vocation and released at age sixteen. But what of the girls? Disfigured and disowned, they had little chance of making it in the outside world.

Music provided the breakthrough. It was at the Pietà that Vivaldi's musical passion and priestly heart found peace with each other. He wrote music and trained the girls to play and sing it, releasing their potential and in the process shaping a new musical period, now known as Baroque for its extravagant ornamentalism. Baroque music swept across Europe and forever changed the world of the arts.

In his *Confessions*, philosopher Jean-Jacques Rousseau (1712–78) describes his firsthand experience listening to the orphans perform. They were without equal, he writes, saying, "I can conceive of nothing more voluptuous nor more touching than this music; the richness of the composition, the exquisite art of the singing, the beauty of the voices, the accuracy of the performance."[2] But because the performers were behind iron latticework, Rousseau could not see who produced such rapturous music. A Pietà employee invited him to meet them. Rousseau was shocked. "'This is Sophie,'—she was crippled. 'This is Cattina,'—she was one-eyed. 'This is Bettina,'—she was disfigured by smallpox. There was hardly a single one that had not some obvious defect."[3]

What a story: beauty meets suffering and changes the world. As Vivaldi wrote pieces to display the talents of his young charges and challenge them to greater heights, he became one of the two most well-known composers of the Baroque period, the other being Johann Sebastian Bach.

Vivaldi composed at a furious pace, crafting more than five hundred concertos (that we know of). In one six-year period, he composed a new piece—complete with orchestral instrumentation—every two weeks. Some of his students became famous. Twenty-eight of Vivaldi's surviving compositions were written specifically for violinist Anna Maria della Pietà. They are intense, says journalist David Epstein, "filled with high-speed passages that require different notes to be played on multiple strings at the same time."[4] In turn, Anna Maria's successor, Chiara della Pietà, "was hailed as the greatest violinist in all of Europe."[5]

"Ugliness does not exclude grace," concluded Rousseau.[6] But surely this crass summation shrouds the full picture of Vivaldi's life's work. As the Anglican priest Samuel Well put it, "He was taking lower-class young girls, with no hopes, prospects, or protectors, giving them a song to sing, and offering them a chance to bring about their own redemption and the liberation of others like them."[7]

Art is the expression of human creativity through which our souls are drawn into a profound understanding of beauty. Jesus followers who pursued Truth shaped the very structure of the visual arts and music. Today's artists stand on their shoulders. We all do.

Most people do not think of themselves as artists, but beauty belongs to each of us. It may lift us up or tear us down, but it always changes us. Perhaps, as we explore its nature and the influence of Jesus followers in the arts, we will find ourselves inspired by a new appreciation of art, the world, and God.

What Is Beauty?

Papua New Guinea forms half of a huge island just a hundred miles off the northern tip of Australia. It boasts twice as many animal species as the United States, even though it is only about 5 percent of its size.

New Guinea's rock star, thanks to a 2015 BBC documentary called *Earth*, is the male flame bowerbird. To attract a mate, the male bowerbird builds an archlike arbor and spends hours decorating it with berries, flowers, shells, and even human-made items such as nails or bottle caps. These it arranges according to size, creating what artists call a "forced perspective" that guides the attention of potential mates. When he attracts their attention, the male flame bowerbird performs an intricate dance of the matador, spreading his wing feathers like a cape, the irises of his eyes pulsating hypnotically.[8]

The male flame bowerbird makes evolutionists' heads spin. Charles Darwin thought that beauty existed in the animal kingdom to ensure reproductive success and pass on good genes. But creating a bower to attract a mate takes an inordinate amount of precious time and energy, and it risks attracting attention from predators as well as from potential mates. It is a dangerous game.

Plus, the evidence for the "good genes hypothesis" is not as strong as Darwin might have hoped. According to science journalist Feris Jabr, a meta-analysis of ninety studies on fifty-five species found only "equivocal" support for the evolutionary relationship between beauty, sexual attractiveness, and fitness for survival.[9] Richard Prum, evolutionary ornithologist at Yale University, admits, "Some of the evolutionary consequences of sexual desire and choice in nature are not adaptive. Some outcomes are truly decadent."[10]

Sometimes beauty exists for its own sake. This makes us wonder, *Why* is the universe so beautiful, and how do we *know* it is beautiful? Holmes Rolston III, a highly respected philosopher, speaks what few people dare: "Such phenomena imply a transcending power adequate to account for these productive workings in the world."[11] In other words, God.

Not only is the universe filled with beauty, but we humans seem uniquely positioned—on *this* planet, in *this* galaxy, with complex, hardwired visual systems—to appreciate it. Some scientists, usually in whispers, talk of the "anthropic principle," that the universe was made in a way that allows us a front-row seat. Robert Jastrow (1925–2008), an astrophysicist instrumental in NASA's development (and an agnostic), wrote, "The anthropic principle . . . seems to say that science itself has proven, as a hard fact, that this universe was made, was designed, for man to live in. It is a very theistic result."[12]

Were we meant to experience beauty? Why do we feel awe when we encounter magnificence? Scholars Dacher Keltner and Jonathan Haidt say that our sense of awe, which is found "in the upper reaches of pleasure and on the boundary of fear," is characterized by two things: *vastness* (we find ourselves overwhelmed) and *accommodation* (we find ourselves changed).[13] Awe leads us, as philosopher Iris Murdoch puts it, to an "unselfing" in which we realize that there is something bigger than us, something we must live for.[14]

But what *is* beauty? History's notable philosophers have described beauty as a harmony that produces a pleasurable sense of longing. The Greek word for "beauty," *kalos*, means "excellent" or "admirable." *Kalos* is often translated as "good" in the New Testament, but not in the sense of good behavior. It is, rather, good in the sense that something blossoms into what it was designed to be.

Beauty exists. We can know it directly and unforgettably. It inspires memory, reminding us of who we are and why we are alive. In this sense, the opposite of beauty is not ugliness but amnesia—a loss of imagination that depletes our desire to grow. A body dies when it stops changing, but physical death is only one way we may pass on. Many whose hearts still beat have stopped being alive to wonder. Is it possible to come back to life? The biblical answer is yes.

A Biblical Understanding of Beauty

Many religious books give an account of beauty, but the Bible uniquely weaves it into the creation narrative itself, into the human condition, and into the hope we may all experience.

In the Genesis account of creation, God inspects his creative work, pronouncing it "good." Our English word *good* simply does not convey the goodness of the Hebrew word used there, *tob* (or *tov*), which means good in every way possible: in beauty, in potential, in wisdom, and in flourishing.[15] God unleashes creation and bids it to abound.[16] The elements of creation announce, in the words of St. Augustine, "'Here we are, look; we're beautiful!' Their beauty is their confession."[17] And that confession points to the beautiful and unchangeable God who made us sub-creators. Every day we can examine our work and call it good, or at least resolve to make it better.

But just as a biblical worldview glories in creation, it also acknowledges that all is not right in the world. In the beginning, God formed living things as a potter forms clay. Humanity's rebellion against God de-forms what God formed.[18] The effects of sin are often reflected in the way beauty is conveyed in art.

Human Sin Twists Beauty into Self-Centeredness

The Truth viewpoint says that we bear God's image, that every human being is a divine masterpiece worthy of honor. The truths viewpoint says that we are "gods" unto ourselves and that beauty is in the eye of the beholder. Yes, people appreciate beauty differently, but today's increasingly bizarre artistic expressions leave the impression that no such thing as beauty exists. I once visited a Pablo Picasso exhibit and found myself distressed at how this brilliant artist increasingly fell into arrogance. In his personal life, Picasso became cruel. In his artistic work, he grew more narcissistic, as if to say, "This is not about beauty. This is about me."

Human Sin Twists Beauty into Rebellion

If you've visited an art gallery, perhaps you've been struck by the contrast between the master works of the medieval and Renaissance periods and those produced in our modern age. I appreciate many works of modern art, but often I'm left wondering what it was about those previous ages that gave us Michelangelo's *David*, while our age's "famous" works include Marcel Duchamp's 1917 display of a urinal titled *Fountain*, symbolizing that everything is waste to be flushed away.[19] It is impossible not to notice the difference. Today's attention-getting art exhibits often feature blank canvases or randomly scattered objects. According to postmodern author Glenn Ward, this is not a lack of skill but an intentional effort to "disrupt bourgeois fantasies about art."[20] It says that "privileged" people have hijacked art to control us. Their efforts must be undone, the thinking goes.

Human Sin Twists Beauty into Cruelty

In 1907, the poet Henry van Dyke wrote the words to "Joyful, Joyful, We Adore Thee" to accompany the final movement of Ludwig van Beethoven's *Ninth Symphony*. It was, perhaps, a way to redeem for spiritual purposes a work Beethoven intended as a political ode to human brotherhood ("Freude! Freude! . . . Alle Menschen warden Brüder"—"Joy! Joy! . . . All men shall become brothers").[21] Unfortunately, van Dyke's efforts fell short, except for the few who remember the old hymn. Though the *Ninth Symphony* has been adopted as the anthem of the European Union (with no words), the piece is forever tainted by its adoration by Adolf Hitler, who demanded that imprisoned musicians perform it to usher inmates into Nazi gas chambers. Hitler perverted its call to universal brotherhood into what music critic John Terauds describes as "a terrifying, sneering parody of all that strives for light in a human soul," gloomily concluding, "we now appreciate more than ever that joy is accessible to everyone only if some people are taking antidepressants."[22]

From self-centeredness to rebellion to cruelty. This is the legacy of sin's encounter with beauty. Is there any rescue?

How Jesus Followers Transformed the Visual Arts

Most of the West's greatest art is about Christian themes—whether icons, religious paintings, sculptures of Mary and Jesus, or the mystical symbolism of Muiredach's Irish High Cross.[23] The great musical works of the past, such as Bach's *St. Matthew's Passion* and Handel's *Messiah*, were written to induce a worshipful attitude among the faithful. Religious themes also dominate great works of literature, such as Dante's *Divine Comedy* and Milton's *Paradise Lost*.

Through their artistic works, Jesus followers portrayed a world made beautiful, harmonious, and meaningful because of Jesus. It is in Christ that all things hold together (Col. 1:17). The great medieval artists could have painted landscapes or bowls of apples or flowers, but they rarely did. Entering into the meaning of the world, not idealizing it, seems to have been their goal. Owen Barfield, a friend and fellow professor of C. S. Lewis, wrote, "Before the scientific revolution the world was more like a garment men wore about them than a stage on which they moved. . . . It was as if the observers themselves were in the picture."[24]

Some medieval masterworks explicitly beckon the viewer to participate. Barna da Siena's *Last Supper* features an open seat at the table, right across from Jesus. It is an invitation: "Please, take a seat and enter into my presence." Tellingly, the open seat is next to Judas. It is impossible to look at the painting and not ask, with a broken heart, "Is it I, Lord? Am I the one who will betray you?"

The medieval age produced a different kind of art because it proceeded from a different worldview. To the medieval mind, everything was connected. The incarnation organizes human history in the same way that planetary motion is the organizing system for testing mathematical proofs. "God and man shared a common reality" is how the late Harvard history professor Steven Ozment (1939–2019) put it.[25] All of the bits and pieces, from theology to geometry to philosophy, come together through Jesus. The incarnation, writes Chris R. Armstrong, professor of church history, "was the linchpin of medieval theology."[26]

Even the ugliness of life is woven into the whole of reality. Medieval paintings vividly portray the suffering of the saints and of everyday people in the light of a suffering Christ. "He had no form or majesty that we should look at him, and no beauty that we should desire him," prophesied Isaiah about the Messiah (Isa. 53:2). Even as his tortured body was taken down from the cross, Christ's loveliness was present in the exquisite way his broken body makes us whole. It was beautiful—*kalos*—because it brought to fullness God's plan. By his stripes we are healed.

As survivors recovered from the plague, medieval art took on a more personal hue. The late Millard Meiss (1904–75), Columbia art historian, wrote that art after the Black Death became more "refined and lyric," expressing "greater animation and spontaneity" and a "more fluid mode of expression."[27] Religious revival broke out, but mystically. Artists portrayed Christ and the saints as ascending above the earth, symbolizing that the viewer, too, may find new hope in the power of the resurrection.[28]

Throughout *Truth Changes Everything*, we've seen that the Black Death in Europe was a turning point in history. It affected the value of human life, medicine, education, science, and the arts. Many have wondered why the trajectory of that age was to move toward God rather than away from him. If God was silent in the face of disaster, ought he not be rejected? This is how we think in our noisy, secular age. Silence is a bad thing. God's silence is an admission that he has nothing to say.

Though it seems strange to us, medieval people viewed heaven's silence as a kind of Sabbath rest; every needful word was uttered by Christ, the Word, on the cross when he cried, "It is finished." A handful of authors have addressed the problem of God's silence in times of trouble. Sir Robert Anderson (1841–1918), a Scotland Yard detective and a real-life Sherlock Holmes, wrote in *The Silence of God* that God's silence is "the silence of a peace which is absolute and profound—a silence which is the public pledge and proof that the way is open for the guiltiest of mankind to draw near to God."[29]

True, Christians like to make noise, as did their Jewish forebears. Psalm 100:1 says, "Make a joyful noise to the LORD, all the earth!" When the people of Jerusalem lifted their voices in praise of Jesus, the Pharisees demanded that he quiet them. Jesus replied, "I tell you, if these were silent, the very stones would cry out" (Luke 19:40).

Yet silence can be a virtue. We sense this in a small way when we enter sacred spaces with hushed voices. Silence is not always proof of absence; often, it is an invitation to presence. The religious themes of late medieval artists invited viewers to experience God's presence through perspective, light, reflectiveness, and vivid depictions of political and philosophical themes. They used their work to communicate that it was God's final Word—Jesus—who gives us hope when our expectations are dashed and we long to find a higher meaning in tragedy. Their innovations shape our understanding of art to this very day.

How Jesus Followers Transformed Music

In 1952, the avant-garde composer John Cage composed—and recorded—*4'33"*, which consists of absolute silence for four minutes and thirty-three seconds. One analyst of the piece noted, with apparent seriousness, that it "is written for any instrument or combination of instruments. It is, however, usually done as a piano piece."[30]

To highlight the playful absurdity of Cage's piece, composer Mike Batt in the early 2000s recorded his own *One Minute Silence*. Incredibly, Cage's publisher claimed royalties. As he stroked a check for 1,000 British pounds, Batt quipped, "John's silence was inferior to mine. My silence was digital and his was analogue. Also, mine was not played by an eight-piece band and his was not played by a solo clarinet."[31]

This royalty battle may have been all in good fun, but it does raise the question "What is music, anyway?" Is music defined by instruments and voices? Are the silent pauses in between the notes part of what makes music meaningful? If so, does not the absence of sound have an artistic value? And if it does, mustn't we rethink what art is?

From a biblical worldview, what makes music beautiful is not just its notes, pauses, meter, and dynamics. As the British philosopher Roger Scruton put it, there is a fittingness or harmony that is the essence of beauty, a context that tells a story about beauty itself.[32]

"Music is the universal language of mankind," wrote the poet Henry Wadsworth Longfellow.[33] New studies reveal that humans do indeed share a deep-seated "musical grammar." Samuel Mehr, director of the Harvard Music Lab, invited his colleagues to compile nearly five thousand descriptions of vocal music written by ethnographers and anthropologists in sixty societies. The group analyzed thousands of songs from eighty-six cultures, focusing on lullabies, healing songs, love songs, and dances. "Music is built from similar, simple building blocks the world over," Mehr concluded.[34]

In many ways, what reaches across cultures musically is the legacy of Jesus followers who pursued Truth. Musical harmony as we know it today developed in the church. Churches sponsored the writing of a vast catalog of chants, motets, cantatas, hymns, and other musical forms that inform musical structure itself. The basic format of these works—beginning in harmony, progressing into tension, and then releasing the tension through melodic resolution—mirrors the glory of creation, the tension of the fall, and the resolution of redemption. As we listen, we are subconsciously reminded of the horror of sin, the honor of self-sacrifice, and the wonder of things made new. Most songs, even those that glorify self or deny Christ, still adhere to this format.

This art of figured song, wrote Johannes Kepler, is modeled on heaven itself. It is designed to "reproduce the continuity of cosmic time . . . to obtain a sample test of the delight of the Divine Creator in His works, and to partake of His joy by making music in the imitation of God."[35]

What Should We Do Now?

If we measure the importance of something by how much Christians write on the subject, we see that art and beauty are difficult things for Christians to accept as important. Christians are good at writing about morality and theology, but books on Christianity and art are rare. They are so rare that even though I've tried to collect them for decades, I have only five good ones in my two-room library of wall-to-wall shelving. And two of those five are so short as to be more like pamphlets than books.

It is easier to talk about how to *be* good than how to *create* good. But God's Truth is no less true in the apologetic of art than it is in the art of apologetics. In the words of David Skeel, beauty "helps us locate what is true."[36] Here are three places we might start. We should do the following:

1. *Appreciate beauty.* As we pay attention to art, music, and architecture, we should ask, "What makes it beautiful? Or what about it subverts beauty? What did the artist intend? What effect does it have? What unexpected insight does it produce?" Put yourself in the work and look out from it. I remember visiting the Martin Luther King Memorial in Washington, DC, on a quiet evening, without crowds. I gazed up at the profile of King, partly chiseled out of a mountain of stone, symbolizing his continually emerging influence. As my eye was drawn up to King's face, I wondered, *What is he looking at?* I turned to follow his gaze across the water to the Thomas Jefferson Memorial. It was as if King were saying, as he did in so many words in his "I Have a Dream" speech, "Mr. Jefferson, you wrote of the right to life, liberty, and the pursuit of happiness. I am here to claim that promise." Stepping into the perspective of the sculpture provided a poignant moment of beauty I will never forget.

2. *Create art.* Art is not just for professionals. We, too, may change culture by what we create. It is never too early to start. Pablo Picasso, T. S. Eliot, Orson Welles, Wolfgang Amadeus Mozart, Frédéric Chopin, and Yo Yo Ma all started early, making major contributions in their twenties. But it's never too late to start either. Poet Robert Frost, at sixty-three, said that while young people glimpse occasional flashes of light, like the stars

of early evening, "it is later in the dark of life that you see forms, constellations."[37] Consider these examples:

- J. R. R. Tolkien was sixty when *Lord of the Rings* was finally published.
- Mary Delany, whose delightful paper cutouts of plants and flowers adorn the British Museum, started at age sixty-eight.
- Grandma Moses, the folk art sensation who once graced the cover of *Time* magazine, began painting in her seventies.
- Impressionist Paul Cézanne was a failed painter in his forties; his career didn't take off until his fifties and sixties.
- Susan Boyle pursued her dream of being an opera singer and at age forty-eight appeared on *Britain's Got Talent*.
- Actor Morgan Freeman was an off-Broadway actor who became internationally known at age fifty-two.
- Louise Bourgeois created her most famous sculpture, *Maman* (a giant spider mom), in her seventies.
- Kathryn Bigelow, director of *Hurt Locker*, which won six Oscars, including best director, was fifty-seven when the movie came out.
- Screenwriter Millard Kaufman published his first novel at ninety-one years of age.

Pick up something new. Take music lessons. Join an art studio. Start a writing group. Writer Joseph Epstein has noted that 81 percent of people believe they have a book in them.[38] Maybe they do, maybe they don't. There is only one way to find out.

3. *Don't ignore the pain.* I've struggled with how to make
this point, but I believe it is important enough to try.
Some believe Christian engagement with art is best
when it is happy: a movie with a fairy-tale ending or
an inspirational quote penned across the surface of
a painting. I love good stories. I love being inspired.
But are these the distinguishing marks of a biblical
Christian worldview? The Bible's expressions of hope
are nearly always nested in pain. David's many heart-
wrenching psalms attest to this, as do the words of
Job: "But when I hoped for good, evil came, and when
I waited for light, darkness came" (Job 30:26). God's
power often manifests as we walk *through* the pain, not
around it. God brings beauty *out of* ashes, gladness *out
of* mourning, and praise *out of* despair (see Isa. 61:3).
The connection between pain and hope occupied much
of my thinking during my cancer battle. It was during
that time that I picked up a heartbreaking biography of
Vincent van Gogh, the artist whose paintings of sun-
flowers and starry nights inspire millions. Van Gogh
grew up in a household of faith but battled mental illness most of his life. He was, as his biographers put
it, "a wayward, battered soul: a stranger in the world,
an exile in his own family, and an enemy to himself."[39]
When a famous art critic sensationalized van Gogh's
work through a glowing review, the artist replied in
despair, "I *ought* to be like that rather than the sad reality of what I feel myself to be."[40] Van Gogh died at age
thirty-seven, penniless. He painted his most famous
work, *Starry Night*, while gazing through the barred
windows of a mental institution. It was in his deepest
despair that van Gogh produced his profoundest works.
Am I suggesting that we revel in our suffering to more

deeply experience beauty? Of course not. But a biblical Christian worldview doesn't hide from pain. Rather, it memorializes it. Truth emerges in the pain, not despite it. This is good news in a time when half of Americans say they feel hopeless several days a week.[41] Your mess is your message, a mentor once told me. When honesty and vulnerability shape our experiences with art, empathy grows in our hearts.

4. *Live artistically.* God is an artist. We bear God's image when we paint a picture but also when we stretch the frame of our lives to include those on the margins. We bear God's image when we hear a symphony rise to its coda but also when we witness others rising to their potential. We bear God's image when we admire a stunning cathedral but also when we invite others to worship in spirit and in truth. We bear God's image when we stand in awe of mighty waves crashing onto the rocks or marvel at a lightning storm but also when we celebrate the triumphs of our fellow image bearers. The art of living is a high form of beauty.

Much of what is beautiful is expressed when we live in community, harmonizing our lives with others in civic society. It's called politics, and it is a worthy form of performance art, though not in the way people usually imagine. Let's turn our attention to it now.

How Jesus Followers Have Changed Politics

The lamp was nearly out of oil. Its soft *whisk whisk* sound had faded, giving way to a steady glow and a thin column of smoke rising to the blackened ceiling. It was okay, though. The manuscript was nearly complete. In the dying light, the writer scratched these words: "All authority in heaven and on earth has been given to me. Go therefore and make disciples of all nations, baptizing them in the name of the Father and of the Son and of the Holy Spirit, teaching them to observe all that I have commanded you. And behold, I am with you always, to the end of the age."[1]

Gently setting down his stylus, Matthew stretched and sighed. There it was. His testimony about Jesus. As he scanned the page, his eye fell on the word *go—poreuthentes*. He smiled. What a perfect way to end his account. How many times had he used that word in his manuscript? Six? Seven? He had lost track. It was the perfect word to describe Jesus. Always on the go.

His mind wandered back to one of Jesus's more notorious "goings," the twenty-six-mile jaunt he had led the disciples on to Caesarea Philippi (see Matt. 16:13–20). "Why are we doing this?" they had wondered aloud, complaining maybe just a bit, as young men will do.

"Because there is something I need to teach you." That's all Jesus had said.

"Well, can't you teach us now so we can turn around and go home?" one of the bolder disciples had asked.

"Nope."

Okay, then. I guess we're hiking.

At last, they arrived. A surprising number of people occupied the space at the foot of the large cliff before them. Some of them were clearly worshipers of the Greek god Pan—what odd people they were, running around in, well, a *panic*. And those schmoozers of the Romans, weren't they a piece of work with all their "Hail Caesar" business?

And there, right at the base of the cliff, was the famous Gates of Hades. Matthew remembered seeing the stream flowing out of the darkness. What was *in* there? The Pan worshipers said it was the entrance to the underworld. How creepy.

That's when Jesus turned around and asked one of his famous questions. "Who do people say that the Son of Man is?" (v. 13).

Matthew chuckled as he remembered looking at the other disciples. Who was going to take this one? And what would they say?

No doubt, it was a question that was on all their minds. Everyone in Galilee wanted to know: "Whose side are you on?" There were oh-so-many sides. Obviously, Jesus was not a Herodian. He had no interest in sucking up to the Romans. And he wasn't a Sadducee either: absolutely nothing about him screamed "spiritual elite."

But was he an Essene? Did he really sympathize with his cousin John the Baptist and his "leave the world behind and head into the desert" crowd? Or perhaps he was secretly a

Zealot, plotting the overthrow of the Romans as a new Elijah, speaking truth to power. Or maybe he was one of the Pharisees, despite the grief he gave them. He *did* talk a lot about obeying God, and his respect for Jeremiah and the prophets was clear.

At last, Simon broke the silence. "Some say John the Baptist, others say Elijah, and others Jeremiah or one of the prophets" (v. 14).

Good answer. But not good enough.

"But who do *you* say that I am?" Jesus pressed (v. 15).

"You are the Christ, the Son of the living God," Simon blurted out (v. 16).

Jesus smiled. "And I also say to you that you are a stone," he said, looking directly at Simon, "and on this rock I will build my church, and the gates of Hades will not overpower it" (v. 18 CSB).

Matthew thought back on that moment. He remembered gazing up at the face of the cliff, trying to make sense of what Jesus had just said. Simon is a little rock. Jesus is going to build his church on the big rock. Nothing that comes out of hell will stop it. And . . . what was that word Jesus had used for church? *Lodoth?* What did that mean exactly? Something like "called out to go out." Confusing.

Sitting there in the growing darkness, Matthew finally understood what Jesus had meant. "As you are going into the world, I am calling you to testify about me wherever people worship power and other false gods." That was a lot of places, but the disciples were doing it. Jerusalem. Athens. Rome. Corinth.

Well, it was late. Time to get a little rest. And then do the only reasonable thing he could do, Matthew realized. Get going.

In this one simple lesson, Jesus rose above political and religious ideologies and offered the disciples a crystal-clear mission: Go, don't stay. Engage, don't escape. Build, don't tear down. Perhaps it was the context of what Jesus said at Caesarea Philippi that caused translators to use the Greek word *ecclesia* to interpret what Jesus had said in Aramaic about the church. But what comes to our minds when we think of church is quite a bit different from what the word *ecclesia* implies, which is more of a gathering of the chosen than a building. As pastor Tony Evans puts it, "To be a part of the church of Jesus Christ, as Jesus defined it, is to be a part of a spiritual legislative body tasked to enact heaven's viewpoint in hell's society."[2]

Wherever and whatever people worship—whether money, fame, power, or sensuality—that is where Jesus intends to build his church. The church is to be at the very heart of the action.

We won't find much about political ideology in the teachings of Jesus. In passages such as Matthew 16, though, we *will* find a clearly articulated theology of engagement. Jesus told the disciples to go out and make more disciples by teaching everyone everywhere to obey God in every area in which Jesus Christ has authority (which is all areas). This command isn't just about "how to get to heaven" but about "how to follow God in all we do."

If we follow God in all we do, then who we are outside the church should be indistinguishable from who we are inside it.

Regardless of your personal political viewpoints, your freedom to express them is a legacy of Jesus followers who gave a biblical shape to our understanding of governance, liberty, and law in the first place. From the formation of the Hebrew republic to Jesus's instructions about engaging culture, a biblical worldview has a great deal to say about politics. To see how this is so, let's begin by defining the word *politics*.

What Is Politics?

Politics is Truth applied to community. *Polis* is the Greek word for "city." *Politics* means "the rule of a city." Politics is not about glitzy rallies or photo ops or the kissing of babies. It is about answering the question "What is the best way to *organize* and *sustain* community so that it promotes human flourishing?"

In answering the question about organizing and sustaining community, politics balances two values: liberty and law. Properly aligned, liberty and law create a stable society. When out of kilter, they end up serving the interests of some while hurting others. So, it is no surprise that liberty and law are both battlegrounds in the conflict between the Truth viewpoint and the truths viewpoint. Let's briefly define each.

Liberty: Freedom from Undue Restraint

In America, the founders believed that the heart of liberty was not freedom to do anything we want but freedom to do as we ought. This was a common understanding of the time, as seen in the writings of Edmund Burke (1729–97), a British statesman who late in his life witnessed the bloody French Revolution. He wrote, "But what is liberty without wisdom and without virtue? It is the greatest of all possible evils; for it is folly, vice, and madness, without tuition or restraint."[3] John Adams, America's second president, wrote to the Massachusetts Militia in 1798, "Avarice, Ambition, Revenge or Galantry, would break the strongest Cords of our Constitution as a Whale goes through a Net. Our Constitution was made only for a moral and religious People. It is wholly inadequate to the government of any other."[4]

Based on their understanding of liberty as the freedom to do as we ought, the founders drew on two traditions that political scientists call negative liberty and positive liberty.

Negative liberty: government secures liberty by removing restraints against it. Negative liberty asks, "What external restraints make it hard to secure liberty, and how might we remove them?" Negative liberty is about negating restraints. Many of America's founders believed that the main threat to liberty is the government, not the people. After much debate, they added a Bill of Rights to the Constitution that compels the federal government to protect people *from itself.* Government may not take away liberty without due process of law.

Positive liberty: government secures liberty by ensuring that the conditions for liberty are present. Positive liberty says that the government should promote liberty by ensuring that it treats people justly. The United States Constitution does this by specifying how laws will be made and enforced, establishing a system of courts, and providing for the national defense. It guarantees several rights, such as the right to a speedy trial and protection against unreasonable search and seizure. Over time, though, positive liberty has taken on an expanded meaning. Most Americans now believe that the government is responsible to make our lives better through infrastructure projects such as public works and transportation. Those with a more progressive mindset believe the government should also add jobs, education, and healthcare to the list of guaranteed rights. Without government intervention, they say, people cannot be truly free. Detractors say that the federal government was never intended to provide for public welfare in these ways or to this extent. Most public policy debates today revolve around this tension. At issue is how far the government should go in ensuring positive liberty.

Law: That Which Constitutes *Orderly* and *Just* Governance

While liberty is concerned with freedom from undue restraint, law is concerned with maintaining public order and justice. What kinds of laws should we have? The answer to this question hinges on where laws come from. Do they come from God, or are they the product of human imagination? Two competing concepts of law vie for our attention.

Natural law: rights come from nature and God. The natural law view says that a government's job is to secure—not invent—rights through a clear, consistent, and well-publicized process. Its laws must be stable, not contradict one another or be beyond the power of people to follow, and be enforced fairly.[5]

Legal positivism: rights are created by human authorities. No one can know the truth for certain, say legal positivists, so the best leaders can do is create rights based on what makes sense to them at the time.

The battle between natural law and legal positivism came to a head in the aftermath of World War II as Nazi leaders were put on trial for their war crimes. The lawyers charged with the prosecution found themselves in a dilemma: If they claimed that what the Nazis had done was wrong, they would have to acknowledge some higher standard of right and wrong. On the other hand, if they claimed that, as the victors, the Allied powers could rightly judge the Nazis, they would essentially be admitting that if the tables had been turned and the Nazis had obtained victory, their murderous actions would have been justified. The trials went forward. Nazi leaders were punished. Yet the underlying question of where right and wrong come from was never fully addressed. Shortly after World War II, the United Nations passed a Universal Declaration of Human Rights to address future atrocities such as those the Nazis had committed. Unlike the American Declaration of Independence, though, the United Nations document still failed to address where these rights came from, other than that there is "recognition" of them by the drafters.[6]

How Does the Battle over Truth Relate to Politics?

Today, advocates of the truths viewpoint insist that God has nothing to do with how we govern ourselves. The secular philosopher Sidney Hook (1902–89) says, "It is not God but the human community that endows its members with rights."[7] Believing that the human community is organized by government, Hook presumably means that government gives rights, and government can take them away.

If we don't have access to Truth, though, how do we even know what rights are? The postmodern professor Stanley Fish, a First Amendment scholar, says that there is no transcendent basis for rights. The best we can do is tell our stories and try to win power. "This is as much of a bottom line as we will ever have," he says.[8] What about the facts? Fish insists that "you *are* entitled to your own facts if you can make your version of them stick."[9] In other words, if you want to secure your rights, learn the art of persuasion.

But why, if no one has direct access to the Truth, should we try to make better arguments? Why would persuasion be a better strategy than force? Because it's nicer? Well, who's to say? If no one has direct access to the Truth, maybe violence is better because it is simpler and it takes less time. Maybe people don't like it, but what if we don't care? Of history's great lessons, this is surely the most chilling: abandoning Truth leads inexorably to injustice and tyranny. And that wide, straight road is paved with good intentions all the way.

A stable society requires more than good stories and wishful thinking. Cheslaw Miłosz, the Nobel Prize–winning Polish poet and critic of Communism, put it this way: "Freedom *from something* is a great deal, yet not enough. It is much less than freedom *for something*."[10] We cannot just clamor to be free; we must discipline ourselves for a citizenly purpose. Marcus Tullius Cicero (106–43 BC) said, "We are slaves of the law so that we may be free."[11] True freedom requires boundaries based on objective reality. The onetime Dutch prime minister Abraham Kuyper wrote, "Unfree, is the fish which though unfettered lies on dry ground; and you make it free precisely by binding and enclosing it in the water."[12]

How do we secure rights without devolving into destructive power struggles? Jesus followers have grappled with this question through the centuries and have offered a nuanced, yet clear understanding of politics based on biblical thinking. Seeing how it might help us in our own time, when many fear an unraveling of civil society, requires a close look at what a biblical view of politics might be.

Politics from a Biblical Worldview

Throughout history, Jesus followers crafted a rational political framework for how human communities should be ruled in a way that ensures liberty and law based on Truth. Let's briefly examine some of the individuals who did this in the Middle Ages, the Enlightenment, and modern times.

A Biblical View of Liberty and Law in the Middle Ages and the Enlightenment

Harvard historian Stephen Ozment says that it was in the Late Middle Ages that the principles of government we recognize today—the separation of church and state, representative government, and the defense of national sovereignty—emerged.[13] He writes, "Many medieval scholars even argue that these centuries were of greater significance for the formation of Western ideas and institutions than the later Italian Renaissance and Protestant Reformation."[14]

Christian legal scholars in the Late Middle Ages synthesized their biblical knowledge with thinking from Greek philosophers such as Aristotle. Most were less interested in reproducing the laws of ancient Israel than in discerning what true principles lay behind the Bible's wisdom. Thomas Aquinas focused on how God's grace as expressed through Jesus applied to society. "Grace does not destroy nature, but completes it," he said.[15]

The pursuit of peace lay at the heart of all this thinking. Earlier in this book, I wrote about the Old Testament word for "peace," *shalom*, meaning "a sense of peace, prosperity, and completeness."[16] Late Middle Age scholars saw peace as an "ontological principle," a divine concept that grounds our being. *The Encyclopedia of Judaism* says, "Peace is the foundation of all being, the principle that harmonizes contending forces within each individual object, and reconciles the separate elements of nature as a whole. Ultimately, peace is the embodiment of the Divine immanence in the world."[17]

What role do everyday people have in developing communities of peace? Let's look to England as an example. Until the Middle Ages, everyday people had little influence. Kings made the decisions. But then the tide shifted. England's barons revolted against King John (1166–1216) and forced him to sign the Magna Carta, an early written constitution granting rights to England's noblemen. This revolt, however, was a case of lesser nobles rebelling against a greater one. It didn't necessarily benefit everyone. In the wake of the Black Death, though, everyday people began growing in influence and wealth. They pushed against royal authority. The royals pushed back. Clearly, the English people needed new thinking about where rights came from and how they ought to be secured before violence broke out (the conflict over rights eventually did turn into a civil war). Let's look at some of the Jesus followers who influenced the discussion based on their biblical beliefs.

William Perkins (1558–1602) was a Cambridge University professor and leading Puritan theologian whose thoughts about the relationship between church, state, and family are not often mentioned in the history of politics. They should be. Perkins used the analogy of a body to explain a well-functioning society. The family is a body, the church is a body, and the government is a body, he wrote. The best possible society arises when each does its job and focuses on the good of the other.[18] Later in the chapter, we'll see how the Dutch reformer Abraham Kuyper built on this concept.

Another influential thinker of the time was Samuel Rutherford (1600–1661), who explained his views in a brief volume titled *Lex Rex (The Law Is King)*.[19] The idea that the law is above the king rather than the king being above the law did not strike England's king as a positive development. Plus, Rutherford published his tract at an awkward time, as Charles II reclaimed the throne of his executed father after a decade of rule by Oliver Cromwell. Charles II set about consolidating his power and persecuting the "Covenanters" who resisted his authority. Rutherford's insistence that the king was not the law infuriated the prickly royal, who insisted that Rutherford appear before Parliament on charges of treason. Rutherford died before he could appear, commenting on his deathbed that he had been summoned by a higher authority. Consequently, Charles II won the battle but lost the war, though he did succeed in persecuting and murdering thousands of reformers. Over time, the power of the monarchy decreased. The stage was set for a new birth of freedom.

Following Rutherford's death, John Locke (1632–1704) expanded on Rutherford's thinking. Humans are born in sin, Locke said, but they have the natural right to life, health, liberty, and possessions. Locke examined Scripture and concluded that all humans are equal heirs of Adam and thus have a right to government by law, not by kings.[20] He wrote, "Political power, then, I take to be a right of making laws . . . in the defense of the commonwealth from foreign injury, and all of this only for the public good."[21] A clear understanding of liberty and a rational basis for good laws would help guard against the corruption caused by human sinfulness.

After Locke's death, though, several influential political thinkers began to reject his Bible-based assessment, setting in motion a conflict that rages to this day. Jean-Jacques Rousseau (1712–78) is one of those who took issue with Locke's approach. Humans are not sinful by nature, he said. Corruption is not an inevitable reality that must be guarded against. Humans are perfectible.

The tension between Locke's and Rousseau's thinking illustrates the difference between a "sin nature" view and a "pure nature" view of the world. To the casual observer, Locke's assessment of the human situation seems dour. Rousseau's is more uplifting. Ironically, though, historical events such as the French Revolution showed that the "pure nature" view was a disaster. Based on Rousseau's teaching, and that of his contemporary Voltaire (1694–1778), French revolutionaries overthrew the monarchy. They assumed that their own motives were pure, and thus justified. Even the killing of opponents was a social good. Maximilien Robespierre (1758–94), one of the French Revolution's most notable leaders, put it this way: the nation "owes nothing to the Enemies of the People but death."[22] Forty thousand people were beheaded by guillotine. Blood stained the streets.

Denis Diderot, author of France's most famous encyclopedia and a supporter of the Revolution, enthused, "Man will never be free until the last king is strangled with the entrails of the last priest."[23] Robespierre called his group of thugs the Committee for Public Safety. It was an early example of political "spin" that gave people a false and deadly sense of security.

For a time, even the revered Thomas Jefferson lent his support to the French Revolution as a positive development for the spread of liberty. Jefferson excused the killings committed by the French revolutionaries by writing, "The tree of liberty must be refreshed from time to time, with the blood of patriots and tyrants. It is its natural manure."[24]

When everyone believes they are pure, chaos results. Eventually, even Robespierre himself was judged by his disciples to be insufficiently pure. He was guillotined without trial. Just like Esther's enemy, Haman, in the Bible, Robespierre died on the gallows he had built for others.

The Oxford-educated social thinker Os Guinness draws a straight line between the French Revolution and the Communist revolutions of the twentieth century, in which tens of millions of people were killed at the hands of their own governments. Guinness personally experienced the terror of the Chinese Communist revolution as the child of missionaries. Two of his brothers died in the ensuing famine.[25]

As we will see shortly, most of America's founders took a very different approach from that of Rousseau and Voltaire. Following the teachings of the Bible and John Locke, they decided that they could not trust even themselves. They knew, as Lord Acton (1834–1902) later phrased it, "Power corrupts, and absolute power corrupts absolutely."[26]

A Biblical View of Liberty and Law in America's Founding

Truth is for all people everywhere. Yet as an American, I find myself most curious about how the battle for Truth intersects with the founding of my own country. People fiercely debate whether America had a Christian founding, but there is little doubt that Jesus followers have exerted a tremendous amount of influence since the nation's infancy.

Of the fifty-six signers of America's Declaration of Independence, fifty-one and possibly fifty-three are known by their writings and histories to have been Christians. In fact, of the larger group of 204 founding fathers, including those who signed the Declaration of Independence and the Articles of Confederation and who attended the Constitutional Convention, all but three or four were members of a Christian denomination.

Of course, it is one thing to be a member of a church and another thing to take the Bible seriously. Though flawed and even personally hypocritical, America's most influential founders treated the principles found in the Bible with the utmost seriousness. John Adams, writing to Thomas Jefferson in 1813, affirmed his belief that the principles of Christianity "are as eternal and immutable, as the Existence and Attributes of God."[27] Noah Webster concurred: "The moral principles and precepts found in the scriptures ought to form the basis of all our civil constitutions and laws. These principles and precepts have truth, immutable truth, for their foundation."[28]

Adams and Webster were not exceptions. Political science professor Donald Lutz examined fifteen thousand documents published in America's early years and found that the Bible was the most cited book, more than all Enlightenment authors put together.[29]

The founders weren't just picking and choosing Bible verses to justify their approach to government. Rather, they looked to the Old Testament narrative about the development of the Hebrew republic. They drew on a hundred years of thinking in what historians Eric Nelson and Michael Walzer call the "Biblical century," in which political theorists explored the Hebrew Torah for insights into godly government.[30]

Based on the sin nature view, America's founders divided political power among three branches of government: the executive, the legislative, and the judicial. They believed that the best constitution was one "built with the crooked timber of selfish humanity in mind," as historian Wilfred M. McClay put it.[31] This vision united landowners and laborers, the noble born and the nobodies.

Despite the documentary evidence and personal testimony, some critics still assert that the founders were not serious Christians but merely deists who believed that God set the world in motion and left the rest up to humanity. These critics cite the influence of Thomas Paine, author of the famous pamphlet *Common Sense*, who wrote that "my own mind is my own church."[32] But a close examination of the beliefs of the founders shows that deism was much rarer than we have been led to believe. The historian Mark David Hall writes, "With the exception of Franklin, Allen, and Paine, I am unaware of any civic leaders who clearly and publicly rejected orthodox Christianity or embraced deism. There may be others, but those who claim the founders were deists give little or no evidence that they exist."[33]

A Biblical View of Liberty and Law in Modern Times

In the last two hundred years, Christian theologians have continued to think through what makes a balanced, well-functioning society. Groen van Prinsterer (1801–76) is an excellent example.

As the royal archivist of the Netherlands, he was concerned about the revolutionary impulse that had destroyed France and was threatening the rest of Europe. Van Prinsterer realized that totalitarian states gain power by destroying attachments to family and religion. Is it possible to have a system that doesn't *force* justice and wise political decision-making but *fosters* them? Finding the answer to this question was van Prinsterer's mission.

One of van Prinsterer's protégés was Abraham Kuyper (1837–1920), a newspaper editor, theologian, and—for a brief time—prime minister of the Netherlands. Kuyper fleshed out van Prinsterer's ideas through what he called "sphere sovereignty." Like the Puritan theologian William Perkins before him, Kuyper saw each sphere of society as united under God but diverse in its service to humans. In 1899, Kuyper gave a series of lectures at Princeton University in which he outlined his thoughts.[34]

Theologians today have expanded on the idea of sphere sovereignty. Depending on their perspective, they include spheres such as education and commerce as well as government, church, and family. Since we've already talked about education in this book and will talk about commerce in a future chapter, let's focus for now on the government, church, and family spheres as outlined by Perkins.

Government. Government's purpose is to secure liberty and make just laws. It pursues justice, secures freedom, and punishes wrongdoing.

Church. The church's purpose is to manifest God's love and grace on earth. It uses persuasion and compassion to foster worship and lift people up, restoring them as image bearers of God.

Family. The family's purpose is to manifest God's community and creativity, including procreativity. It influences the world by raising children who will make a positive contribution to society.

These three spheres balance one another. Picture three balloons in a box. If one is overinflated, the other two get squeezed. Though it isn't the purpose of this book to go into detail about how the three spheres are balanced at the present time, a majority (55 percent) of Americans say the government has too much power. Only 7 percent say it has too little.[35] This concern should be taken seriously. One cannot easily opt out of a government. It influences everything one does.

If the government attempts to regulate or replace the functions of the church and family, all of society suffers. Healthy families and churches are an important counterbalance in a time when the role of government has expanded dramatically.

What Should We Do Now?

A healthy nation demands involvement. We may love our families and attend church, but we also ought to teach, coach, serve on boards, volunteer, and share ideas with others. In addition, we ought to be involved in politics. When we fail to take our citizenship responsibilities seriously, government can get out of bounds, harming the very people it is sworn to protect.

Here are two principles we can learn from Jesus followers who influenced politics. We should do the following:

1. *Worship God yet hold government accountable.* Everything good in life requires allegiance to something. A good spouse does not say, "I consider myself married three days a week, but not the other four." A good soldier does not say, "I'm going to be a faithful soldier when I am on duty, but in my free time, I will fight for whomever I please." In the same way, it is disloyal for a Christian to say, "I will think Christianly about

my church and family, but how I vote is not a faith decision."

From Christianity's earliest days, leaders such as Augustine of Hippo (354–430) consistently called civic authorities to account. They insisted that Christians speak the truth, even when it was unpopular.[36] In his book *City of God*, Augustine contrasted what it meant to be citizens of the earthly city versus the heavenly one. The earthly city makes false gods of everything, even human beings. "The heavenly one, on the other hand, living like a wayfarer in this world, makes no false gods for herself," he wrote. "On the contrary, she herself is made by the true God that she may be herself a true sacrifice to Him."[37]

Think about it this way: If the earthly city is worshiped as God and it goes astray—which the sin nature view says is inevitable—who will hold it accountable? The citizens of the heavenly city make good citizens in the earthly city precisely because they have a higher allegiance.

As of this writing, in America, seven in ten people think the United States is going in the wrong direction.[38] But we must resist the temptation to cast ourselves as victims. In the 1970s and 1980s, Pope John Paul II made it a priority to visit and encourage the oppressed. His message was not "I feel sorry for you." Rather, he called his audiences to overcome fear and step up to their responsibility. On his trip to Cuba, he told people harassed by a Communist regime, "You are and must be the principled agents of your own personal and national history."[39]

2. *Keep our priorities straight.* One thing I've discerned from the writings of America's founders is that there is a flow of political engagement from principles to

policies to personalities, not the other way around. If we start with principles, we can develop rational policies that guide our interactions, even with those who rub us the wrong way.

If we focus on personality first by avoiding candidates whose personalities we don't like, we end up with a whiplash approach to policy: "I'm for whatever my hated candidate is against." In this situation, there is almost no chance we can arrive at principled leadership.

Therefore, I tell my students at Summit Ministries, "Start with principles, not personalities." The founders started with principles ("We hold these truths to be self-evident"), then developed policies (such as the government consisting of three branches). With these firmly in place, they gained perspective for the personality clashes that would inevitably arise.

What principles should Christians apply? Here is my thinking:

- Actively oppose evil. My friend Kevin Bywater from the Oxford Study Centre points out that when we vote and get involved, we're not merely choosing the lesser of two evils. Evil is everywhere—even in our own hearts. We should ask, "How do we protect the vulnerable and cultivate freedom so that people can lift themselves up?" Personally, asking the question "How might I lessen evil through my vote?" leads me to put issues such as the protection of innocent life and economic opportunity at the center of my political thinking.
- Keep the leash tight. Our founders recognized that government's power must be firmly kept in balance with our other priorities. Is government taking over

responsibilities that families should share? Is government hurting religious freedom and denying religious expression? Which candidates seem to grasp that these are serious questions? They're the ones I look at first.

- Focus on local issues as well as national ones. The leaders who can best solve problems are those closest to the problems themselves, not those in a far-off capitol issuing one-size-fits-all regulations. Plus, local leaders are easier to hold accountable. We can meet with them and admonish them to do what is right.

Ultimately, though, we cannot stand publicly for what we do not first cherish in our hearts. Judge Learned Hand (1872–1961), a highly respected jurist, said, "Liberty lies in the hearts of men and women; when it dies there, no constitution, no law, no court can even do much to help it. While it lies there it needs no constitution, no law, no court to save it."[40]

Liberty and law are vital. But there is a third leg of the stool: justice. In the next chapter, we'll turn our attention to Truth-focused Jesus followers and investigate how they transformed our understanding of how to set things right.

How Jesus Followers Have Changed the Pursuit of Justice

Corrie had just finished helping six people scramble into the hidden room. As she closed the hidden panel behind them, a heavyset, pale-faced gestapo officer stormed in.

"What's your name?"

"Cornelia ten Boom."

"So you're the ring leader! Tell me now, where are you hiding the Jews?"

"I don't know what you're talking about," Corrie replied calmly.

The man struck her hard across the face.

"Where are the Jews?" he demanded.

Looking him in the eye, Corrie replied, "There aren't any Jews here."[1]

Searching as thoroughly as they could, the gestapo could not find the hidden room. Frustrated, they took Corrie, her sister Betsie, and their father, Casper, into custody. Ten days later, Casper died. Corrie and Betsie were sent to the Ravensbruck concentration camp, where Betsie also perished. Corrie was released, due to a clerical error, just one week before the Nazis sent all the women her age to the gas chambers. She wrote about her experiences in *The Hiding Place* and carried on a worldwide ministry until her death at age ninety-one.

Corrie's story has inspired millions with a message of courage and forgiveness, yet some are bothered by the fact that the ten Booms—and many other believers—deceived government authorities in their efforts to help those in their care. Did these efforts come at the cost of Truth? Is there ever a case in which the Truth demands deception?

Christians have debated these questions for centuries. Some say that we must always speak accurately and accept the consequences. Others say that unjust authorities are not *owed* the Truth. Either way, we must grapple with questions of justice, authority, and our obligations in society. We need clarity if we are to stand for what is right and love our neighbor as ourselves.

"We must obey God rather than men," the apostle Peter says in Acts 5:29. Put on trial and beaten for his faith, Peter counted it an honor to suffer for Jesus. Christians through the ages have been similarly harassed, imprisoned, and treated in grotesquely inhumane ways because they put God first.

The pursuit of justice upsets people. It often defies the will of authority figures who benefit from keeping things as they are. How can we be sure that justice is genuinely based in Truth and not in our personal preferences? Let's seek an answer by defining justice, looking at its biblical roots, and exploring how Jesus followers transformed our understanding of justice through their love of Truth.

What Is Justice?

Justice means setting things right. Whereas politics is Truth applied to community, justice is Truth applied to conflict. A biblical worldview treats justice as something knowable because it proceeds from the nature and character of God. We cannot conduct an archaeological dig and find "justice" buried in the sands of time. Rather, we must use our minds to seek an objective and transcultural standard by which we can reliably make judgments. Justice requires facts, not opinions. Take the crime of murder as an example. In a just system, a person accused of murder cannot be condemned on the word of a government official. Nor can they get off the hook by "speaking their truth." How the public "feels" about the charges is irrelevant. Justice is done when evidence is presented to an impartial jury, which renders a verdict in the presence of a judge who makes sure the proceedings are fair. Many things can go wrong, and do, but because we can know what justice is, we can support a process that substantially increases its chances of being upheld.

The truths viewpoint disagrees with the idea that we can know what justice is. It says that the best we can do is gain power and get others to see things our way. But what if this leads to the very kind of misery that a system of justice is supposed to prevent? The Truth viewpoint and the truths viewpoint battle over what justice is, where it comes from, and how to secure it. There is much at stake.

Justice from a Biblical Worldview

Peace, safety, decency, and freedom are not "things" like money and products. They are immaterial. By saying that no one can know what is ultimately real, the truths viewpoint cannot account for them.

Here is a very important point that many people fail to consider: Unlike material things, immaterial values are abundant. Money is limited, but wealth is not. There may be only a certain number of products for sale, but a good idea can have infinite potential.

As an immaterial value, justice is theoretically unlimited; it can grow more widespread and valuable over time. You don't have to take justice away from one person to give it to someone else. There is enough for everyone. The reason it often does not seem this way, according to a biblical worldview, is human sinfulness. Humans act unjustly and pretend that their actions are just. They ignore injustice when it is convenient to do so. They allow injustice to remain out of fear that doing what is just might have negative consequences for them personally.

Justice is secured through constant vigilance. If just a tiny percentage of the population decides to break the law, the system unravels. One tragic example of this is human trafficking. The United Nations defines human trafficking as "a process by which people are recruited in their community and exploited by traffickers using deception and/or some form of coercion to lure and control them."[2] Every nation in the United Nations prohibits slavery, but it is estimated that forty million people are enslaved through human trafficking today. Sex trafficking is the organized exploitation of women and girls, though men and boys are often victims as well.[3] Only a few hundred sex traffickers are convicted each year in the United States. The crimes of most traffickers go unreported because victims are afraid that law enforcement will not adequately protect them. This emboldens exploiters. Human trafficking is a global catastrophe committed by a minute fraction of the population.

God cares a great deal about justice. Leviticus 19:15 says, "You shall do no injustice in court. You shall not be partial to the poor or defer to the great, but in righteousness shall you judge your neighbor." Psalm 33:5 says, "[God] loves righteousness and justice; the earth is full of the steadfast love of the LORD." Two Hebrew words for justice appear repeatedly throughout the Old Testament of the Bible: *tzadeqah* refers to the state of a society in which justice reigns; *mishpat* refers to what is needed to restore justice.

The Bible assumes that justice is a knowable reality that comes from God. Isaiah 33:5 says, "The LORD is exalted, for he dwells on high; he will fill Zion with justice [*mishpat*] and righteousness [*tzadeqah*]." The systems of justice we have today can be traced back to the efforts of Truth-seeking Jesus followers.

How Jesus Followers Restored Justice

Let's look at five ways believers have pursued justice based on a biblical worldview: property rights, criminal justice, international law, just war, and administrative law.

Property Rights

In the thirteenth century, an English Franciscan friar named William of Ockham (1285–1347) found himself frustrated by laws that were too theoretical. Going back to the story of the garden of Eden, William reasoned that in having the right to enjoy the fruits of their labors, Adam and Eve had been given the right to property. Later Scripture passages forbidding theft ("You shall not steal" [Exod. 20:15]) and promoting the validity of contracts ("You shall not bear false witness" [20:16]) reinforced William's view. Property is a tangible basis for rights, he surmised.[4]

William was followed by other Christian thinkers such as the brilliant Dutch lawyer Hugo Grotius (1585–1645), who obtained his doctorate at age fifteen and wrote several books defending the truth of Christianity. Grotius's extensive writings on property law influenced John Locke, who in turn influenced America's founders, who in turn included the right to property in the Constitution. Many other nations have similar laws. Those that do not, find themselves mired in poverty and corruption. The Harvard professor Richard Pipes has pointed out that nations whose legal systems effectively protect the right to property have nearly ten times the average income as nations that do not protect such rights.[5]

On the opposite side of these thinkers is the atheistic Karl Marx (1818–83), whose ideas are enjoying a resurgence today. Marx believed in abolishing private property. In the 1920s and 1930s, Soviet leaders put Marx's ideas into practice. They seized farms and starved, deported to labor camps, and executed farmers as enemies of the state.[6]

These policies had horrifying consequences: twenty to sixty million people lost their lives in Soviet purges or intentional campaigns of isolation and starvation.[7] In China, forty to seventy million people lost their lives—in peacetime—through Chairman Mao's application of Marxist policies.[8] Many other nations followed suit, with similarly disastrous results. The deliberate rejection of God and biblical morality led to the forced abolition of private property, which in turn led to the most destructive social experiment in history.

Criminal Justice

The truths viewpoint often leads to a naive understanding of justice. Those who want to "defund the police," a legacy of Marxist ideology, assert that law enforcement programs are the problem, not the solution to the crises we face. Jacob Tobia, who calls himself a "gender queer author-performer," said in a 2019 *Vice* article that he envisions a world "without prisons and without cops, so cops are just these community members who don't even need night sticks because they just give people emotional support."[9] While Tobia is being intentionally provocative, his viewpoint is widely shared.

Jesus followers acknowledge that because of human sinfulness, inequities in the justice system do exist. They must be addressed. Yet we must be realistic. It is not true that no one chooses to do wrong, as some thinkers such as the spiritual teacher Eckhart Tolle claim. Tolle asserts that a proper justice system will recognize that people are not responsible for the evil they do. Rather, their "pain-body" is responsible. Tolle longs for the day when a legitimate defense in court would be, "My client's pain-body was activated, and he did not know what he was doing. In fact, he didn't do it. His pain-body did."[10]

From the perspective of Truth, as well as the sweep of human history, I find Tolle's view impossibly naive. If Truth cannot be known, all we have are truths based on individual self-perception. Further, if Truth cannot be known, justice is not a category of meaning that exists and may be discovered. Relativistic kind of thinking threatens the very foundation of justice, wrote Harold Berman, a longtime Harvard Law School professor and Jewish convert to Christianity. As law loses its religious and transcendent qualities, Berman warned, "the historical soil of the Western legal tradition is being washed away . . . and the tradition itself is threatened with collapse."[11]

Based on the belief that Truth exists and justice is real and discoverable, Jesus followers in history have sought to reform the justice system. According to historian Philip Jenkins, it was Christian thinkers who injected compassion into brutal systems of criminal law. The idea that offenders should be reformed came from a Christian understanding of redemption. In the 1700s, first-time offenders could "plead their clergy" to receive lighter punishment. Priests implemented an annual "Love Day" on which enemies were encouraged to reconcile with one another rather than engage in deadly feuds. They even developed liturgies in which sworn enemies could enter into blood brotherhood with one another. Today's renewed emphasis on reconciliation (meetings in which perpetrators express sorrow and victims extend personal forgiveness), mediation (victims and perpetrators meeting to satisfy justice and seek restoration), and arbitration (people in conflict meeting with a neutral third party to work out disputes) can be traced back to these innovations.[12]

International Law

The United Nations Universal Declaration of Human Rights of 1948 recognizes that all human beings are born free and equal in dignity and rights; that everyone has the right to life, liberty, and security of person; and that no one shall be held in slavery or servitude or be subject to torture or cruel, degrading, or inhumane treatment. As we have seen in the last several chapters, these rights are biblically based, though the United Nations did not acknowledge this foundation.

With so little attention given to the biblical basis for rights, it is not surprising that few people realize the impact Jesus followers have had in the field of international law.[13] Here is one story demonstrating that impact. As a young man, Bartolomé de Las Casas (1484–1556) came to the New World, where he participated in the abuse of Native Americans. Challenged by other Catholic leaders, Las Casas repented and dedicated his life to fighting for the rights of natives. He lobbied the royal court of Spain to end their enslavement. Initially, Las Casas advocated for the use of African slaves, though he later changed course and worked to protect them as well. Las Casas was motivated by his faith. Along with everything else, he was concerned about evangelizing the natives and knew they would be receptive if they were freed from coercion and abuse. The gospel should be freely preached and freely accepted or rejected.[14] His work led to new laws—laws that became the first examples of international law. Hugo Grotius (1583–1645), the child-prodigy-turned-legal-expert also exerted tremendous influence with his writings on how nations should relate to one another. For his contributions, Grotius has been called the "father of international law."

Just War

"Blessed are the peacemakers," Jesus said (Matt. 5:9). But as the prophet Jeremiah warned, "'Peace, peace,' when there is no peace" is to heal a wound lightly (Jer. 6:14). Peace dies when evil reigns.

Many Christians in history, especially those of Amish, Mennonite, and Quaker backgrounds, have embraced nonresistance and pacifism as the best paths to peace. They do not believe in serving in the military or in law enforcement, where their jobs might require them to commit violence. But nonresistance and pacifism are personal stances. What should a political leader do when facing aggression from other nations?

Sometimes war is necessary to restore peace. The question is not whether war is evil—it is. The question is how to minimize evil when war becomes unavoidable. Augustine of Hippo and Thomas Aquinas thought deeply about this and formed the "just war" tradition. We looked at this tradition briefly in chapter 5 when examining the value of human life. Based on a view of humans as God's image bearers, seven commonsense criteria for a just war have been developed:

1. Just cause. All aggression is condemned; only defensive war is legitimate.
2. Just intention. The goal is to secure a just peace. This is the *only* legitimate goal. It is never right to wage war to secure revenge, to conquer for the purpose of economic gain, or to prove that your side is superior.

3. Last resort. War may be waged only when every other path—such as negotiation and compromise—has failed.

4. Formal declaration. War may be waged only by government, not private individuals, and the government's highest authorities must officially declare their government's intentions.

5. Limited objectives. The purpose of war is to win peace. It is never right to destroy the enemy's economic or political institutions.

6. Proportionate means. The weaponry and the force used should be limited to what is needed to repel the aggression and deter future attacks.

7. Noncombatant immunity. Since war is an official act of government, only those who are officially agents of government may fight, and individuals not actively contributing to the conflict should be immune from attack.[15]

These seven points are not a checklist.[16] The goal is not to justify war but to secure justice. If every nation refused to wage wars of aggression, stayed focused on securing a just peace, used war only as a last resort, formally declared war with limited objectives, and used only proportionate means while protecting noncombatants, war as we have known it would be very rare.

How does just war theory square with Matthew 5:39, where Jesus says that if someone slaps you on the cheek, you should "turn to him the other also"? The philosopher Arthur Holmes (1924–2011) maintained that the context of that verse refers to individuals, not to governments or churches.[17] "It means that as an individual I do not take the law into my own hands," he said.[18] The pursuit of justice permits national defense and law enforcement, Holmes argued, but not personal vengeance.

Administrative Law

One of the most important aspects of justice is how laws ought to be justly administered. It is an aspect of law that many people find baffling, and yet our everyday lives would be dramatically different if we didn't have it.

Think of it this way. If I'm thirsty, I turn on the tap to get a drink of water and seldom consider all the work it takes to make this simple act possible. A water source must be identified. Dams and aqueducts must be built and maintained. These things take money, which requires legislation to authorize a system of assessing, billing, receiving taxes, and distributing the proceeds. Legal codes, courts, and penalties must be established to protect property rights and prosecute those who fail to pay.

All of this must be done before I get a single drop of water. Then the water must be tested, pressurized, and pushed through hundreds of miles of pipes to deliver it to buildings engineered in accordance with standardized codes to keep people safe and limit property damage. Rights of way must be established and mapped. Teams of engineers and construction workers must be hired, and equipment must be purchased to carry out the work. This is all enormously expensive and demands a taxing district, established through clear laws, that authorizes and collects tax proceeds. And don't forget all the pipes, pumps, taps, and installation equipment that must be manufactured from raw materials as well.

Not only must water be safely delivered, but waste products must also be disposed of in a sanitary fashion. This requires another system in reverse—hundreds more miles of pipes and a water treatment facility where waste water can be recycled or treated and released. The system often breaks down, which requires yet more mapping processes, construction teams, and communication systems.

That drink of water I take for granted results from decades of work by scores of people whose coordinated efforts make my life much easier. Administrative law makes all of this happen. Administrators figure out how to put laws into practice through (hopefully) fair regulations, trained personnel, and accountability systems that minimize corruption.

Considering how difficult it is to justly administer laws, the ancient legal system handed down by Moses seems brilliantly ahead of its time. It specifies a system of courts and legislative bodies that regulate community life. These regulations include defining and securing the boundaries of towns, protecting property holdings, recording economic transactions, providing food safety and the disposal of waste, handling public health crises, resolving disputes, and ensuring worker safety.

Up against the complexity of forming and enforcing just laws, the truths viewpoint seems absurd in the extreme. Postmodern rhetoric of "my truth" and "your truth" cannot maintain a just legal system, or even make sense of how we ought to live together in community. Unless someone in the process believes that reality is real, we'd better get used to being thirsty.

Even with a commitment to Truth, administrative law is fraught with difficulties. In the United States Constitution, the founders charged Congress with making laws. Imagine the immense responsibility members of Congress bear. Every year Congress convenes more than 200 committees and subcommittees to consider 9,500 bills totaling 110,000 pages, which would be a stack of paper 36 feet high.

Then, when Congress passes laws and turns them over to government departments to administer, things become even more complex. The Internal Revenue Service regulations run to seventy-five hundred pages of legalese, and the IRS is just one of more than four hundred federal agencies. Take that times fifty states, hundreds of county commissions, thousands of municipalities, and thousands of other governing bodies such as school districts, and you can see the problems that might emerge.

One problem is that those who administer the laws are not accountable to the people in the way that elected officials are. We don't get to vote for who operates the Department of Motor Vehicles or how they operate it. There is very little room for appeal when things go wrong.

A second problem is that some administrators of laws have used their power to undermine law. The Fifteenth Amendment to the Constitution specifically states that the right to vote will not be denied or abridged based on race, color, or previous condition of servitude. Yet the Jim Crow laws of the twentieth century did exactly that, placing barriers between people and their right to vote. How did this happen? Because administrators wrote voting regulations in such a way that rights were denied.[19]

A third problem is that administrative law can become a criminal justice issue. Many regulations involve criminal penalties for violators. There are more than four thousand federal crimes on the books and thousands more in each of the fifty states. These laws often conflict with one another. Attorney Harvey Silverglate estimates that the average American unwittingly commits three felony crimes every day because of vague laws.[20] A felony is a serious crime for which a person could go to prison, be deprived of certain rights, and be taken out of the market for good jobs.

Fourth, burdensome bureaucracy can be used as a tool of persecution. I once visited a country where the government assumes that every native person is born a Muslim. This is listed on citizens' national identity cards. If a person becomes a Christian and wants to change their card, they will be buried in years of paperwork. They'll be discriminated against and forced to pay bribes to corrupt officials. To my knowledge, Christians in that nation are not being beaten and tortured by the government. Rather, they are persecuted by being buried in bureaucracy in a way that makes it difficult for them to exercise their freedom of conscience.

Despite the importance of administrative law and its origins in the law of Moses, I am not aware of any current resources that offer a biblical worldview of administrative law beyond warning of how its abuse can diminish God-given freedoms.[21]

Still, many Jesus followers through history have offered biblical insight into what makes for good political leadership, which is essential to just administration. Take John Calvin (1509–64) as an example. Though he is seen as a polarizing figure by many, Calvin's sage advice for "civil magistrates" deserves consideration. In his *Institutes of the Christian Religion*, Calvin says that God ordained government and that magistrates are ordained by him. As God's representatives, "they should watch with all care, earnestness, and diligence, to represent in themselves to men some image of divine providence, protection, goodness, benevolence, and justice."[22] Calvin discusses the difference between the judicial, ceremonial, and moral laws of the Old Testament. He offers guidance for how to engage with the courts, how to handle unjust rulers, and so much more. As a professor, I once led a study group in reading the section of the *Institutes* devoted to government. Many of my students admitted to being surprised at the practical, almost fatherly, guidance Calvin offered. This is especially amazing given that Calvin published his first draft of the *Institutes* at age twenty-seven!

What Should We Do Now?

We have covered a lot of ground in this chapter. Maybe your mind is spinning with the complexity of it all. What should Christians do? I suggest we begin in these four places. We should do the following:

1. *Start with what God says.* We can summarize a biblical worldview of politics and justice in seven points:

   - We are social. Humans are created as social beings (Gen. 2:20). Society exists because we are relational.
   - We are to serve. Up against the haughty, elite-driven cultures of Greece and Rome, Jesus taught that "the last will be first, and the first last" (Matt. 20:16; cf. Mark 10:43; Luke 22:27).
   - Both the individual and society are valuable. We start with the value of every person and on that basis learn to live in community and challenge unjust laws when necessary.
   - Society's institutions must be respected and balanced. The family, church, and state all contribute to stability. All must be carefully nurtured.
   - Government is a noble endeavor. Even though leaders often make poor decisions, we should pray for them and hold them accountable. Christians must be good citizens.
   - Family and sexual integrity must be preserved. In ancient Greece and Rome, sexual perversion was common. Only with Christianity, says the legendary historian Will Durant, did sexual fidelity become a virtue.[23] This encouraged the kind of family stability that undergirds a good society.
   - Church is essential. The role of the church is to proclaim the Truth regarding sin, repentance, and salvation. Churches are to model what it looks like to love our neighbors as ourselves. The church is the conscience of a nation. The church models God's kingdom values on earth.

In advocating these seven points, we may find ourselves at odds with governmental leaders. What should we do in such situations? Usually, there is a process by which we can advocate for change. But what if there isn't? Andrew van der Bijl, known as Brother Andrew, has dedicated his life to smuggling Bibles into closed countries. When challenged about whether this was ethical, van der Bijl replied with this question: Should anti-God forces be allowed to win by default? He reasoned as follows: Christians are to be subject to the governing authorities (Rom. 13:1). They must love all (Matt. 5:44). They must live at peace with all (Rom. 12:18). If our leaders have made themselves enemies of God, though, we are not to let them win. We are not to be conquered by evil (12:21).

If justice were easy, everyone would pursue it. If the cost were low, everyone would pay it. Standing for justice requires us to have a firm grasp of Truth and a willingness to stand for what is right, even at great personal risk.

2. *Champion religious freedom.* In the US Constitution's Bill of Rights, religious freedom is the first right protected. It is mentioned before freedom of speech, freedom of the press, the right to peaceably assemble, and the right to petition government for the redress of grievances. In the United States, current law says that the federal government must protect religious freedom, except in extreme cases where the government has a compelling interest in restricting it—for example, if a religious group calls for violence against the citizenry.

Most people don't think much about religious freedom. "You have the right to go to church," they reason, "so what are you complaining about?" But religious freedom is so much more than the freedom to worship. According to government professor Timothy Shah, a commitment to religious freedom has led to economic development, political freedom, civil liberties, gender empowerment, reduction of poverty, and the stability of government.[24] Sociologists Brian J. Grim and Roger Finke additionally point out the direct link between governmental and social restrictions on religion and religious persecution and conflict. Government restriction on religion signals anti-religious groups that they are free to attack those with whom they disagree.[25]

Be a defender of religious freedom, here and abroad, and not just for people you agree with.

3. *Support justice initiatives.* America's founders believed that by outlining the principles of liberty, they could set in motion a process through which America could grow to become a beacon of freedom and justice. They envisioned equal opportunity for all.

If you are concerned about social justice, there are many excellent initiatives to support. Each year *World Magazine* highlights ministries that serve the marginalized in Jesus's name. Pick one and get involved. Consider especially supporting initiatives that restore people to full functioning in society. One example is the InnerChange Freedom Initiative (IFI), which helps ex-convicts reintegrate into their communities. Sociologist Byron R. Johnson spent six years interviewing ex-convicts, people for whom society holds little hope. The IFI program, he found, changed participants from the inside out. "I'm not who I used to be" became their common refrain as they became new creations in Christ (see 2 Cor. 5:17).[26]

4. *Keep our wits about us.* In 2 Timothy 4:5, the apostle Paul tells his protégé, "Always be sober-minded." In

other words, keep your wits about you. Evil never stops trying to eat away at what is good. Jesus followers committed to Truth may have restored justice in the past, but injustice still threatens to prevail. It is tempting to give up. When I get discouraged, I remember a scene from J. R. R. Tolkien's *The Two Towers* in which the hobbits Pippin and Merry entreat Treebeard, the leader of the peace-loving Ents, ancient tree-like creatures, to join the battle against the forces of the evil Sauron. When the Ents refuse, Pippin tries to comfort Merry by saying, "Maybe Treebeard is right. We don't belong here, Merry. This is too big for us. What can we do in the end? We've got the Shire. Maybe we should go home." Merry replies with desperation in his voice, "The fires of Isengard will spread, and the woods of Tribru and Buckland will burn. And all that was once great and good in this world will be gone."[27]

What Merry understood is a lesson for contemporary society. When we fail to promote Truth through freedom and justice, there may come a day when we no longer have the freedom to act justly. Injustice reigns in many places. What responsibility do we have to God and to future generations to stand for Truth and fight against evil and injustice in our time? This is a vital question we must all answer.

So far, we've examined the impact of Jesus followers on the value of human life, caring, education, science, art, politics, and justice. But one thing that ties these Jesus followers together is their commitment to hard work. As we will see in the next chapter, even here—in the world of vocation and economic productivity—Jesus followers have exerted tremendous influence.

How Jesus Followers Have Changed How We Work

La Sagrada Familia, Church of the Holy Family, in Barcelona, Spain, is a place of worship unlike any other. It winds, undulates, and ripples. The interior makes worshipers feel as if they are in a forest, with branches stretching upward and enormous stained glass windows filtering light as through fluttering leaves in the breeze. Louis Sullivan, the father of the skyscraper, called it "spirit symbolized in stone."[1] He considered it one of the greatest pieces of architecture he had seen.

Millions of people visit La Sagrada Familia each year. Not all have been fans. George Orwell called it "one of the most hideous buildings in the world" and thought that the Anarchists had shown bad taste in "not blowing it up when they had the chance."[2]

Love it or hate it, La Sagrada Familia is a story of a man transformed by the work of building, even as he challenged the public's understanding of what a building could be. It is the story of the work we do—even tasks as unexciting as pouring concrete and putting one brick on top of another. The work we do is a subplot in the story God is telling in the world.

La Sagrada Familia's architect was the quirky Antoni Gaudi (1852–1926). Upon Gaudi's graduation from architecture school, the school's director said, "Today we have granted this degree to either a madman, or a genius. Time will tell which."[3]

In commissioning Gaudi to build La Sagrada Familia, philanthropist José Maria Bocabella placed his bet on the genius. Yet he was concerned by Gaudi's lack of interest in spiritual things. Bocabella assigned his protégé devotional texts to inspire him artistically and draw him closer to God. The more Gaudi built, the more his heart warmed to the spiritual themes of the humility of Jesus's birth and the cruelty of his death on the cross. He found himself elatedly meditating on Jesus's exaltation to glory. His student Cesar Martinell (1888–1973) wrote that Gaudi "wanted the stones placed one on top of another to form verses of a magnificent poem which would be perceived by the eyes of the people and repeated through the centuries."[4]

From age thirty to the end of his life, Gaudi obsessed over converting his newfound spiritual sensitivity into the architectural masterpiece La Sagrada Familia would become.[5] He lived as a pauper, seeking no economic reward. "Gaudi's peculiar Christian humility understood that we should all try, each within the bounds of our own gifts or limitations, to play a part in God's greater design; however large or small that might be," noted his biographer Gijs Van Hensbergen.[6]

"Beauty is the radiance of Truth," Gaudi told his students.[7] The mission of the La Sagrada Familia project, he said, was to capture in a building what God had made in creation. God did not create in straight lines or sharp corners, Gaudi observed, so buildings should not be made that way either. Yet Gaudi's dreamlike style is not random. Its whimsy conceals intricate geometric designs and mathematical precision. La Sagrada

Familia's interior, for example, is a series of interconnected catenary arches, which are the kinds of arches you would have if you hung weights on a series of cables and then inverted them. Essentially, Gaudi imagined the entire interior of the church upside down and then flipped it over. Today, La Sagrada Familia's architects and engineers employ powerful computer-aided design programs to decipher Gaudi's vision and bring it to completion. Gaudi died without finishing his great work (it is scheduled for completion in 2026, at which point it will have been under construction for 144 years).

Gaudi never wrote a book, but what he penned in stone connected Truth with everyday work. "Without truth there is no complete art," he said.[8] As the first spires were being completed, Gaudi placed the words "Hosanna in Excelsis" at their top, too high for worshipers to see with the naked eye. The angels would see it, he said, and they would rejoice.

For Gaudi, work was worship. He believed, therefore he worked. This is God's way. The God of the Bible is a working God. He worked in creation, and he continues his work today.

Yet most of us wonder about the value of the work we do. A 2021 Gallup World Poll of workers in 160 countries found that seven in ten employees are "struggling or suffering, rather than thriving, in their overall lives." Eighty percent lack engagement, which Gallup defines as involvement in, enthusiasm about, and commitment to their work and workplace.[9] These problems are not just COVID-19 related. According to Gallup chairman and CEO Jim Clifton, workplace dissatisfaction has been rising for a decade.[10] What most people do with their waking hours sucks the life out of them. Clifton finds himself deeply troubled by this. "Imagine a worldwide Venezuela," he says, calling to mind the heartbreaking collapse of an economically prosperous nation through misguided socialist policies and corruption.[11]

Is it possible to reclaim work as an act of worship? That's the million-dollar question. Or more accurately, the trillion-dollar question. The Gallup organization estimated in 2017 that low employee engagement costs the global economy seven trillion dollars a year due to lost productivity.[12]

The Christian philosopher Søren Kierkegaard (1813–55) mused, "What I really need is to arrive at a clear comprehension of what I am to do . . . to find the idea for which I am willing to live and to die."[13] Kierkegaard longed for the "Archemedian point," a reference to the Greek mathematician Archemedes, who said, "Give me a lever long enough and a fulcrum on which to place it, and I shall move the world."[14] Kierkegaard believed that if only he could look back and see the world from God's viewpoint, he would gain the leverage needed to live forward and change the world.

The truths viewpoint cannot satisfy Kierkegaard's quest. If nothing can be known for certain, we are at the mercy of our external circumstances. We are victims. In history, Jesus followers rejected this way of seeing the world. Their faith offered them a worldview of work that made life meaningful here and now, not just in the hereafter. Work is, as John Calvin put it, a "sentry post" God has given us so that we "may not heedlessly wander about through life."[15]

The biblical story of work is not about giving in to what is *outside* us but about cultivating what is *inside* us—the image of God. It affects everything from how we apply ourselves in our labor to how we rest from it.

What Is Work?

A biblical worldview is a worldview of work. Yes, we are theological beings who live in a God-saturated world. But we are also scientific and political and artistic beings. Importantly, we are also economic beings. The word *economics* comes from the Greek words for "household" and "rule." We were designed to steward God's creation by taking initiative and being productive. We were made for work.

Even our most mundane tasks take on meaning when we consider them through a biblical perspective on work. Sor Juana Ines De La Cruz (1648/51–95), a writer who was a Mexican nun, wryly observed that "one can perfectly well philosophize while cooking supper. And I am always saying, when I observe these small details: If Aristotle had been a cook, he would have written much more."[16]

Modern life provides us with economic advantages that would have been unthinkable just a few hundred years ago. This is largely due to Jesus followers who reasoned biblically about work. In 1776, just four months before the American founders signed the Declaration of Independence, moral philosopher Adam Smith (1723–90) published *Wealth of Nations*, drawing the title from passages in Isaiah such as 66:12: "I will make peace flow to her like a river, and the wealth of nations like a flood" (CSB). Smith showed how market forces could free the world from the mercantilist idea that the total amount of wealth was fixed. When each person is free to pursue their own calling, markets serve as an "invisible hand"; they create abundance, benefiting all of us.

The economic transformation that Smith documented has thoroughly changed life on this planet. The Brookings Institution says that as the twenty-first century accelerates, more than 50 percent of the world's population lives in households that are middle class or rich. They have income to buy things like household appliances, go on vacation, and cushion an economic downturn. This has never before been the case in the history of civilization.[17]

Growing wealth has brought unprecedented relief from poverty. Matt Ridley, British journalist and member of Great Britain's

House of Lords, wrote in 2019 that extreme poverty has fallen to historic lows, as has child mortality. Famines are rare. Diseases such as malaria, polio, and heart disease are all declining. In countries with strong economic growth, the use of natural resources such as minerals, metals, and fossil fuels has dropped by a third in the last ten years. Efficient technologies have reduced household electrical consumption. Farmers use 65 percent less land to produce the same quantity of food as they did fifty years ago. Tree density is growing. Animal populations are thriving. Wealth made this possible.[18]

For most of history, people saw survival as life's goal. A few, such as the Greek philosopher Lucretius (99–55 BC), thought that absorbing the teachings of the wise would free people from pain, fear, and struggle.[19] But this had little impact on their material existence. Humanity's only hope was to be transported beyond the cares of life. In the Middle Ages, this mentality dramatically shifted.

How the Middle Ages Transformed Work as We Know It

Before the Middle Ages, most people lived hand to mouth. Their work was backbreaking and tedious. In the Middle Ages, technological innovation increased productivity and made work easier. An example of early technology was the invention of water wheels, which appeared in Irish monasteries of the 600s. Water wheels made it possible to efficiently grind grain, clean newly woven cloth, power bellows and trip hammers in blacksmith shops, saw lumber, and make paper.[20] Windmills performed a similar function in places that lacked flowing streams.

Other labor-saving devices invented in the Middle Ages include the heavy wheeled plow, the horseshoe, the horse collar, the scythe, the chimney, the blast furnace, the suction pump, the grinding wheel, the wheelbarrow, the horizontal loom, the cog, the compass, the hourglass, the mechanical clock, eyeglasses, soap, the wine press, and plate armor.[21] In the medieval world, workers formed into professional guilds for nearly every kind of work. Large cities might have had a hundred such guilds, which included religious duties and were dedicated to patron saints.

Global trade boomed along with population growth. The Black Death, which struck for the first time in the mid-1300s, threatened to bring this economic transformation to a halt. But strangely, the opposite happened. After examining letters, books, and other records of the time, historian John Aberth concluded that the Black Death formed the crucible in which Europe's rebirth was forged.[22]

What specifically happened? Harvard historian Steven Ozment says that in the Black Death's aftermath, the scarcity of workers led to higher wages, which in turn brought independence to people who had previously believed that God had ordained them to be poor.[23] The nobility's heavy-handed economic control was shattered. "The peasant's gain was the lord's loss," says historian David Routt.[24]

This new independence led to property ownership, manufacturing, and banking. According to Ozment, "The Later Middle Ages also saw the development of a money economy. . . . The division between capital and labor that characterizes modern capitalism established itself at this time."[25] People lived longer and ate better.[26] The growing wealth, according to art historian Millard Meiss, led to large donations to churches, which fostered architecture, arts, and music.[27]

The transition to independence, property ownership, and growing wealth for the working class was not smooth. Landowners, desperate to retain their wealth, sought to artificially freeze wages and increase taxes on peasants. This led to peasant revolts in France, Italy, and England, making the fourteenth century the most violent century until the twentieth.[28] As the industrial economy boomed, many working families were hard hit. Children often bore the brunt of this impact, forced to work slavish hours in deplorable conditions. Many Jesus followers tried to soften the blow. Cloth miller John Wood, a devout Christian, set an example for other factories by limiting the workday and establishing a school for the children. Anglican priest George Bull and member of the British Parliament Michael Sadler battled a reluctant Parliament to establish more reasonable work hours and provide education to children forced to work.[29] For many, though, it was too little, too late. The whole system, they came to believe, needed to be overthrown.

The Rise of Marxism

In the 1800s, worker discontent sparked a revolutionary fervor across Europe. In 1848, Karl Marx published *The Communist Manifesto*, in which he enthused, "Let the ruling classes tremble at a communist revolution. The proletarians have nothing to lose but their chains. They have a world to win. Proletarians of all countries, unite!"[30]

For oppressed people, these seemed like words of hope. What is in the earth—natural resources—is all we can count on, Marx believed. History is defined by who controls these resources. Marx theorized that employers take advantage of their employees by abusing their labor without sharing the profits. The rich have taken more than their fair share. It must be taken back, by force if necessary.[31]

As we've seen in earlier chapters, Marxist ideas led to catastrophe. Yet vestiges of Marx's thinking still define our relationship with work today. Many believe that the conflict between the workers (proletariats) and the owners of the means of production (bourgeoisie) is inevitable.[32] A study jointly conducted by the Barna Research Group and Summit Ministries found that 83 percent of Christian, church-attending millennials strongly agree or agree somewhat that the root of society's problems is that rich people exploit the system in a way that hurts the working class.[33]

Can a biblical worldview speak into this conflict? What, exactly, is God's design for work?

Work from a Biblical Worldview

A biblical worldview says we were made to work. Novelist Dorothy L. Sayers (1893–1957) said, "Man is a maker. . . . He is made in the image of the Maker, and he must himself create or become something less than a man."[34]

The impulse to make things, to be productive, is often cast in its basest form. The German sociologist Max Weber (1864–1920) concluded that Protestant Christians invented modern capitalism because they believed that wealth was a sign of God's favor on their work. At the same time, they felt guilty buying nice things, so they saved and invested. This generated capital that led to the Industrial Revolution. By the end of the nineteenth century, according to Weber, the pursuit of wealth became separated from the pursuit of calling. Wealth was pursued for wealth's sake—as a way to win rather than a way to witness to God's power.[35]

A biblical worldview says that work cannot be fully explained by a fear of God's displeasure, greed, or a desire to win. Instead, it makes three basic observations: we were made to work, to risk, and to rest.

We Were Made to Work

Genesis 2:15 says, "The LORD God took the man and put him in the garden of Eden to work it and keep it." The Hebrew word for "work" is *abad*, meaning "to tend" or "to serve in a worshipful way." Work is a form of worship in which we serve God by taking care of what he has made.

The children of Israel were the creation story's original audience. As they came out of Egypt to establish a new nation, the Israelites needed to know their story as image bearers of God. They had been miraculously rescued from oppression, but that did not mean their lives would be easy. Surviving in the promised land would involve building homes, digging wells, planting crops, raising animals, and defending their families from outside enemies. Freedom from slavery did not mean freedom from work. Rather, it was a move from work done in painful obedience to a human king to work done in joyful obedience to the King of Kings.

We are designed for work. Brain research is now showing that work we find ourselves absorbed in seems to trigger key neural networks in the brain associated with alertness, rewards, and having a sense of control over our lives.[36]

Work's value is found not only in how it changes the world but also in how it changes us as worshipers. Karol Wojtyła (1920–2005), who became Pope John Paul II, reflected a great deal throughout his life on the relationship between work and worship. As a young man, he wrote a poem about the deeper meaning of his work in a rock quarry:

> Listen: the even knocking of hammers,
> so much their own,
> I project on to the people
> to test the strength of each blow.
> Listen now: electric current
> cuts through a river of rock
> And a thought grows in me day after day:
> the greatness of work is inside man.[37]

Recent research affirms the relationship between work and worship. Neuroscientist Andrew Newberg of the University of Pennsylvania School of Medicine used various imaging systems to study the brains of people as they meditated or prayed. He found that meditation and prayer activate the frontal lobe—which is associated with concentration and attention—and decrease activity in the parietal lobe, the part of the brain that orients us to space and time. In worship, we touch eternity.[38]

Newberg's description of what happens during worship is directly tied to what happens to people during meaningful experiences of work. In my decades of working with young adults, I've asked thousands of students if they've ever had the kind of experience Newberg describes. Some recall times of intense worship in a church service or at a retreat. Many more describe times of working on something they found so fascinating that they lost track of time and space. What's more, they recall such experiences from early childhood, whether it involved making a drawing, crafting a story, building a fort, or creating an imaginary play world. They were expending effort, but it seemed more like worship than work.

Our work-worship orientation reflects God's image in us. Even in a sinful world, as Wojtyła affirmed, the greatness of work is inside a person. It isn't just what we produce that is important; it is what is produced in us. We are fallen but great. Our work matters.

We Were Made to Risk

The Genesis account showcases the God who moves his creation from formlessness to order and from a void to abundance. God made us not merely to survive but to be fruitful, multiply, and fill the earth. This mindset would have been utterly unfamiliar to the children of Israel, bound as they had been to Egyptian servitude. The primary Egyptian religious text, the

Book of the Dead, pictures the world as unpredictable and cruel. Beyond the order of Egypt, people believed, was only chaos. According to history professor W. M. Spellman, Egyptians viewed the "journey" as a thing to be feared. To journey into the wilderness for three days was unthinkable. To go into the wilderness forever was completely absurd.[39]

To embrace their freedom, the children of Israel needed release from the story of chaos and scarcity they had internalized in Egypt. By hearing the Genesis account, they would have learned that God had made them in his image to work, that sin had tainted the world, and that God had chosen them as agents of redemption.

To move toward order and abundance, the children of Israel had to risk something. They had to journey into the wilderness, rejecting the familiar and embracing the unknown. They had to learn that the enemy inside—the one that kept them stuck—was a harsher master than the wilderness ever would be. Perhaps that is why "fear not" is the most repeated command in the Scriptures. The good life is risky.

We Were Made to Rest

Just as we were made to work, as God does, we were also made to rest, as God did. Genesis 2:1–2 states, "Thus the heavens and the earth were finished, and all the host of them. And on the seventh day God finished his work that he had done, and he rested on the seventh day from all his work that he had done." The word for "rest" in Hebrew is *shabbat*, or *sabbath*, which means "to cease or neglect."

To even know what it means to *have* a seventh day requires taking on God's perspective. Most time cycles occur in nature. A year is the time it takes for the earth to make a complete orbit around the sun. A day is one revolution of the earth. But a week of seven days, said the Jewish philosopher Abraham

Joshua Heschel (1907–72), is unrelated to these natural cycles. It exists in the mind of God. God set an example for rest and invented the seven-day week to show us how to do it. The sabbath, Heschel said, "is a day on which we are called upon to share in what is eternal in time, to turn from the results of creation to the mystery of creation; from the world of creation to the creation of the world."[40]

Rest is an essential aspect of work that turns our attention away from our out-of-control-ness to God's in-charge-ness. The Anglican *Book of Common Prayer* teaches worshipers this end-of-the-day prayer as they cease from their labors: "Be present, O merciful God, and protect us through the silent hours of this night, so that we who are wearied by the work and the changes of this fleeting world may rest upon Thy eternal changelessness; through Jesus Christ our Lord. Amen."[41]

Once God's people were freed from slavery, a biblical worldview enabled them to bear God's image through work, be rewarded for the risks they took, and find rest and balance. Their work was something more than toil; it was a God-given vocation that gave meaning to every area of life.

How Jesus Followers Explained the Meaning of Work

First Corinthians 7:17 says, "Only let each person lead the life that the Lord has assigned to him, and to which God has called him." The Greek word for "call" is *klesis*. It was translated into Latin as *vocare*, from which we get our word *vocation*. The Puritan philosopher William Perkins (1558–1602) said, "Every person, of every degree, state, sex, or condition without exception, must have some personal and particular calling to walk in."[42] The true end of our lives—the reason we are here—is to serve God by serving others through our vocation.[43]

Of course, a vocation and a job are not the same thing. A vocation is a lens through which we view our life's work. John Henry Newman (1801–90) said, "For in truth we are not called once only, but many times; all through our life Christ is calling us."[44]

Notable Christian thinkers have written extensively about how we work, what our work means to us and to our families, and what to do when our earthly vocation comes into conflict with our heavenly one.

Early Christian thinkers seemed to believe that the best vocation was the "contemplative life"—*viva contemplativa*—rather than the "active life"—*viva activa*. Bernard of Clairvaux (1090–1153), writing to a young protégé named Walter, chided the young man for staying home to care for his mother rather than joining the monastery. "You use such great endowments to serve not Christ their giver, but transitory things," he wrote.[45] To another young correspondent, Bernard wrote, "Now, as fire and water cannot be together, so the delights of the spirit and those of the flesh are incompatible."[46]

To be sure, the contemplative life was not an idle one. All the church fathers (and mothers, such as Christine de Pasan [ca. 1365–1430]), condemned idleness. Christine quotes St. Bernard: "Idleness is the mother of all error and the wicked stepmother of the virtues."[47] Thomas à Kempis (1380–1471) wrote that idleness makes it boring to be alive.[48]

In his extensive writing, Thomas Aquinas (1225–74) began challenging what he saw as an artificial barrier between the active life and the contemplative life. Quoting St. Gregory, he wrote, "Those who wish to hold the fortress of contemplation must first of all train in the camp of action."[49] Work is done out of love. God does not need our work, but our neighbor does.

Martin Luther (1483–1546) built on Aquinas's observations. In "An Open Letter to the Christian Nobility of the German

Nation Concerning the Reform of the Christian Estate," he challenged the idea that pastors, priests, monks, and nuns had a vocation, while the rest just had jobs.[50] According to the Lutheran scholar Gene Edward Veith, Luther rejected the distinction between "those who prayed, those who ruled, and those who worked." All are called to prayer. All are called to be citizens. All are called to productive work.[51]

Our work is meaningful not just because of what we produce and how we bear God's image in producing it. Our work is a spiritual calling.

What Should We Do Now?

Many assume that work is hard and hard is bad. A biblical worldview rejects this assumption, showing us a working God who made us in his image. It celebrates productivity. We use our minds to come up with new ideas. With just laws and a secure right to property, we can multiply wealth and opportunity. This creates options that make us better off so we can be generous with what we've received. I weave these thoughts together with this sentence: Minds with property multiply options and give. Let's look briefly at each of these five aspects of work.

Minds

The human mind has created more wealth than all the world's natural resources. Of the world's twenty wealthiest companies, only two derive their profits primarily from natural resources such as oil. The other companies are mind-focused. They develop computer programs, make financial arrangements, and develop systems to efficiently deliver consumer products. The top job creators and innovators of today don't mine things out of the ground; they employ their minds to bring value.

Minds matter. As a high school student, I worked in a super-market, which seemed at the time like a low-level job compared to the jobs of some of my friends, who helped out in law firms or caddied at the country club. When I expressed my frustration to my father, he challenged my thinking. "Your physical circumstances do not control you," he said. "You have a choice." My father was right. Every day I had to choose to take pride in my mopping and cleaning. I had to choose to help our customers enjoy their experience in our store. I had to choose to encourage my fellow employees. I didn't end up going into the grocery business, but the lessons I learned there have helped me succeed in the jobs I've held since and in businesses I've started. It isn't anyone else's responsibility to engage me. I must use my mind to give meaning to my circumstances.

Property

The right to own the source of our value encourages productivity. As we learned in the chapter on justice, this right is rooted in the right to private property. Data shows that nations that strongly protect private property, rather than try to abolish it, have a substantially higher standard of living.[52] Yet what makes the right to property meaningful is not how many square feet of earth we control. It is about creating value. It is about ideas.

I am old enough to remember having to buy a Microsoft Windows operating system in a box containing a booklet and a CD-ROM. The box, CD-ROM, and booklet probably had a physical cost of a dollar, and yet the package cost a hundred times that much. Why? Because it contained a computer code—a sequence of ideas—that would help me use my computer more productively. Bill Gates became one of the wealthiest people in the world because of his ideas, not because of his access to mineral wealth.

Right now, I'm thinking of the wealthiest people I know. Many of them own a great deal of property, but that is not the source of their economic value. Rather, their value is in their willingness to learn, their focused effort, their cultivation of a network, and their problem-solving ability. Those are values in which each of us can grow.

Multiply

The scarcity mindset says that there is only so much to go around. It is like a pie that must be divided into smaller and smaller pieces as more people populate the planet. The abundance mindset, on the other hand, says we should multiply, not divide. Instead of handing out smaller and smaller pieces of pie, we should make more pies! As the traditional Kenyan proverb puts it, "You can count the number of seeds in a mango, but you cannot count the number of mangos in a seed."[53]

Here's an example of the power of multiplication. Programmers say they could re-create the Uber rideshare app for a million dollars or so. But as a company, Uber has a market capitalization of $64 billion. This makes it more valuable than Ford, Fiat-Chrysler, General Motors, or even FedEx.[54] Uber has its problems, as all companies do, but more than a million people use the app to earn an average of 50 percent more than the federal minimum wage by driving others around. They use their private vehicles to create economic value for themselves and provide a valuable service to consumers. Most of the Uber drivers I've spoken to work part-time, using their free hours to make a little extra money to pay down student loans, live in a little nicer apartment, or pay for their children's educational activities. The point is that they work as much or as little as they want, when they want, and use their own property to generate income.

Once, after I explained the multiply principle to a group of high school students, a young woman approached me in frustration. "I have a dog-walking business," she said. "I charge $10 an hour. There are only so many hours in a day. So how does the multiply principle apply to me?" Suddenly, her eyes lit up. "Wait. Who says I must walk only one dog at a time? Or that I have to be the only person doing the walking?" This young woman quickly saw that she could multiply the fruit of her labors by changing her thinking. It is a simple example, but I've thought about it many times. I've learned to ask, "How can I be a better steward of my time and resources in this situation?"

Options

Work is most profitable when people have options. Sometimes options are overwhelming, like when trying to choose from among hundreds of kinds of breakfast cereal at a supermarket. But as anyone who lives in a country where the shelves are bare will tell you, having options is better than not having them.

One way to multiply options, especially for vulnerable populations, is to support small businesses. African American business owners have twelve times more wealth than African Americans who do not own businesses.[55] In the last decade, more than 50 percent of the two million new businesses started in the United States were minority owned. These businesses created 4.7 million jobs. Minority-owned businesses add $700 billion annually to the economy.[56]

Give

We don't just work for our own benefit. Work creates wealth and opportunity, which may be shared with others. Proverbs 11:25 says, "The generous will prosper; those who refresh others will themselves be refreshed" (NLT).

Giving brings pleasure. A study conducted by the National Institutes of Health showed that when people were given $100 to spend however they pleased, donating a portion of their windfall activated the pleasure centers in their brains.[57] Giving also motivates others. Ironically, it also increases wealth: people who give more manage their budgets more carefully to make room for giving, a habit that improves their overall accumulation of wealth.[58]

People of faith get this. As we saw in chapter 3, the value of services performed and contributions made just by Americans of faith is in the trillions of dollars each year, representing more than 10 percent of America's annual economic value.

The more I use my mind, the more value I create. The more value I create, the more options I multiply for myself and others. This generates more time, talent, and treasure for me to share with others. Through work we can see a strong connection between loving God by bearing his image as hard workers and loving our neighbors by creating value for their lives.

Jesus followers from history help us see work as something we do as image bearers of God. Work grows us in character and in spiritual calling. It is an act of worship.

Through their work, Jesus followers changed the world's understanding of human value, advanced medical care, fostered education, gave birth to science, created beautiful art, and set the world on a path to liberty. At the end of the last several chapters, I speculated about how we might apply the lessons we've learned from the lives of these Jesus followers. In the next chapter, I'd like to add to these observations by speculating about how we might communicate differently every day based on Truth.

How to Tell the Truth and Be Nice at the Same Time

In the past, the truths viewpoint led to a soft tolerance that said that individual truth claims must be accepted unless they directly harm others. This has changed in the last half century with the teachings of scholars like Herbert Marcuse (1898–1979), a Marxist professor and the popularizer of critical theory. To Marcuse, intolerance is a virtue and tolerance is a vice. Tolerance legitimizes viewpoints that should not be tolerated. Tolerance is "serving the cause of oppression," he says.[1]

As more people embrace the truths viewpoint, traditional protections of tolerance, such as freedom of speech and freedom of the press, are coming under attack. Fifty-one percent of Americans now say that the First Amendment, which guarantees the right to freedom of speech and freedom of religion, is outdated and should be rewritten to prevent hate speech and better reflect the cultural mores of the times.[2] In the truths viewpoint, psychology replaces logic. Carl R. Trueman says, "Once harm and oppression are regarded as being primarily psychological categories, freedom of speech then becomes part of the problem, not the solution, because words become potential weapons."[3]

Many worldviews do, by their nature and the example of their leaders, weaponize language to demean others. Take, for example, the Marxist worldview and one of its heroes, Vladimir Lenin (1870–1924). Biographer Victor Sebestyen notes that Lenin carefully crafted a harsh and abusive way of making his arguments and as a result "almost single-handedly . . . changed the language on the revolutionary Left." His opponents weren't just wrong. They were "scoundrels," "philistines," "cretins," "filthy scum," or other names that are too profane to mention here.[4] One of Lenin's close associates, Moishe Olgin, remarked, "He does not reply to an opponent. He vivisects him. . . . He ridicules his opponent. He castigates him. He makes you feel that his victim is an ignoramus, a fool, a presumptuous nonentity."[5]

Even after the fall of the Soviet Union, Sebestyen says, Communists everywhere "learned that it made sense to play the man, not the ball—and how to do it with ruthless efficiency." It became "settled Bolshevik practice."[6]

Saul Alinsky's bestselling book, *Rules for Radicals*, carried Lenin's death-dealing rhetoric into American life. "Ridicule is man's most potent weapon," he gloats. "There is no defense. It is almost impossible to counterattack ridicule. Also it infuriates the opposition, who then react to your advantage."[7]

Christians often feel especially targeted. Social commentator Rod Dreher says that "a progressive—and profoundly anti-Christian militancy—is steadily overtaking society . . . empowered by unprecedented technological capabilities to surveil private life. There is virtually nowhere left to hide."[8]

Some Christians I have talked to believe the only way Truth can "win" is to fight fire with fire. In the Summit Ministries program, we've tried to teach and model a different way: telling the Truth while being gracious.

Admittedly, the fight-fire-with-fire strategy draws more attention. "Watch person X humiliate person Y in three sentences" is a social media link that will get more traction than "Watch person X respond to person Y with Truth and grace." Yet the Jesus follower should have more than an immediate victory in mind. We may find those we disagree with irritating (they may feel the same way about us), but they still have dignity as image bearers of God with eternal souls. Here are four steps I hope and pray are making a difference in my own life and in the lives of those I communicate with.

First, speak up. If the Truth is true at every moment, then at every moment we must proclaim it. A culture dies, said famed psychologist Philip Rieff, "when its normative institutions fail to communicate ideals in ways that remain inwardly compelling."[9]

The antidote to culture-depleting indoctrination is to tell people the Truth, expose the lies that would deceive them, show them how to refute those lies, and prepare them with the thinking skills necessary to resist falsehood. Speaking up doesn't just mean saying words. It certainly doesn't mean yelling back at those who yelled first. Our words ought to radiate Truth from beginning to end.

Second, be personal. People most clearly see the Truth found in the person of Jesus when we respect their personhood and interact in a personal way. Truth rarely hits people over the head. More often, it dawns on them. "A soft answer turns away wrath" (Prov. 15:1). How do we communicate softly? At Summit Ministries, we teach students to engage in conversation and ask good questions. As Emily Dickinson says, "The truth must dazzle gradually, or every man be blind."[10] In this chapter, I'll share specific ways I am trying to practice this.

I've found that stories of personal experiences that reflect the goodness of creation, the tragedy of fallenness, and the hope of redemption can be very effective in shining the light of Truth.

We are storytelling creatures. Screenwriting instructor Robert McKee says, "When culture repeatedly experiences glossy, hollowed-out, pseudo-stories, it degenerates. We need true satires and tragedies, dramas and comedies that shine a clean light into the dingy corners of the human psyche and society."[11] Screenwriter and novelist Brian Godawa agrees. "Movies may be about story, but those stories are finally, centrally, crucially, primarily, *mostly* about redemption," he says.[12]

Third, build trust. People have lost trust in one another. That's the conclusion of a recent study by the Pew Research Center. Seventy percent think there is less confidence in one another than twenty years ago.[13] Much of the distrust is based on fear of harm. Three-quarters of conservatives and half of liberals say they hold opinions they are afraid to share because they might face public shame or even lose their jobs.[14]

Many lay the blame for today's distrust at the feet of social media. Instagram, Twitter, and Facebook are boxing rings that earn much of their profit by cashing in on divisiveness. Posts expressing "indignant disagreement" receive twice as many "likes" and "shares" on Facebook.[15] The angrier people get, the more time they spend on social media, searching for evidence confirming their viewpoints and putting others down. And social media companies feed them advertisements the entire time.

If social media is often a barrier to trust, personal interaction is a bridge to it. A friend of mine who works in a high-conflict environment has learned to build trust and diffuse tension by saying, "Can I take you to coffee and hear your viewpoint and share mine?"

Fourth, practice. The Polish poet and artist Cyprian Kamil Norwid speaks of "a nation bleeding only because for the past hundred years its every action came too early and every book came too late."[16] We rarely get to choose the timing of our opportunities to speak Truth. We must be ready when the moment arises. This means we need to have a few basic habits of conversation in mind, such as how to ask good questions, how to affirm others' search for Truth, and what to do if the conversation becomes hostile.

The good news is that most people want to get along and build trusting relationships. A recent survey found that 93 percent believe that it is very important or somewhat important to improve the level of confidence we have in one another.[17] In recent months, Summit Ministries has conducted nationwide polling to help our team better understand this cultural moment. Our research shows that despite the conflict-inducing communication strategies of many media platforms, most people claim to not take the bait. Yes, some get angry and want to cut others out of their lives, but they are an extreme minority. Less than 5 percent of people say they get triggered in this way.[18]

We cannot let the worst among us dictate how we seek the best between us. It's time to talk.

Fourteen Ways to Practice Speaking Up, Personally, in a Way That Builds Trust

In the last several chapters, we talked about how Jesus followers have changed the world for good because of their belief that Jesus is the Truth. True confession: I find myself intimidated by many of the stories I've shared. I haven't built any cathedrals or made any breakthroughs in chemistry. I didn't publish a famous theological work at age twenty-seven or discover dinosaur bones at age twelve. I have never translated an astronomy textbook into Mandarin or produced a concerto in two weeks (or ever). I love telling these stories, but I find it overwhelming to think about how they might apply to my own life.

So how might we be Truth-tellers in our own time? Given the number of people in the world who claim to be Jesus followers, if we simply discipline ourselves to communicate in a way that breathes life into others, we will quickly notice a dramatic change. This can happen one conversation at a time. Here are some of the practices I seek to intentionally embrace:

1. *Use five conversation-altering words.* "Tell me more about that." When I get confused about the Truth, I feel disoriented. I try to let my default be to express interest in the person, not just the point they're making. I want to be curious.

2. *Ask questions.* Sometimes nerves get the better of me. I don't know what to say when confronted. I shut down. It helps immensely to memorize a handful of questions and keep them in my back pocket. For example:

   - What do you mean? Defining terms is paramount. If someone says, "Evolution proves that the Bible is untrue," I ask what they mean by "evolution," "proof," and "truth." If someone says, "There is no God," I ask what they mean by "God."

   - How did you arrive at that conclusion? I'm learning to seek to understand the backstory behind why people say what they say. Passionately expressed viewpoints often mask a painful story. If someone says, "I could never believe in a God who would allow evil," I say, "It sounds like there is a story behind that. Would you be willing to share it with me?"

   - How do you know what you believe is true? Often people simply assume, without evidence, that what they are saying is true. If someone says something like, "Sexuality is determined at birth, but gender is a choice," I want to express curiosity by replying, "That's interesting. I've heard the theory that sexuality and gender are different things, but how do you know it is true that this difference is actually real?"

- What happens if you're wrong? Even if I don't have the opportunity to express my viewpoint, I can still leave the other person thinking. To understand the following example, you need to know something about me. I have a strong personal conviction that I should never vote for someone who publicly favors unrestricted elective abortion. I have received a lot of criticism for this view. None of it has changed my mind. The way I see it, those who are willing to publicly defend the taking of innocent life have automatically disqualified themselves for public office. As you can imagine, this leads to tension in many conversations. If someone says, "It doesn't matter whether the person I vote for is pro-life. Elected officials can't do anything about abortion anyway," I respond, "I'd like to push back for a moment. What if you are wrong and the advocacy of an elected official does matter, as well as the example they set for all those who are watching?"

3. *Show caring.* It's important to use my whole being to express caring. Psychologist Albert Mehrabian found that 55 percent of our communication is *visual*, through our posture and facial expressions, 38 percent is *vocal*, through our tone of voice, and only 7 percent is *verbal*, through our words.[19] (This is why it is a bad idea to have an argument through text messaging, social media posts, or email—only 7 percent of your message is getting through.) No matter what I say, I want the other person to hear this: "I care about you, I care

about our country, and I care about doing what makes sense."

4. *Keep the message clear.* No matter the setting, a well-communicated message has four qualities:

- It gets the attention of the other person based on what is important to them.
- It shows the need, the core problem that needs to be addressed.
- It provides a solution to the problem.
- It asks for action, a change of mind or specific set of steps.[20]

5. *Avoid creating unsolvable fear.* In 2021 Chapman University surveyed adults on ninety-five fears such as government corruption, environmental disaster, and loss of health and death.[21] It turns out that the majority of Americans suffer from tremendous fear. Many—perhaps as high as 85 percent of the population—live with a sense of impending doom—a classic indication of clinical anxiety.[22] For 70 percent of Gen Z, the top fear is being alone.[23] If I present a fear and do not show how it can be effectively relieved, the result is counterproductive.[24] In presentations and conversation, I often say something like, "I am concerned about what is happening in the world, but we are not helpless."

6. *Acknowledge the need for social validation.* People want to feel that what they believe is plausible—that it makes sense to those whose opinions they value. The famed psychologist Stanley Milgram studied the power of social validation by placing people on a busy street corner of a large city and telling them to suddenly turn their gaze upward. When only one person looked up,

4 percent of the onlookers also looked up. When five people suddenly looked up, 18 percent of those around did so as well. When fifteen people suddenly turned their gaze skyward, 40 percent of those around also looked up.[25] I can acknowledge the need for social validation by saying, "I know how important it is to know that you're in good company. You might be surprised by the number of people who find what I am saying plausible."

7. *Get to know them.* People want to find agreement with those they like. Persuasion researcher Robert B. Cialdini says that in negotiations and sales situations, people who take time to get to know one another have greater success. Discussing a study of online negotiation, Cialdini says that 30 percent of the time, the negotiation fails to reach a satisfactory agreement. When participants share personal information about their interests and families to create a connection, the failure rate dropped to 6 percent.[26] Simply being likeable and expressing interest significantly increased the success of the negotiations. Keep in mind, when talking about deep convictions or highly controversial issues, this may mean months or years rather than just a few extra minutes or hours.

8. *Offer a way to be consistent.* A poll conducted on behalf of Summit Ministries by a national polling firm demonstrated that 81 percent of people prefer to listen respectfully and engage in dialogue when talking with someone with whom they disagree.[27] In difficult conversations, most people—nearly all—are amiable. I can affirm this by saying, "You are a good listener. Thank you for your willingness to talk about difficult subjects

with me. I want you to know that I would stand up for your freedom to say what you think, and I hope you would do the same for me." As a follow-up comment, I can say, "I would like to know if you disagree. Will you reach out to me directly if you find yourself irritated by something I say?"

9. *Deflect hostility.* In those rare situations when the person I'm talking with becomes hostile, I must avoid responding in kind. Here are some steps I try to take to settle the conversation down:

- Acknowledge differences. "We have differences and that's okay."
- Legitimize having differences. "Having differences is normal."
- Focus on commonalities. "We also have more in common than we realize. We both care about making life better for those around us."
- Avoid focusing on personality issues. "We may not end up agreeing, but I still respect your right to say what you think."
- Avoid stereotypes. "I know we're supposed to simplify our views and fight over our differences, but hopefully we'll find that we can listen to each other, even when our disagreement is strong."
- Be friendly, but don't grovel or compromise. "I know we don't see eye to eye on this, but you've given me a lot to think about and I hope you feel the same."

10. *Encourage feedback.* Actual *feedback* is more important to whether a person is persuaded by an argument than their *belief* that the argument is persuasive.[28] Encouraging the other person to get feedback about what

I'm saying is a key step in furthering the conversation and coming to agreement. I say something like, "Why don't you take this argument to your friends and get their feedback? See if they have any good responses and share them with me." It sounds odd, but persuasion research shows that inviting feedback is itself persuasive in getting others to consider your viewpoint.

11. *Don't be discouraged by resistance.* As I shared in chapter 3, many people, especially younger adults, believe that if what they say might offend someone or hurt their feelings, it is wrong. [29] It's a misguided belief that stops short many discussions about Truth. Resistance to persuasion is an important step in the persuasion process. People resist for many reasons—loss of status, security, or comfort. This resistance is healthy. It brings energy that helps overcome apathy. It helps counteract groupthink and encourages creative alternatives. At some point in difficult conversations, I try to say something like, "Thinking this through with you makes both of us stronger." [30]

12. *Ask for change.* The persuasion expert mentioned earlier, Robert Cialdini, once conducted a study in which he had his associates randomly approach people on the street and say, "Excuse me, I am enlisting volunteers to chaperone juvenile detention center inmates on a trip to the zoo. Would you be willing to do that?" Only 17 percent of people said yes (still a very high number, given the random nature of the request). A second group of associates asked, "Would you be willing to serve as an unpaid counselor at the juvenile detention center for two hours a week for the next two years?" Predictably, all of the respondents declined the offer.

But then the associates asked, "If you can't do that, would you be willing to chaperone juvenile detention center inmates on a trip to the zoo?" Incredibly, 50 percent said yes. That's almost triple the number who said yes to the original question.[31] Here's the takeaway from Cialdini: the more people were asked for initially, the more they ultimately agreed to do. People engage more when they believe that their contribution matters and disengage when they don't see how it does. Researchers call this "social loafing." The same thing applies in conversation. In our Summit Ministries programs, I ask students, "What are the barriers that would stop you personally from living a life that is fully committed to Christ?" It's a huge question to ask, but I don't just want students to merely think that being committed to Jesus is a good idea; I want them to experience change. Boldly asking the question is itself a persuasive act.

13. *Be comfortable with silence.* Certainly, there are times when words are demanded. Silence in the face of evil is no virtue. But there are also many times when our words get in the way of God's message. James 1:19 says, "Let every person be quick to hear, slow to speak, slow to anger." Proverbs 10:19 says, "When words are many, transgression is not lacking, but whoever restrains his lips is prudent." Upon witnessing Job's suffering, his friends sat with him in silence (Job 2:13). Isaiah prophesied of the Messiah, "He was oppressed, and he was afflicted, yet he opened not his mouth" (Isa. 53:7). A silent witness—especially in the face of suffering or as a way to rein in the ego-driven impulse to defend ourselves at every turn—can be an eloquent witness to God's power.

14. *Keep your mood positive!* People who are energetic and have a positive attitude lead others to be positive. Conversely, people who are energetic and negative lead others to be negative.[32] Several years ago, I consulted with an activist group struggling to involve young adults in their work. I found myself baffled by this until I met with the group's leaders in person. They were stressed and angry. I could easily see why young adults would not want to be like them, or even be around them. As the group's leaders changed their attitude from reacting cynically to current events to empowering young adults to be leaders for their generation, things turned around. Now the group has many active young adults organized in college campus chapters around the US.

The Way to Walk

"This is the way, walk in it," God says (Isa. 30:21). Through Jesus, we can "abhor what is evil" and "hold fast to what is good" (Rom. 12:9). We cannot push the responsibility for communicating the Truth of Jesus onto others ("I just gave up on them," or "I told them the brutal truth—they just didn't want to hear it"). God perceives what is in our hearts (Prov. 24:12).

It takes constant prayer and discipline to communicate the Truth *in the way Jesus wants it communicated.* Zechariah 8:16–17 is a good watchword: "'These are the things you must do: Speak truth to one another; make true and sound decisions within your city gates. Do not plot evil in your hearts against your neighbor, and do not love perjury, for I hate all this'—this is the LORD's declaration" (CSB).

Truth Really Does Change Everything

Three friends paced along the path through the trees, the River Cherwell quietly gurgling alongside them. They loved walking here late at night, striding to and fro, arguing for hours.

"Tollers, what you're saying about Christianity can't be true," said one of the men.

"Why not, Jack?"

Jack sighed. He had gained quite a reputation at Oxford University as the resident expert on the history of the English language. He enjoyed decoding ancient Norse languages and translating Norse mythology into English. He loved storytelling.

As he argued about the Christian faith with his two friends, Jack concluded in exasperation, "Myths are lies, and ultimately, they are worthless."

"You're wrong," Tollers insisted. "They are not lies."

"What do you mean?" asked Jack.

Tollers explained. Myths are stories that ring true because they grasp for fulfillment through Christianity.[1] Humans distort them into lies, but all ideas originate with God.[2]

Suddenly, a breeze blew and the men stopped, watching leaves cascade to the ground, glimmering silver in the moonlight. After a moment, Tollers continued. "Jack, is it possible that Christianity is the great story behind all great stories? The one story that came true in real life?"

Shortly after this late-night conversation, Jack became a Christian. Soon, he and Tollers would invent magical realms populated with fantastical beasts and brave souls, worlds in which myths came to life. Tollers's story told of a small, furry-footed creature called a hobbit, who set off on a great adventure. Jack's work, sometime later, centered around an enchanted world called Narnia.

C. S. "Jack" Lewis and J. R. R. Tolkien, whom Lewis called Tollers, both gained fame through their fiction. But their stories weren't just stories. As Christians, they understood that all stories point somewhere. Good stories reveal Truth.

Of course, Truth can be revealed only if it is real in the first place. A biblical worldview says that it is, and that the Bible, like a compass, points us to it. Theologian Michael Goheen explains that the Bible's story "tells us the way the world really is." It isn't tied to local legend or narrow tribal interests. Rather, says Goheen, "It makes a factual claim about the world as a whole: it is public truth":

> The biblical story encompasses all of reality—north, south, east, west, past, present, and future. It begins with the creation of all things and ends with the renewal of all things. In between it offers an interpretation of the meaning of cosmic history.[3]

All worldviews claim to identify the source of humanity's brokenness. All offer a plan of salvation, whether it is through God, human effort, or achieving oneness with all things. All worldviews have prophets, high priests, and holy texts. Among these, a biblical worldview claims to be universal. It says that the Truth about Jesus is true about everything, everywhere, all the time. It says that Christ died to redeem the *whole world* from the *universal* condition of sin. Christians are to love God with *all* their heart, soul, mind, and strength and love *all* their fellow human beings. God created the *whole universe*, and this design is observable by *everyone*, even those who suppress that Truth through other commitments.

In *Truth Changes Everything*, we've looked at the epic battle between the Truth viewpoint and the truths viewpoint. We've explored how those who embraced Jesus as Truth changed the world in understanding the value of human life, charity, medicine, education, science, art, politics, justice, and even the meaning of our everyday work. We've looked at creative ways to communicate Truth with those around us, even in a hostile environment.

As I reflect on the difference Truth-seeking Jesus followers made even in times of crisis, I'm struck by how creative they were. They did not seem interested in turning back the clock or reclaiming the glory of a previous era. They were innovators. Their fidelity—faithfulness—to Truth grounded their efforts and made them possible. This shouldn't have surprised me. "Fidelity to roots," Pope John Paul II insisted, "does not mean a mechanical copying of the past. Fidelity to roots is always creative."[4]

By committing to an unchangeable Truth in a constantly changing culture, the Jesus followers we've studied gained insight into the future and courage for the troubling now.

Three Takeaways about Truth

What was it about the unchangeable Truth that made this insight and courage possible? Three takeaways come to mind.

Takeaway #1: Truth Is a Person

I remember hiking through a developing country on a footpath that passed by a very modest home. I could see the resident wearily standing inside the doorway. We smiled and waved at her as our group walked by.

Later, passing by the same spot, we saw the same woman standing in the doorway, still barefoot but wearing a dress. She smiled and waved as we passed. My heart was quietly subdued. This woman's poverty did not diminish her dignity. Indeed, it accented it. Deep inside I knew, and hoped that she knew as well, that her value came not from her circumstances but from being an image bearer of God.

If there is no Truth, but only the stories we tell, then the life of this poverty-stricken woman means little in the greater scheme of things. If she speaks her truth, who will hear?

But the central implication of a biblical worldview is that Truth is not just told by persons. It *is* a person, Jesus. Because of Jesus, we are much more than our individual self-perceptions or the stories we use to persuade others of our value. We are not merely helpless animals clinging to a spinning hunk of rock as it hurtles through space. We are not just "wetware," as Silicon Valley software engineers describe human beings.[5]

C. S. Lewis pointed out that atheists may think that "nations, classes, civilizations must be more important than individuals" because "individuals live only seventy odd years each and the group may last for centuries." To the Christian, though, "individuals are more important, for they live eternally; and races, civilizations and the like are in comparison the creatures of a day."[6]

Denying the value of every person is at the root of humanity's most shameful moments, from oppression of native people to the genocide of Jews, Armenians, Tutsis, or the unborn.

Some of those who committed these atrocities considered themselves Christians, even though they lived in a way that was diametrically opposed to everything Jesus taught. Jesus himself predicted that this would happen (Matt. 7:21–23). These individuals forgot—or ignored—the Bible's central focus on all people as image bearers of God.

If Truth is a person, though, then focusing on the value of each person is a holy, heroic act. At Summit Ministries, our staff has learned to picture Truth and relationship as two strands of a DNA double-helix. Both are vital. Truth without relationship leads to arrogance. Relationship without Truth leads to indifference. God's Truth, on the other hand, is personal, caring, and focused on flourishing.

Truth is a very human enterprise.

Takeaway #2: Truth Is Life

The Bible is not just a collection of moral commandments such as "You shall not steal" and "You shall not covet." God isn't the kind of deity who shows up to spank us for our bad deeds and then returns to his heavenly home. The whole story of the Bible is that Jesus is *life* (John 10:10; 14:6). God straightens what sin has bent, unearths the treasures of meaning, and assures us of a love beyond description.

In the little hippie town where Summit Ministries is located, a guy walked past my house shaking a stick and proclaiming, "Love! Peace! Happiness!" When he saw my bewildered expression, he shyly held out the stick, saying, "I just made a new wand and I'm casting happy spells on the neighborhood." I smiled and said, "Thank you." In a way that made sense to his new spiritualist worldview, the man was trying to breathe life into our neighborhood.

Looking back, I wish I had had the presence of mind to share this thought with my wand-waving neighbor: love, peace, and happiness don't appear through magic; they arise as we breathe life into our circumstances through seeking, growing, and maturing. I doubt that any of the Jesus followers we've met in this book had any idea of the impact they would ultimately have. They just loved Jesus and lived out the Truth as best they could.

Dionysius the Areopagite, thought to be a disciple of the apostle Paul, said, "The divine longing is Good seeking good for the sake of the good."[7] This good is secured by inviting personal contact, not cutting it off. African American sociologist George Yancey discusses empirical research on the "contact hypothesis," that "when we share an overarching identity with those we're in contact with, we begin to see them as part of our group. At that point our biases are dramatically reduced."[8]

In his book *Challenging Conversations*, author Jason Jimenez observes that most conversations about tough topics fall along a single-dimensional line from *avoidance* ("You have your truth and I have mine") to *aggression* ("I just dropped the mic—you should be speechless and ashamed"). Jimenez says we ought to add another dimension, forming a triangle. At the top of the triangle is *advocacy*. A Truth-based, Jesus-centered worldview advocates for both the Truth and the other person.[9] Instead of imagining ourselves knocking heads with others, we might imagine walking side by side with them, seeking the Truth.

Takeaway #3: Truth Is Eternal

The truths viewpoint says that we "win" in life by telling stories that help us survive as long as possible. A biblical worldview, on the other hand, calls for something more. Thomas à Kempis (1380–1471) wrote, "How great a vanity it also is to desire a long life and to care little for a good life."[10] The fullest life is not one that ignores eternity but one that lives in light of it. As mathematician Blaise Pascal (1623–62) put it, our wants and desires are an "infinite abyss" that "can be filled only with an infinite and immutable object; in other words by God himself."[11]

In a biblical worldview, Truth means seeing everything from God's perspective. My daily prayer is "God, show me what you see. Let me hear what you hear. Let me do what you would do." Second Corinthians 4:18 says, "We look not to the things that are seen but to the things that are unseen. For the things that are seen are transient, but the things that are unseen are eternal."

What we see is not all there is. Human institutions are important, but they don't last forever. In my recent journey through cancer, I realized in a new way how frightfully transitory life is. Human institutions, not just our individual lives, are more fragile than we realize. Even the most powerful human institutions can falter and die. Of the largest companies in 1955, only sixty remained on the *Fortune* 500 list in 2017.[12] Have you heard of American Motors, Brown Shoe, Studebaker, Collins Radio, or Zenith Electronics lately? In 1955, they were among America's most popular brands. They no longer exist. Now the most well-known companies are Tesla, Amazon, Facebook, Microsoft, Google, and Netflix.[13] Only one of the founders of these six companies was even *alive* in 1955 (Bill Gates of Microsoft was born in October of that year). Someday we'll likely look back on these massive brands with nostalgia. I imagine my children someday pulling their children close and saying, "When I was a kid, we had this thing called Facebook . . ."

How do we find meaning in a fleeting life? The agnostic philosopher Richard Rorty admitted, "I came to realize that the search of the philosophers for a grand scheme that would encompass everything was illusory. Only a theism that combined a God with equal measures of truth, love, and justice, could do the trick."[14] Sadly, Rorty rejected the obvious path because he could not imagine himself being religious.

Made for This Moment

After his visit to America, French sociologist Alexis de Tocqueville (1805–59) chillingly described a future devoid of Truth: "Some people may let the torch be snatched from their hands, but others stamp it out themselves."[15]

Every moment of our lives is a moment of choosing. Will we hold high the torch of Truth *in this moment*? Will we live in every moment the conviction that Jesus is the Truth? The Jesus followers we've met in this book point the way. Will we emulate their dogged determination and their out-of-the-box solution-finding? I doubt that any of them believed their individual actions would change the world, and yet they did. If there was ever a time to commit ourselves to that kind of life, it is now. In the past, Truth changed everything. It still does today.

Acknowledgments

The bulk of *Truth Changes Everything* (*TCE*) was written over a ten-month period when I was fighting and recovering from cancer, but it took the better part of three years to conceptualize, secure a publisher, research, write, and edit. During these years, many hands made light work.

My wife and best friend, Stephanie, encouraged the writing process during my cancer journey by listening to me read chapter drafts. Over and over again. This is true love.

Alex Field from The Bindery Agency believed in the vision of *TCE*, supporting and championing it from day one.

Aaron Zubia wrote *TCE* research reports while finishing his PhD at Columbia, carrying out a postdoctoral fellowship at Princeton, nurturing his young family, and preparing for a professorship. I miss the old days of brainstorming together about a biblical worldview of everything.

Summit Ministries' vice president of program services, Jason Graham, and director of publishing, Aaron Klemm, helped nurture *TCE* from concept to editing to marketing. They are "all in," and I'm grateful. I'm grateful as well for the amazing creativity of the Summit Ministries marketing team, headed by Rajeev Shaw.

Tosha Payne has been an awesome executive assistant over the last eleven years. During the writing process, she gracefully coordinated my schedule, served as a sounding board, and tracked down books and research articles on the most random topics.

The nurses and doctors at the Rocky Mountain Cancer Center took an interest in my writing and even helped spread the word about the new podcast I was launching. It was a special grace.

Thank you to Elizabeth Angier for the conversation and research on Vivaldi's epic story.

Some serendipitous *TCE* encounters will remain in my heart forever, such as the conversation with my cancer surgeon about Kant, Aquinas, and the soul. Of course, I was being sedated at the time, so my memory is fuzzy. I hope it was an interesting dialogue.

It is an immense privilege to work and live in community with so many Jesus followers who believe that Truth really does change everything. It is one of the greatest blessings of my life.

Notes

Chapter 1 The Point of No Return

1. See Nancy Pearcey, *Total Truth: Liberating Christianity from Its Cultural Captivity* (Wheaton: Crossway, 2008); Francis Schaeffer, *The God Who Is There: 30th Anniversary Edition* (Downers Grove, IL: InterVarsity, 2008); and Dallas Willard, *Renewing the Christian Mind: Essays, Interviews, and Talks* (New York: HarperOne, 2016). See also Donald Williams, "True Truth: Francis Schaeffer's Enduring Legacy," The Calvinist International, September 24, 2014, https://calvinistinternational.com/2014/09/24/true-truth-francis-schaeffers-enduring-legacy/; Dallas A. Willard, "Truth in the Fire: C. S. Lewis and Pursuit of Truth Today," Independent Institute, July 21, 1998, https://www.independent.org/publications/article.asp?id=1669.

2. Philosophers usually call this the "correspondence theory of truth." The truths viewpoint, on the other hand, holds to "anti-realism" (we cannot know that reality exists) or "relativism" (what we call reality depends on its relationship to us personally or to our society).

3. George Barna, "American Worldview Inventory 2020—At a Glance," Cultural Research Center, May 19, 2020, https://www.arizonachristian.edu/wp-content/uploads/2020/05/AWVI-2020-Release-05-Perceptions-of-Truth.pdf.

4. George Barna, "Millennials in America: New Insights into the Generation of Growing Influence," Cultural Research Center, October 2021, https://www.arizonachristian.edu/wp-content/uploads/2021/10/George-Barna-Millennial-Report-2021-FINAL-Web.pdf.

Chapter 2 The End of Time; the Dawn of Hope

1. "Adam Schall von Bell: German Missionary," *Encyclopedia Britannica*, accessed February 18, 2022, https://www.britannica.com/biography/Adam-Schall-von-Bell.

2. Stefano Salvia, "The Battle of the Astronomers: Johann Adam Schall von Bell and Ferdinand Verbiest at the Court of the Celestial Emperors (1660–1670)," *Physics in Perspective* 22 (2020): 81–109, https://doi.org/10.1007/s00016-020-00254-0. See also "Ferdinand Verbiest (1623–1688)," Family pedia, accessed February 18, 2022, https://familypedia.fandom.com/wiki/Ferdinand_Verbiest_(1623-1688).

3. Christopher Cullen and Catherine Jami, "Christmas 1668 and After: How Jesuit Astronomy Was Restored to Power in Beijing," *Journal for the History of Astronomy*, February 3, 2020, https://doi.org/10.1177/0021828620901887.

4. Cullen and Jami, "Christmas 1668."

5. Salvia, "Battle of the Astronomers," 96.

6. Quoted in Augustin Udías, "Jesuit Astronomers in China, India and Other Missions (1540–1773)," in *Searching the Heavens and the Earth: The History of Jesuit Observatories*, Astrophysics and Space Science Library, vol. 286 (Dordrecht: Springer, 2003), https://doi.org/10.1007/978-94-017-0349-9_3.

7. Janet Nguyen, "Americans on Shaky Ground Financially, Speaking Out More on Racism, Poll Finds," Marketplace, October 15, 2020, https://www.marketplace.org/2020/10/15/americans-on-shaky-ground-financially-speaking-out-more-on-racism-covid-19-pandemic/; Alessandra Malito, "Only 37% of Americans Believe Today's Children Will Grow Up to Be Better Off," MarketWatch, August 23, 2017, https://www.marketwatch.com/story/only-37-of-americans-believe-todays-children-will-grow-up-to-be-better-off-2017-08-22; and "Trust in Government 1972–2020," Gallup, https://news.gallup.com/poll/5392/trust-government.aspx.

8. Di Minardi, "The Grim Fate That Could Be 'Worse Than Extinction,'" BBC, October 15, 2020, https://www.bbc.com/future/article/20201014-totalitarian-world-in-chains-artificial-intelligence.

9. Sebastian Farquhar, John Halstead, Owen Cotton-Barratt, Stefan Schubert, Haydn Belfield, and Andrew Snyder-Beattie, "Existential Risk: Diplomacy and Governance," Global Priorities Project 2017, http://globalprioritiesproject.org/2017/02/existential-risk-diplomacy-and-governance/.

10. "The End of Absolutes: America's New Moral Code," Barna, May 25, 2016, https://www.barna.com/research/the-end-of-absolutes-americas-new-moral-code/.

Chapter 3 Does the Truth Matter?

1. Josh Shepherd, "New Netflix Miniseries Is More Mess Than Messianic," *The Federalist*, January 6, 2020, https://thefederalist.com/2020/01/06/new-netflix-miniseries-is-more-mess-than-messianic/.

2. According to the poll conducted in 2017, 29 percent of churchgoing Christians under forty-five strongly agreed with this statement. Just 8 percent

of churchgoing Christians over forty-five agreed. See https://www.barna.com/research/competing-worldviews-influence-todays-christians/.

3. "Americans Are Most Likely to Base Truth on Feelings," Barna, February 12, 2002, https://www.barna.com/research/americans-are-most-likely-to-base-truth-on-feelings/.

4. Angela Sailor, "Republicans and Democrats Agree on Need to Cancel 'Cancel Culture,'" Heritage Foundation, July 31, 2020, https://www.heritage.org/civil-society/commentary/republicans-and-democrats-agree-need-cancel-cancel-culture.

5. Kevin Roose, "How the Biden Administration Can Help Solve Our Reality Crisis," *New York Times*, February 2, 2021, https://www.nytimes.com/2021/02/02/technology/biden-reality-crisis-misinformation.html.

6. Will Durant and Ariel Durant, *The Story of Civilization: Caesar and Christ* (New York: Simon & Schuster, 1935), 665.

7. For more on this perspective, see Samuel P. Huntington, *The Clash of Civilizations: The Debate* (New York: Foreign Affairs, 2010), 1.

8. Pitirim A. Sorokin, *The Crisis of Our Age: The Social and Cultural Outlook* (New York: Dutton, 1957), 163.

9. Alexandr Solzhenitsyn, "'Men Have Forgotten God': Aleksandr Solzhenitsyn's 1983 Templeton Address," *National Review*, December 11, 2018, https://www.nationalreview.com/2018/12/aleksandr-solzhenitsyn-men-have-forgotten-god-speech/.

10. Francis A. Schaeffer, *How Should We Then Live? (L'Abri 50th Anniversary Edition): The Rise and Decline of Western Thought and Culture* (Wheaton: Crossway, 2005).

11. Jeremiah Johnston, *Unimaginable: What Our World Would Be Like without Christianity* (Bloomington, MN: Bethany House, 2017), 152–53.

12. Scott Todd, *Fast Living: How the Church Will End Extreme Poverty* (Colorado Springs: Compassion International, 2011), 37.

13. "Water, Sanitation and Hygiene (WASH)," World Health Organization, accessed March 21, 2021, https://www.who.int/health-topics/water-sanitation-and-hygiene-wash.

14. J. R. R. Tolkien, *The Fellowship of the Ring* (London: George Allen & Unwin, 1954), 151.

15. Personal conversation with Bill Brown.

16. Oprah Winfrey, Golden Globe Awards, broadcast January 7, 2018.

17. Quoted in Scott Consigny, "Nietzsche's Reading of the Sophists," *Rhetoric Review* 13, no. 1 (1994): 7.

18. Daniel Stoljar and Nic Damnjanovic, "The Deflationary Theory of Truth," *Stanford Encyclopedia of Philosophy*, revised December 14, 2021, https://plato.stanford.edu/entries/truth-deflationary/.

19. William James, *Pragmatism: A New Name for Some Old Ways of Thinking* (Cambridge, MA: Harvard University Press, 1975), 97.

20. See Richard Rorty, *Philosophy and the Mirror of Nature* (Princeton: Princeton University Press, 1979).

21. John Capps, "The Pragmatic Theory of Truth," *Stanford Encyclopedia of Philosophy*, March 21, 2019, https://plato.stanford.edu/entries/truth-pragmatic/.

22. Simon Blackburn, *Being Good: An Introduction to Ethics* (New York: Oxford University Press, 2002), 23–24.

23. Quoted in Scott Sheeran and Sir Nigel Rodley, eds., *Routledge Handbook of International Human Rights Law* (Abington, UK: Taylor and Francis, 2014), 31.

24. Umberto Eco, *The Name of the Rose* (Boston: Mariner, 1983), 527.

Chapter 4 Can Truth Be Known, and How Would We Know It?

1. R. Scott Smith says that "on a naturalistic, evolutionary account of human nature, there are no essences." R. Scott Smith, *In Search of Moral Knowledge: Rethinking Ethics and the Fact-Value Dichotomy* (Downers Grove, IL: InterVarsity, 2014), 142. To postmodernists, it is possible to *describe* what you think people agree on, but you cannot say that anything is actually "true" or "false" or "good" or "evil."

2. Edmund Husserl, *Logical Investigations*, vol. 2, trans. J. N. Findlay (London: Routledge and Kegan Paul, 1970), 2:603.

3. The celebrated postmodernist English professor Stanley Fish makes this point in his many books, especially *Winning Arguments: What Works and Doesn't Work in Politics, the Bedroom, the Courtroom, and the Classroom* (New York: Harper, 2017).

4. See William Brennan, *Dehumanizing the Vulnerable: When Word Games Take Lives* (Fort Collins, CO: Life Cycle Books, 2000).

5. "Lecture: Dr. Michael Bauman 'The Meaning of Meaning,'" Summit Ministries, posted November 24, 2009, https://www.summit.org/resources/videos/the-meaning-of-meaning/.

6. See Professor Justin McBrayer's controversial yet insightful essay, "Why Our Children Don't Think There Are Moral Facts," *New York Times*, March 2, 2015, https://opinionator.blogs.nytimes.com/2015/03/02/why-our-children-dont-think-there-are-moral-facts/.

7. Richard H. Beis, "Some Contributions of Anthropology to Ethics," *The Thomist* 27, no. 2 (April 1964): 174–223, quoted in William D. Gairdner, *The Book of Absolutes* (Montreal: McGill-Queen's University Press, 2008), 198–200.

8. Flannery O'Connor, *The Habit of Being: Letters of Flannery O'Connor*, ed. Sally Fitzgerald (New York: Farrar, Straus & Giroux, 1979), 100.

9. In a PhilPapers survey from 2009, faculty members in ninety-nine university departments were asked to respond to the following question: "Truth: correspondence, deflationary, or epistemic?" The responses were as follows:

50.8 percent accepted or leaned toward correspondence, 24.8 percent toward deflationary, 17.5 percent toward other, 6.9 percent toward epistemic. This poll is mentioned in Marian David, "The Correspondence Theory of Truth," *Stanford Encyclopedia of Philosophy*, revised May 28, 2015, https://plato .stanford.edu/entries/truth-correspondence/.

10. Moran Gershoni and Shmuel Pietrokovski, "The Landscape of Sex-Differential Transcriptome and Its Consequent Selection in Human Adults," *BMC Biology* 15, no. 1 (2017), https://bmcbiol.biomedcentral.com/articles /10.1186/s12915-017-0352-z.

11. Quoted in J. P. Moreland and Kai Nielsen, *Does God Exist? The Great Debate* (Nashville: Thomas Nelson, 1990), 211.

12. Thank you to Frank Turek for helping me communicate this point.

13. David Allen Clark, Donald A. Koch, and Mark R. Harris, "A Strange Way to Save the World," copyright Universal Music Publishing Group, 1993.

14. See, for example, Gary Habermas, *Risen Indeed: A Historical Investigation into the Resurrection of Jesus* (Bellingham, WA: Lexham Academic, 2021).

15. Jim Clifton, *The Coming Jobs War* (New York: Gallup Press, 2011), 51.

16. Kai-man Kwan, professor of religion and theology at Hong Kong Baptist University, in studying verbal reports of people's conversion experiences, concludes that such people are not having isolated, delusional experiences. Kwan says religious experiences can be studied for their validity if they are (1) shared experiences that happen over and over again, across cultures and time, (2) common in their ontology in that the experiences reported by people occur around certain things, processes, or properties, and (3) conceptually coherent in that they are describable in a coherent way. See Kai-man Kwan, "The Argument from Religious Experience," in *The Blackwell Companion to Natural Theology*, ed. William Lane Craig and J. P. Moreland (Malden, MA: Wiley-Blackwell), 511.

17. C. D. Broad, *Religion, Philosophy and Psychical Research* (London: Routledge and Kegan Paul, 1953), 197, quoted in Kwan, "Argument from Religious Experience," 502.

Chapter 5 How Jesus Followers Have Changed How We Value Human Life

1. Many online resources tell of the life of Catherine. A good place to start is "Catherine of Siena: Mystic and Political Activist," *Christianity Today*, accessed February 18, 2022, https://www.christianitytoday.com/history/people /innertravelers/catherine-of-siena.html; and J. D. Long-Garcia, "Why You Should Read St. Catherine of Siena—in Her Own Words—During the Coronavirus Pandemic," *America*, April 29, 2020, https://www.americamagazine.org /faith/2020/04/29/why-you-should-read-st-catherine-siena-her-own-words -during-coronavirus-pandemic.

2. You can find Catherine of Siena's letters in many places on the internet, including in a PDF download called "Dialogue of St. Catherine of Siena," hosted on a website called "The Four Kingdoms" by the Dominican Sisters, a religious society of the Roman Catholic Church: http://www.4kingdoms .com/dialogue_of_st_catherine_of_siena_chapter_14_newest.pdf.

3. Catherine of Siena, "Dialogue of St. Catherine of Siena," The Four Kingdoms, trans. Suzanne Noffke, n.d., http://www.4kingdoms.com/dia logue_of_st_catherine_of_siena_chapter_14_newest.pdf.

4. Quoted in Trevin Wax, *Rethink Your Self: The Power of Looking Up before Looking In* (Nashville: B & H, 2020), 35.

5. Edward O. Wilson, *On Human Nature* (Cambridge, MA: Harvard University Press, 2004), 2.

6. Rollo May, *Psychology and the Human Dilemma* (Princeton: D. Van Nostrand Company, 1967), 188.

7. Dallas Willard, "What Does It Mean to Be Human?" (lecture, Ohio State University Veritas Forum, November 2002).

8. *Avengers: Infinity War*, directed by Anthony Russo and Joe Russo (Burbank, CA: Marvel Studios and Walt Disney Studios Motion Pictures, 2018).

9. Julian L. Simon, *Population Matters: People, Resources, Environment, and Immigration* (New Brunswick, NJ: Transaction Publishers, 1990), 169.

10. "Editorial: Nobel Committee Honors Pro-Growth Economists, Including Colorado's Paul Romer," *Colorado Springs Gazette*, October 9, 2018, https://gazette.com/opinion/editorial-nobel-committee-honors-pro -growth-economists-including-colorado-s/article_3cad368c-cb75-11e8-b581 -ff3cf7f71398.html.

11. I'm sure I didn't invent this comparison, but I don't remember where I first heard it.

12. See Barry Asmus and Wayne Grudem, *The Poverty of Nations: A Sustainable Solution* (Wheaton: Crossway, 2013).

13. E. Calvin Beisner, "What Is the Most Important Environmental Task Facing American Christians Today?," *Mount Nebo Papers* 1 (Spring 2008): 11, https://theird.org/publication/mount-nebo-papers-spring-2008/.

14. Beisner, "What Is the Most Important Environmental Task," 13.

15. N. T. Wright, *Broken Signposts: How Christianity Makes Sense of the World* (New York: HarperOne, 2020), 147.

16. Chris R. Armstrong, *Medieval Wisdom for Modern Christians: Finding Authentic Faith in a Forgotten Age with C. S. Lewis* (Grand Rapids: Brazos, 2016), 82.

17. Thomas Aquinas, *Summa Theologica: Complete English Edition in Five Volumes*, trans. Fathers of the English Dominican Province, Volume One, Question 93, Second Article, "Whether the Image of God Is to Be Found in Irrational Creatures" (Notre Dame, IN: Christian Classics, 1948), 470.

18. See J. P. Moreland, *The Soul: How We Know It's Real and Why It Matters* (Chicago: Moody, 2014), especially 109–10, 120–21.

19. Quoted in Armstrong, *Medieval Wisdom for Modern Christians*, 63.

20. See, for example, Tom Kane, *Bad Church, Good Church: A Memoir of a Former Catholic Priest* (New York: Primus Publications, 2010), where he shares why as a priest he counseled a young couple to have an abortion.

21. Robert P. George and Christopher Tollefsen, *Embryo: A Defense of Human Life* (New York: Doubleday, 2008), 39.

22. Theodore Seuss Geisel, *Horton Hears a Who* (New York: Random House, 2020), n.p.

23. Francis J. Beckwith, *Defending Life: A Moral and Legal Case against Abortion Choice* (New York: Cambridge University Press, 2007), 65.

24. Peter Singer, *Practical Ethics*, 2nd ed. (New York: Cambridge University Press, 1993), 85–86.

25. From "Humanist Ethics: The Groundwork," quoted in Morris B. Storer, *Humanist Ethics: Dialogue on Basics* (Buffalo: Prometheus Books, 1980), 255.

26. The Dalai Lama, *A Profound Mind* (New York: Three Rivers, 2011), ix.

27. Steven Levy, "Marvin Minsky's Marvelous Meat Machine," *Wired*, January 26, 2016, https://www.wired.com/2016/01/marvin-minskys-marvelous-meat-machine/.

28. Herbert S. Terrace, "Why Chimpanzees Can't Learn Language: 1," *Psychology Today*, October 2, 2019, https://psychologytoday.com/us/blog/the-origin-words/201910/why-chimpanzees-cant-learn-language-1.

29. As an example, the chimpanzees under observation, while curious and bright, could not master the sequential nature of human language (they could not distinguish between "the dog bit the lady" and "the lady bit the dog," for example). "Memory for Stimulus Sequences Distinguishes Humans from Other Animals," *Science Daily*, June 20, 2017, www.sciencedaily.com/releases/2017/06/170620200012.htm.

30. See Mortimer J. Adler, "The Confusion of the Animalists," Radical Academy, accessed February 18, 2022, https://radicalacademy.org/adleranimalists.html.

31. Moreland references the Christian philosopher St. Augustine of Hippo (354–430). See Moreland, *Soul*, 144–45.

32. In discussing this seeming quirk of the Hebrew language and mode of thought, Owen Barfield—a professor and friend of C. S. Lewis—wrote, "It was the logic of their whole development that the cosmos of wisdom should henceforth have its perennial source, not without, and behind the appearances, but within the consciousness of man." Owen Barfield, *Saving the Appearances: A Study in Idolatry* (Middletown, CT: Wesleyan University Press, 1988), 155.

33. Aquinas, following Aristotle, wrote that the soul comes into an unborn child when it is "animated." Aristotle taught that this happens for boys forty days after gestation and for girls eighty days after gestation. Aquinas followed this line of thinking, which seems strange to us in the scientific age. When Aquinas wrote,

it was assumed that long-established sources such as Aristotle should be trusted unless there was good reason not to trust them, and the tools for discerning the nature of the unborn child were not developed until hundreds of years later. In the last half of the twentieth century, writers seeking to overturn the Catholic Church's stance against abortion (a stance that Aquinas fully embraced), sought to use Aquinas's thoughts on "delayed animation" to argue that until a child is "animated," it does not have a soul, and thus abortion on demand is not the killing of a human person. This interpretation has been rejected by the Catholic Church, and from his writings, we know that Aquinas would have rejected it as well. He believed that abortion at any stage of fetal development was a grave sin.

34. See Jonathan Burnside, *God, Justice, and Society: Aspects of Law and Legality in the Bible* (New York: Oxford University Press, 2011).

35. Nicholas Wolterstorff, *Justice: Rights and Wrongs* (Princeton: Princeton University Press, 2008), 29.

36. Jürgen Habermas, *Time of Transition* (Hoboken, NJ: Polity Press, 2006), 150–51 (translation of an interview from 1999).

37. Robert D. Woodberry, "The Missionary Roots of Liberal Democracy," *American Political Science Review* 106, no. 2 (May 2012): 244.

38. Gary B. Ferngren, *Medicine and Health Care in Early Christianity* (Baltimore: Johns Hopkins University Press, 2009), 102.

39. Ferngren, *Medicine and Health Care*, 99.

40. Quoted in Timothy S. Miller, "Basil's House of Healing," *Christian History Magazine*, Issue 101: Healthcare and Hospitals in the Mission of the Church, 14.

41. Miller, "Basil's House of Healing," 15.

42. Dennis Prager, *The Rational Bible: Genesis—God, Creation, and Destruction* (Washington, DC: Regnery Faith, 2019), 70.

43. See Richard Weikart, *From Darwin to Hitler: Evolutionary Ethics, Eugenics, and Racism in Germany* (New York: Palgrave Macmillan, 2004).

44. Will and Ariel Durant, "The History of War," in *The Lessons of History* (New York: Simon & Schuster, 2012), 81.

45. Aquinas, *Summa Theologica*.

46. The just war tradition is not the only approach to war that Christians have advocated based on a biblical understanding. Others have embraced biblical nonresistance (turning the other cheek), pacifism (no participation in war), and preventative war (preemptive aggression to stop further aggression). For a discussion of these four Christian views of war, see Robert G. Clouse, ed., *War: Four Christian Views* (Downers Grove, IL: InterVarsity, 1991).

47. Kelly DeVries, "Medieval Warfare and the Value of a Human Life," Medievalists.net, June 20, 2015, https://www.medievalists.net/2015/06/medieval-warfare-and-the-value-of-a-human-life/. Full text available at https://web.archive.org/web/20130207150851/http://eres.lndproxy.org/edoc/FacPubs/loy/DeVriesK/MedievalWarfare-06.pdf.

48. Peter J. Leithart, *Theopolitan Reading* (West Monroe, LA: Athanasius Press, 2020), 30.

49. Richard Swinburne, *The Evolution of the Soul* (Oxford: Oxford University Press, 1986), see chapter five, "Purposes."

50. Quoted in D. James Kennedy and Jerry Newcombe, *What If Jesus Had Never Been Born?* (Nashville: Thomas Nelson, 1994), 238.

Chapter 6 How Jesus Followers Have Changed How We Care for One Another

1. "The Divine Call: Carrie A. Nation," in *American Spiritualities: A Reader*, ed. Catherine L. Albanese (Bloomington: Indiana University Press, 2001), 321.

2. Ronald D. Utt, *Ships of Oak, Guns of Iron: The War of 1812 and the Forging of the American Navy* (Washington, DC: Regnery History, 2012), 119.

3. Friedrich Nietzsche, *Twilight of the Idols*, trans. Judith Norman (New York: Cambridge University Press, 2005), 219.

4. Nietzsche, *Twilight of the Idols*, 33.

5. Quoted in George Weigel, *Witness to Hope: The Biography of Pope John Paul II* (New York: Harper Perennial, 2005), 857.

6. Gary B. Ferngren, "A New Era in Roman Healthcare," *Christian History Magazine*, Issue 101: Healthcare and Hospitals in the Mission of the Church, 7.

7. Rodney Stark, *The Rise of Christianity: A Sociologist Reconsiders History* (Princeton: Princeton University Press, 1996), 212. Stark references the work of historian Edwin A. Judge.

8. Lucian of Samosata, "The Passing of Peregrinus," Early Christian Writings, accessed February 18, 2022, http://www.earlychristianwritings.com/text/peregrinus.html.

9. Quoted in John Foster, *Church History: The First Advance, AD 29–500* (London: Society for Promoting Christian Knowledge, 1977), 28.

10. Ferngren, "New Era in Roman Healthcare," 11.

11. Yaron Ayalon, "1-The Black Death and the Rise of the Ottomans," Cambridge Core, December 5, 2014, 21–60, https://www.cambridge.org/core/books/natural-disasters-in-the-ottoman-empire/black-death-and-the-rise-of-the-ottomans/D83E412C0BB3C092E79683722AFFFC33/core-reader.

12. From Wendell Berry, *What Are People For?*, quoted in Joel Shuman and Brian Volck, *Reclaiming the Body* (Grand Rapids: Brazos, 2006), 95.

13. Lawrence Wright, "How Pandemics Wreak Havok—and Open Minds," *New Yorker*, July 13, 2020, https://www.newyorker.com/magazine/2020/07/20/how-pandemics-wreak-havoc-and-open-minds.

14. Ayalon, "1-The Black Death," full text available at https://www.cambridge.org/core/books/natural-disasters-in-the-ottoman-empire/black-death

-and-the-rise-of-the-ottomans/D83E412C0BB3C092E79683722AFFFC33/core-reader.

15. Adam Davis, "The Charitable Revolution," *Christian History Magazine*, Issue 101: Healthcare and Hospitals in the Mission of the Church, 34.

16. Davis, "Charitable Revolution," 35.

17. Karl Zinmeister, "Less God, Less Giving? Religion and Generosity Feed Each Other in Fascinating Ways," Philanthropy Roundtable, Winter 2019, https://www.philanthropyroundtable.org/philanthropy-magazine/less-god-less-giving.

18. Quoted in Emerson Thomas McMullen, "No Vein Inquiry," *Christian History* 76 (2002): 41. See https://christianhistoryinstitute.org/magazine/article/no-vein-inquiry/.

19. Quoted in Joseph Needham, *A History of Embryology* (Cambridge, UK: Cambridge University Press, 1934), 41.

20. "The Study of Anatomy," Khan Academy, accessed March 21, 2022, https://www.khanacademy.org/humanities/renaissance-reformation/early-renaissance1/beginners-renaissance-florence/a/the-study-of-anatomy.

21. Andrew D. White *A History of the Warfare of Science with Theology in Christendom* (New York: D. Appleton and Company, 1908), 31–36.

22. Lawrence G. Duggan, "Armsbearing by the Clergy and the Fourth Lateran Council," in *The Fourth Lateran Council and the Development of Canon Law*, ed. Atria Larson and Andrea Massaroni (Turnhout, Belgium: Brepois, 2018), 63–75.

23. James J. Walsh, *The Popes and Science: The History of the Papal Relations to Science during the Middle Ages and Down to Our Own Time* (New York: Fordham University Press, 1915), https://www.gutenberg.org/files/34019/34019-h/34019-h.htm#1.

24. Mondino de Luzzi (1270–1326), Andreas Vesalius (1514–64), Leonardo da Vinci (1452–1519), Michelangelo Buanorotti (1475–1564), Baccio Bandinelli (1493–1560), Guy de Chauliac (1300–1368), and Gabriele Falloppio (1523–62) all carried out studies of the human body to advance scientific knowledge. Sanjib Kumar Ghosh, "Human Cadaveric Dissection: A Historical Account from Ancient Greece to the Modern Era," *Anatomy and Cell Biology* 48, no. 3 (September 2015): 153–69, https://www.ncbi.nlm.nih.gov/pmc/articles/PMC4582158/#.

25. Walsh, *Popes and Science.*

26. William L. Minkowsli, "Women Healers of the Middle Ages: Selected Aspects of Their History," *American Journal of Public Health* 82, no. 2 (February 1992): 288–95, https://ajph.aphapublications.org/doi/pdf/10.2105/AJPH.82.2.288. See also Muriel Joy Hughes, *Women Healers in Medieval Life and Literature* (Freeport, NY: Books for Libraries Press, 1943), 116.

27. From "Concerning Certain Medical Women of the Late Middle Ages," *Med Life* 42 (1934): 111–28, quoted in Minkowsli, "Women Healers of the Middle Ages," 288.

28. Quoted in Maya Schwayder, "Debunking a Myth," *Harvard Gazette*, April 7, 2011, https://news.harvard.edu/gazette/story/2011/04/debunking-a-myth/.

29. Andrew Gregory, "William Harvey: English Physician," *Britannica*, accessed February 18, 2022, https://www.britannica.com/biography/William-Harvey. For a lengthier discussion of witch trials, see Jeff Myers, "Is God a Mean Bully?," in *Understanding the Faith: A Survey of Christian Apologetics* (Colorado Springs: David C. Cook, 2016).

30. Philip Birnbaum, "Shalom," in *Encyclopedia of Jewish Concepts* (New York: Hebrew Publishing Company, 1991), 601–2.

31. Robert Putnam, *Bowling Alone: The Collapse and Revival of American Community* (New York: Simon & Schuster, 2000), 19.

32. Substance Abuse and Mental Health Services Administration, "Key Substance Use and Mental Health Indicators in the United States: Results from the 2018 National Survey on Drug Use and Health," HHS Publication no. PEP19-5068, NSDUH Series H-54 (Rockville, MD: Center for Behavioral Health Statistics and Quality, Substance Abuse and Mental Health Services Administration, 2019), https://www.samhsa.gov/data/.

33. American Medical Association Advocacy Resource Center, "Issue Brief: Nation's Drug-Related Overdose and Death Epidemic Continues to Worsen," November 12, 2021, https://www.ama-assn.org/system/files/issue-brief-increases-in-opioid-related-overdose.pdf.

34. Nirmita Panchal, Rabah Kamal, Cynthia Cox, and Rachel Garfield, "The Implications of COVID-19 for Mental Health and Substance Use," Kaiser Family Foundation, February 10, 2021, https://www.kff.org/coronavirus-covid-19/issue-brief/the-implications-of-covid-19-for-mental-health-and-substance-use/.

35. William L. White, *Pathways from the Culture of Addiction to the Culture of Recovery: A Travel Guide for Addiction Professionals* (Center City, MN: Hazelden, 1996), 54.

36. Jeremy E. Uecker, Mark D. Regnerus, and Margaret L. Vaaler, "Losing My Religion: The Social Sources of Religious Decline in Early Adulthood," *Social Forces* 85, no. 4 (June 2007): 1667–92.

37. Henri J. M. Nouwen, *The Wounded Healer: Ministry in Contemporary Society* (New York: Image Books, 1972).

38. Anjali Talchekar, "Timeline: History of Addiction Treatment," American Addiction Centers, January 2020, https://www.recovery.org/drug-treatment/history/.

39. Brian J. Grim and Melissa E. Grim, "Belief, Behavior, and Belonging: How Faith Is Indispensable in Preventing and Recovering from Substance Abuse," *Journal of Religious Health* 58, no. 5 (2019): 1713–50, https://link.springer.com/article/10.1007%2Fs10943-019-00876-w.

40. Jeremiah Johnston, *Unimaginable: What Our World Would Be Like without Christianity* (Bloomington, MN: Bethany House, 2017), 152–53.

41. Glenn Sunshine, "Shi Meiyu (1873–1954)," April 15, 2013, Colson Center. See also "Kang Cheng and Shi Meiyu: The University of Michigan's First Chinese Students," in David Ward and Eugene Chen, *The University of Michigan in China* (Ann Arbor, MI: Maize Books, 2017), https://quod.lib .umich.edu/m/maize/mpub9885197/1:7/--university-of-michigan-in-china?rgn =div1;view=fulltext.

42. Zinmeister, "Less God, Less Giving?"

43. Scott Todd, *Fast Living: How the Church Will End Extreme Poverty* (Colorado Springs: Compassion International, 2011), 37.

44. "Water, Sanitation and Hygiene (WASH)," World Health Organization, accessed March 21, 2022, https://www.who.int/health-topics/water-sani tation-and-hygiene-wash.

45. Michael Zigarelli, "Gratitude: Pathway to Permanent Change," Christianity 9 to 5, accessed February 18, 2022, http://www.christianity9to5.org /gratitude-pathway-to-permanent-change/.

46. Robert Emmons, "Pay It Forward," *Greater Good Magazine*, June 1, 2007, https://greatergood.berkeley.edu/article/item/pay_it_forward.

47. James H. Fowler and Nicholas A. Christakis, "Cooperative Behavior Cascades in Human Social Networks," *Proceedings of the National Academy of Science* 107, no. 4 (March 8, 2010), https://www.pnas.org/doi/10.1073 /pnas.0913149107.

48. For more about the relationship between brokenness and our ability to help the poor, see Steve Corbett and Brian Fikkert, *When Helping Hurts: How to Alleviate Poverty without Hurting the Poor . . . Or Yourself* (Chicago: Moody, 2009).

49. See, for example, Kent Berghuis, "Fasting through the Patristic Era," in *Christian Fasting: A Theological Approach* (PhD diss., Trinity International University, 2002), https://bible.org/seriespage/chapter-3-fasting-through-patris tic-era#P705_293859.

50. Quoted in Michael Lundy, *Depression, Anxiety, and the Christian Life: Practical Wisdom from Richard Baxter* (Wheaton: Crossway, 2018), 173.

Chapter 7 How Jesus Followers Have Changed How We Learn and Grow

1. Mark A. Noll, *Princeton and the Republic, 1768–1822* (Vancouver: Regent College Press, 1989), 28.

2. John Witherspoon, quoted in Buckner F. Melton Jr., ed., *The Quotable Founding Fathers: A Treasury of 2,500 Wise and Witty Quotations from the Men and Women Who Created America* (Washington, DC: Brassey's, 2004), 249.

3. John Witherspoon, *The Works of the Rev. John Witherspoon to Which Is Prefixed an Account of the Author's Life, in a Sermon Occasioned by His Death* (Boston: William W. Woodward, 1802), 3:563.

4. Noll, *Princeton and the Republic*, 29.

5. Jeffry H. Morrison, *John Witherspoon and the Founding of the American Republic* (Notre Dame, IN: University of Notre Dame Press, 2005), 4.

6. See Helen Pluckrose and James Lindsay, *Cynical Theories: How Activist Scholarship Made Everything about Race, Gender, and Identity—and Why This Harms Everybody* (Durham, NC: Pitchstone, 2020).

7. Melville Herskovits, *Cultural Relativism* (New York: Vintage Books, 1972), 15.

8. Gary M. Galles, "Is Math Racist? That Does Not Compute," Mises Institute, February 16, 2021, https://mises.org/wire/math-racist-does-not -compute.

9. Jonathan Sacks, "The Far Horizon: Bo 5781," Jonathan Sacks: The Rabbi Sacks Legacy Trust, January 18, 2021, https://rabbisacks.org/bo-5781/.

10. Augustine, *On Free Will*, trans. Thomas Williams (Indianapolis: Hackett, 1993), 2.16.

11. G. K. Chesterton, *Heretics / Orthodoxy* (Nashville: Thomas Nelson, 2000), 81–82.

12. Tom Holland, *Dominion: How the Christian Revolution Remade the World* (New York: Basic Books, 2019), 540–41.

13. J. P. Louw and E. A. Nida, *Greek-English Lexicon of the New Testament: Based on Semantic Domains*, 2nd ed. (New York: United Bible Societies, 1996), 1:366.

14. Rachel E. Stark, "Infant Vocalization: A Comprehensive View," *Infant Mental Health Journal* 2, no. 2 (Summer 1981): 118–28.

15. Christiane A. M. Baltaxe, "Vocal Communication of Affect and Its Perception in Three- to Four-Year-Old Children," *Perceptual and Motor Skills* 72 (1991): 1188.

16. See Jay Belsky, "Mother-Father-Infant Interaction: A Naturalistic Observational Study," *Developmental Psychology* 15, no. 6 (1979): 601–7; and Elissa L. Newport, Henry Gleitman, and Lila Gleitman, "Mother, I'd Rather Do It Myself: Some Effects and Non-Effects of Maternal Speech Style," in *Talking to Children: Language Input and Acquisition*, ed. Catherine E. Snow and Charles A. Ferguson (Cambridge: Cambridge University Press, 1977).

17. Ann D. Murray, Jeanne Johnson, and Jo Peters, "Fine-Tuning of Utterance Length to Preverbal Infants: Effects on Later Language Development," *Journal of Child Language* 17 (1990): 511–25; Deborah G. Nelson, Kathy Hirsh-Pasek, Peter W. Jusczyk, and Kimberly Wright Cassidy, "How the Prosodic Cues in Motherese Might Assist Language Learning," *Journal of Child Language* 16 (1989): 55–68; Ann E. McCabe, "Differential Language Learning Styles in Young Children: The Importance of Context," *Developmental Review* 9 (1989): 1–20; and Catherine E. Snow, "The Role of Social Interaction in Language Acquisition," in *Children's Language and Communication: The Minnesota Symposia on Child Psychology*, vol. 12, ed. W. Andrew Collins (Hillsdale, NJ: Lawrence Erlbaum Associates, 1979), 157–82.

18. Sara Mannle, Michelle Barton, and Michael Tomasello, "Two-Year-Olds' Conversations with Their Mothers and Preschool-Aged Siblings," *First Language* 12 (1991): 57–71.

19. Mihaly Csikszentmihalyi, *Finding Flow* (New York: Basic Books, 1998), 69. In case you're curious, as I was, *Csikszentmihalyi* is pronounced Chick-SENT-me-high.

20. See, for example, Miya Narushima, Jian Liu, and Naomi Diestelkamp, "Lifelong Learning in Active Ageing Discourse: Its Conserving Effect on Wellbeing, Health and Vulnerability," *Ageing and Society* 38, no. 4 (April 2018): 651–75.

21. Pope Benedict XVI, "The Cathedral from the Romanesque to the Gothic Architecture: The Theological Background," General Audience, November 18, 2009, http://www.vatican.va/content/benedict-xvi/en/audiences /2009/documents/hf_ben-xvi_aud_20091118.html.

22. The historian Francis Woodman referred to King's College Chapel as "the English building of the late Middle Ages, every element capturing the artistic and political revolution of its time." See Julia Vitullo-Martin, "What the Late Middle Ages Wrought," *Wall Street Journal*, December 19, 2009, https://www.wsj.com/articles/SB10001424052748704517504574590023741272370.

23. Other languages feature a similar number of sounds. Some, like Mandarin Chinese, feature fewer sounds but several tones, which make them more complicated to learn.

24. See, for example, Charles F. Hockett, "The Origins of Speech," *Scientific American* 203, no. 3 (1960): 89–96; and Frank E. X. Dance and Carl E. Larson, *Speech Communication: Concept and Behavior* (New York: Harper & Row, 1972), 35.

25. Frank E. X. Dance, "The Centrality of the Spoken Word," *Central States Speech Journal* 23 (1977): 200.

26. Dyson Hague, *The Life and Work of John Wycliffe* (Oxford: Oxford University Press, 1935), 94.

27. See "English Words/Phrases from Early Translations," Houston Baptist University, accessed February 18, 2022, https://hbu.edu/museums/dunham -bible-museum/influence-in-history-and-culture/english-wordsphrases-from -early-translations/; "Learning English Timeline," British Library, accessed February 18, 2022, https://www.bl.uk/learning/timeline/item126567.html; and Youngjoo Lee, "The Lexical Contribution of Wycliffe's Bible English to the History of the English Language," https://citeseerx.ist.psu.edu/viewdoc /download?doi=10.1.1.617.7828&rep=rep1&type=pdf.

28. David Lyle Jeffrey, "Where Would Civilization Be Without Christianity? The Gift of Literacy," *Christianity Today*, December 6, 1999, https:// www.christianitytoday.com/ct/1999/december6/9te054.html.

29. "Our Impact," Wycliffe Bible Translators, accessed February 18, 2022, https://www.wycliffe.org.uk/about/our-impact/.

30. T. S. Eliot, *The Rock: A Pageant Play, Written for Performance at Sadler's Wells Theatre 28 May to 9 June 1934 on Behalf of the Forty-Five Churches Fund of the Diocese of London* (New York: Harcourt, Brace, 1934), 7.

31. Dorothy L. Sayers, "The Lost Tools of Learning" (paper read at a Vacation Course in Education, Oxford University, 1947), https://www.pccs.org/wp-content/uploads/2016/06/LostToolsOfLearning-DorothySayers.pdf.

32. See Brian D. Yurochko, "Cultural and Intellectual Response to the Black Death" (master's thesis, Duquesne University, 2009), https://dsc.duq.edu/cgi/viewcontent.cgi?article=2412&context=etd.

33. Charles Dickens, *Dombey and Son* (Boston: Bradbury and Guild, 1848), 275.

34. C. S. Lewis, *English Literature in the Sixteenth Century, Excluding Drama* (Oxford, UK: Clarendon, 1954), 62.

35. J. Warner Wallace, *Person of Interest: Why Jesus Still Matters in a World That Rejects the Bible* (Grand Rapids: Zondervan, 2021), 171–72.

36. Quoted in Daniel P. Kinkade, "Destination on Right: The Influence of Dr. Gladys West," Gideons International, May 3, 2019, https://www.gideons.org/blog/dr_gladys_west.

37. Horace Mann, "Extract from Twelfth Report on Schools in Massachusetts by Horace Mann," in *Acts and Resolves of the General Assembly of the State of Rhode Island and Providence Plantation, Passed at the January Session, 1855* (Providence: Knowles and Anthony, State Printers, 1855), 218.

38. Mann, "Extract from Twelfth Report," 218.

39. Richard Paul and Linda Elder, *The Thinker's Guide to Fallacies: The Art of Mental Trickery and Manipulation* (Dillon Beach, CA: Foundation for Critical Thinking Press, 2006), 7–8.

40. Ralph Waldo Emerson, "Compensation," 1841, The Literature Page, http://www.literaturepage.com/read/emersonessays1-51.html.

41. John Dewey, *A Common Faith* (New Haven: Yale University Press, 1962), 84.

42. Leon Kass, *Founding God's Nation: Reading Exodus* (New Haven: Yale University Press, 2021), 604.

Chapter 8 How Jesus Followers Have Changed the World of Science

1. Jonathan Sacks, "Rabbi Sacks on 'The Great Partnership,'" Jonathan Sacks: The Rabbi Sacks Legacy Trust, June 7, 2018, https://rabbisacks.org/great-partnership/.

2. Maltbie D. Babcock, "This Is My Father's World," 1901, emphasis added.

3. Fulget Master (Circle of Neri da Rimini), *King David in an Initial D*, https://www.christianiconography.info/metropolitan/december2009/davidCallFulget.html.

4. C. S. Lewis, *The Discarded Image* (Cambridge: Cambridge University Press, 2012), 112.

5. Thomas Browne, *Religio Medici: Letter to a Friend etc. and Christian Morals*, part 2, section 9, ed. W. A. Greenhill (London: Macmillan, 1881), 111.

6. Dan McCollam, "The God Vibration," Heaven's Physics, accessed February 18, 2022, http://heavensphysics.com/chapter8/.

7. C. S. Lewis, *The Magician's Nephew* (New York: HarperCollins, 2008), 106.

8. Steven Weinberg, "Elementary Particles and the Laws of Physics. The 1986 Dirac Memorial Lectures," Internet Archive, accessed February 18, 2022, https://archive.org/stream/B-001-000-178/B-001-000-178_djvu.txt.

9. *New World Encyclopedia*, s.v. "Johannes Kepler," accessed March 21, 2022, https://www.newworldencyclopedia.org/entry/Johannes_Kepler.

10. See William A. Wilson, "Scientific Regress," *First Things*, May 2016, https://www.firstthings.com/article/2016/05/scientific-regress.

11. National Academy of Sciences, *Science, Evolution, and Creationism* (Washington, DC: National Academy Press, 2008), 10.

12. Quoted in Peter Harrison, *Territories of Science and Religion* (Chicago: University of Chicago Press, 2015), 60.

13. Quoted in Lee Strobel, *The Case for Faith: A Journalist Investigates the Toughest Objections to Christianity* (Grand Rapids: Zondervan, 2000), 111.

14. Francis Collins, *The Language of God: A Scientist Presents Evidence for Belief* (New York: Free Press, 2006), 233.

15. Hildegard of Bingen (1098–1179), founder of scientific natural history; Robert Grosseteste (1175–1253), founder of scientific thought; Nicole Oresme (1323–82), discoverer of the curvature of light through atmospheric refraction; Otto Brunfels (1488–1534), father of botany; John Ray (1627–1705), inventor of the concept of species; Antonie van Leeuwenhoek (1632–1723), father of microbiology; Albrecht von Haller (1708–77), father of modern physiology; Mikhail Lomonosov (1711–65), formulated the law of conservation of mass in chemical reactions; Antoine Lavoisier (1743–94), father of modern chemistry; Carl Linnaeus (1707–78), father of modern taxonomy; Joseph Priestley (1733–1804), discoverer of oxygen; Alessandro Volta (1745–1827), inventor of the first electric battery; George Cuvier (1769–1832), father of paleontology; Andre Marie Ampere (1775–1836), one of the founders of classical electromagnetism; Benjamin Silliman (1779–1864), first person to distill petroleum; William Whewell (1794–1866), coined the terms *scientist* and *physicist*; Michael Faraday (1791–1867), founder of electromagnetic theory; Charles Babbage (1791–1871), originated the idea of a programmable computer; Gregor Mendel (1822–84), father of modern genetics; Louis Pasteur (1822–95), discoverer of vaccination and pasteurization; James Prescott Joule (1818–89), discoverer of the first law of thermodynamics; Joseph Lister (1827–1912), pioneer of antiseptic surgery; J. J. Thomson (1856–1940), discoverer of the electron; Giuseppe Mercalli (1850–1914), developer of the scale for measuring the intensity of earthquakes; Guglielmo Marconi (1874–1937),

developer of long-distance radio transmission; William Williams Keen (1837–1932), first brain surgeon in the United States; Georges Lemaitre (1894–1966), first to propose Big Bang theory; Werner Heisenberg (1901–76), creator of quantum mechanics; Wernher von Braun (1912–77), developer of modern rocketry; Joseph Murray (1919–2012), pioneer of transplant surgery. For more names, see "List of Christians in Science and Technology," Wikipedia, last edited February 2, 2022, https://en.wikipedia.org/wiki/List_of_Christians _in_science_and_technology.

16. "How Many Nobel Prize Winners Believed in God?," John Lennox, January 23, 2019, https://www.johnlennox.org/resources/145/how-many-nobel -prize-winners.

17. Rodney Stark outlines his methodology in "God's Handiwork: The Religious Origins of Science," in *For the Glory of God: How Monotheism Led to Reformations, Science, Witch-Hunts, and the End of Slavery* (Princeton: Princeton University Press, 2003), 160–63. Of the fifty-two scientists Stark examined, half were Catholic and half were Protestant. Only two, Edmund Halley and Paracelsus, qualified as skeptics. Stark concludes that Halley was probably an atheist.

18. Quoted in Collins, *Language of God*, 231.

19. Quoted in David Berlinski, *Newton's Gift: How Sir Isaac Newton Unlocked the System of the World* (New York: Free Press, 2000), 172.

20. Nicolas Fuss, "Eulogy of Leonhard Euler," trans. John S. D. Glaus, April 2005, http://eulerarchive.maa.org/historica/fuss.html.

21. "Most Influential Women in British Science History," The Royal Society, accessed February 18, 2022, https://royalsociety.org/topics-policy/diver sity-in-science/influential-british-women-science/.

22. Quoted in Matthew Stanley, "Religious Lives," in *Huxley's Church and Maxwell's Demon: From Theistic Science to Naturalistic Science* (Chicago: University of Chicago Press, 2015), 18.

23. Pew Research Center, "Scientists and Belief," November 5, 2009, https:// www.pewforum.org/2009/11/05/scientists-and-belief/.

24. Steven Shapin, *Never Pure: Historical Studies of Science as if It Was Produced by People with Bodies, Situated in Time, Space, Culture, and Society, and Struggling for Credibility and Authority* (Baltimore: Johns Hopkins Press, 2010), 48–50.

25. Jonathan Sacks, *Radical Then, Radical Now: The Legacy of the World's Oldest Religion* (New York: HarperCollins, 2001), 68.

26. This brief list is wonderfully explained, illustrated, and footnoted in Nancy Pearcey and Charles Thaxton, *The Soul of Science: Christian Faith and Natural Philosophy* (Wheaton: Crossway, 1994), 21–37.

27. Robert C. Koons, "Science and Theism: Concord, Not Conflict," in *The Rationality of Theism*, ed. Paul Copan and Paul K. Moser (London: Routledge, 2003), 82.

28. Quoted in Shapin, *Never Pure*, 165.

29. Quoted in Shapin, *Never Pure*, 251.

30. Shapin, *Never Pure*, 197–99.

31. Ian G. Barbour, *Religion and Science: Historical and Contemporary Issues* (San Francisco: HarperSanFrancisco, 1997), 19–20.

32. Robert Boyle, *The Christian Virtuoso; Shewing, That by Being Addicted to Experimental Philosophy, a Man Is Rather Assisted, Than Indisposed, to Be a Good Christian* (London: Edward Jones, 1690), 3.

33. Boyle, *Christian Virtuoso*, 39.

34. Boyle, *Christian Virtuoso*, 19.

35. Boyle, *Christian Virtuoso*, 44.

36. Richard Feynman, with Robert B. Leighton and Matthew Sands, *Six Easy Pieces: Essentials of Physics Explained by Its Most Brilliant Teacher* (New York: Basic Books, 2011), 2, 44, 83, 113, 135.

37. Quoted in Bridget O'Brien, "Prof. Stuart Firestein Explains Why Ignorance Is Central to Scientific Discovery," *Columbia News*, May 8, 2012, https://news.columbia.edu/news/prof-stuart-firestein-explains-why-ignorance-central-scientific-discovery.

38. See Prov. 3:34; 11:22; 15:33; 18:12; 22:4; Isa. 57:15; Mic. 6:8; Matt. 23:12; Col. 3:12; James 4:10; 1 Pet. 5:5–6. A search of terms related to "humility" yields more than one hundred results.

39. See "Pump and Circumstance: Robert Boyle's Literary Technology," in Shapin, *Never Pure*, 89–116.

40. Shapin, *Never Pure*, 48.

41. Rhonda Martens, *Kepler's Philosophy and the New Astronomy* (Princeton: Princeton University Press, 2000), 78.

42. Steinar Thorvaldsen and Ola Hossjer, "Using Statistical Methods to Model the Fine-Tuning of Molecular Machines and Systems," *Journal of Theoretical Biology* 501 (2020): 110–352, https://www.sciencedirect.com/science/article/pii/S0022519320302071.

43. Glenn Myers, "Naturalist and Apothecary," *Christian History Magazine*, Issue 134: How the Church Fostered Science and Technology, 15.

44. Linda O. McMurry, *George Washington Carver: Scientist and Symbol* (Oxford: Oxford University Press, 1981), 306.

45. Ted Davis, "The Faith of a Great Scientist: Robert Boyle's Religious Life, Attitudes, and Vocation," Biologos, August 8, 2013, https://biologos.org/articles/the-faith-of-a-great-scientist-robert-boyles-religious-life-attitudes-and-vocation.

Chapter 9 How Jesus Followers Have Changed the World of the Arts

1. Quoted in Frederick J. Crowest, *A Book of Musical Anecdote: From Every Available Source* (London: R. Bentley and Son, 1878), 2:128–29.

2. Jean-Jacques Rousseau, *Confessions* (New York: Oxford University Press, 2000), 306.

3. Rousseau, *Confessions*, 306.

4. David Epstein, *Range: Why Generalists Triumph in a Specialized World* (New York: Riverhead Books, 2019), 57.

5. Epstein, *Range*, 60.

6. Rousseau, *Confessions*, 306.

7. Samuel Wells, "Vivaldi's Business Plan," *Christian Century*, February 25, 2014, https://www.christiancentury.org/article/2014-02/vivaldi-s-business-plan.

8. Feris Jabr, "How Beauty Is Making Scientists Rethink Evolution," *New York Times Magazine*, January 9, 2019, https://www.nytimes.com/2019/01/09/magazine/beauty-evolution-animal.html.

9. Jabr, "How Beauty Is Making Scientists Rethink Evolution."

10. Quoted in Jabr, "How Beauty Is Making Scientists Rethink Evolution."

11. Holmes Rolston III, *Science and Religion: A Critical Survey* (San Diego: Harcourt Brace, 1987), 39.

12. Robert Jastrow, "A Scientist Caught between Two Faiths," *Christianity Today*, August 6, 1982, quoted in Norman Geisler, *Systematic Theology* (Bloomington, MN: Bethany House), 2:591.

13. Dacher Keltner and Jonathan Haidt, "Approaching Awe, a Moral, Spiritual, and Aesthetic Emotion," *Cognition and Emotion* 17, no. 2 (2003): 297.

14. See Iris Murdoch, *Existentialists and Mystics: Writings on Philosophy and Literature* (New York: Penguin Books, 1950), 369.

15. *Strong's Lexicon*, s.v. "tob," accessed March 22, 2022, https://www.blueletterbible.org/lexicon/h2896/kjv/wlc/0-1/.

16. For a thought-provoking discussion of beauty, art, and culture, see Andy Crouch, *Culture Making: Recovering Our Creative Calling* (Downers Grove, IL: InterVarsity, 2008).

17. Augustine of Hippo, *The Works of Saint Augustine: A Translation for the 21st Century*, trans. Edmund Hill, ed. John E. Rotelle (New Rochelle, NY: New City Press, 1993), 71.

18. See Gen. 3; Rom. 1:18–31.

19. Stephen R. C. Hicks, *Explaining Postmodernism: Skepticism and Socialism from Rousseau to Foucault* (Tempe, AZ: Scholargy Publishing, 2004), 196.

20. Glenn Ward, *Postmodernism* (Chicago: McGraw-Hill, 2003), 51.

21. Kendall Todd, "Bernstein, Beethoven, and the Berlin Wall," WCRB, August 25, 2017, https://www.classicalwcrb.org/blog/2017-08-25/bernstein-beethoven-and-the-berlin-wall.

22. John Terauds, "'Ode to Joy' Has an Odious History. Let's Give Beethoven's Most Overplayed Symphony a Rest," *Toronto Star*, June 26, 2018, https://www.thestar.com/entertainment/music/opinion/2018/06/26/ode-to-joy-has-an-odious-history-lets-give-beethovens-most-overplayed-symphony-a-rest.html.

23. Glenn Sunshine, "Muiredach's Cross," Every Square Inch Ministries, November 4, 2020, https://www.esquareinch.com/muiredachs-cross/.

24. Owen Barfield, *Saving the Appearances: A Study in Idolatry* (Middletown, CT: Wesleyan University Press, 1988), 44–45.

25. Steven Ozment, *The Age of Reform, 1250–1550: An Intellectual and Religious History of Late Medieval and Reformation Europe* (New Haven: Yale University Press, 1980), 55.

26. Chris R. Armstrong, *Medieval Wisdom for Modern Christians: Finding Authentic Faith in a Forgotten Age with C. S. Lewis* (Grand Rapids: Brazos, 2016), 144.

27. Millard Meiss, *Painting in Florence and Siena after the Black Death: The Arts, Religion and Society in the Mid-Fourteenth Century* (Princeton: Princeton University Press, 1979), 6.

28. Meiss, *Painting in Florence*, 41.

29. See Sir Robert Anderson, *The Silence of God* (Grand Rapids: Kregel, 1965), chap. 13.

30. Larry J. Solomon, "The Sounds of Silence: John Cage and 4'33"," accessed March 22, 2022, https://web.archive.org/web/20180109031457/http://solomonsmusic.net/4min33se.htm.

31. Quoted in Jeremy Phillips, "The Price of Silence and the Myth of the Batt Cage," IPKat, April 19, 2012, https://ipkitten.blogspot.com/2012/04/price-of-silence-and-myth-of-batt-cage.html?m=0#:~:text=Way%2C%20way%20back%20in%202004,33%20seconds%20of%20absolute%20silence.

32. Roger Scruton, *Beauty: A Very Short Introduction* (Oxford: Oxford University Press, 2011), 10.

33. Quoted in Jed Gottlieb, "Music Everywhere," *The Harvard Gazette*, November 21, 2019, https://news.harvard.edu/gazette/story/2019/11/new-harvard-study-establishes-music-is-universal/.

34. Quoted in Jim Daley, "What Makes a Song? It's the Same Recipe in Every Culture," *Scientific American*, November 21, 2019, https://www.scientificamerican.com/article/what-makes-a-song-its-the-same-recipe-in-every-culture/.

35. Quoted in Arthur Koestler, *The Sleepwalkers: A History of Man's Changing Vision of the Universe* (New York: Penguin, 1990), 398.

36. Quoted in Elaine Scarry, *On Beauty: And Being Just* (Princeton: Princeton University Press, 1999), 31.

37. Quoted in Lesley Lee Francis, *You Come Too: My Journey with Robert Frost* (Charlottesville: University of Virginia Press, 2015), n.p.

38. Joseph Epstein, "Think You Have a Book in You? Think Again," *New York Times*, September 28, 2002, https://www.nytimes.com/2002/09/28/opinion/think-you-have-a-book-in-you-think-again.html.

39. Steven Naifeh and Gregory White Smith, *Van Gogh: The Life* (New York: Random House, 2011), 3–4.

40. Naifeh and Smith, *Van Gogh*, 811.

41. USA Facts, "48% of Americans Are Feeling Down, Depressed, or Hopeless During the COVID-19 Pandemic," September 22, 2020, https://usafacts .org/articles/45-americans-are-feeling-down-depressed-or-hopeless-during -covid-19-pandemic/; and Abigail Johnson Hess, "51% of Young Americans Say They Feel Down, Depressed or Hopeless—Here's How Advocates Are Trying to Help," CNBC, May 10, 2021, https://www.cnbc.com/2021/05/10/51per cent-of-young-americans-say-they-feel-down-depressed-or-hopeless.html.

Chapter 10 How Jesus Followers Have Changed Politics

1. Matt. 28:18–20.

2. Tony Evans, *Oneness Embraced: Reconciliation, the Kingdom, and How We Are Stronger Together* (Chicago: Moody, 2011), 251.

3. Edmund Burke, *Reflections on the Revolution in France* (New York: Library of Liberal Arts, 1955), 288.

4. "From John Adams to the Massachusetts Militia, October 11, 1798," National Archives, accessed February 18, 2022, https://founders.archives.gov /documents/Adams/99-02-02-3102.

5. Lon Luvois Fuller, *The Morality of Law* (New Haven: Yale University Press, 1964), 33–38.

6. Universal Declaration of Human Rights, United Nations General Assembly Resolution 217A, December 10, 1948.

7. Sidney Hook, "Solzhenitsyn and Secular Humanism: A Response," *The Humanist*, November/December 1978, 6.

8. Stanley Fish, *The First: How to Think about Hate Speech, Campus Speech, Religious Speech, Fake News, Post-Truth, and Donald Trump* (New York: Atria/One Signal Publishers, 2020), 176.

9. Fish, *The First*, 170, emphasis added.

10. Cheslaw Miłosz, *The Captive Mind* (New York: Penguin, 2007), 35.

11. Marcus Tullii Cicero, *Orationes*, ed. George Long and A. J. Macleane (London: Whittaker, 1855), 2:353.

12. Quoted in Roger Henderson, "The Development of the Principle of Distributed Authority, or Sphere Sovereignty," *Philosophia Reformata* 82 (2017): 85.

13. Steven Ozment, *The Age of Reform, 1250–1550: An Intellectual and Religious History of Late Medieval and Reformation Europe* (New Haven: Yale University Press, 1980), 4–5.

14. Ozment, *The Age of Reform*, 5.

15. Quoted in Paul E. Sigmund, ed., *St. Thomas Aquinas on Politics and Ethics* (New York: Norton, 1988), xix.

16. "Shalom," Hebrew 8934, in James A. Swanson, *A Dictionary of Biblical Languages with Semantic Domains: Hebrew Old Testament* (Oak Harbor, WA: Logos Research Systems, 1997).

17. Geoffrey Wigoder, ed., *The Encyclopedia of Judaism* (New York: Macmillan, 1989), 544.

18. Perkins writes, "Now all societies of men are bodies, a family is a body, and so is every particular Church a body, and the Commonwealth also; and in these bodies there be several members, which are men walking in several callings and offices, the execution whereof must tend to the happy and good estate of the rest, yea of all men everywhere, as much as possible is." William Perkins, with C. Matthew McMahon, *Glorifying God in Our Jobs* (Crossville, TN: Puritan Publications, 2015), 26–27.

19. The full title of Rutherford's book is *Lex Rex, Or The Law and the Prince; A dispute for The Just Prerogative of King and People: containing the reasons and causes of the most necessary defensive wars of the Kingdom of Scotland, and of their Expedition for the aid and help of their dear brethren of England; in which their innocency is asserted, and a full answer is given to a seditious pamphlet, entitled, "SACRO-SANCTA REGUM MAJESTAS," or The Sacred and Royal Prerogative of Christian Kings; under the name of J. A., but penned by John Maxwell, the excommunicate Popish Prelate; with a scriptural confutation of the ruinous grounds of W. Barclay, H. Grotius, H. Arnisæus, Ant. de Domi. popish Bishop of Spilato, and of other late anti-magitratical royalists, as the author of Ossorianum, Dr. Ferne, E. Symmons, the Doctors of Aberdeen, etc. In Forty-four Questions.*

20. For a full text, see John Locke, "A Letter concerning Toleration (1689)," Lonang Institute, http://www.lonang.com/exlibris/locke/.

21. John Locke, *Of Civil Government* (London: Dent, 1924), 118.

22. Maximilien Robespierre, "On the Principles of Revolutionary Government," speech by Robespierre to the Committee on Public Safety, December 25, 1793, in *From Enlightenment to Romanticism*, ed. Ian Donnachie and Carmen Lavin (Manchester, UK: Manchester University Press, 2003), 97.

23. Quoted in Ronald Hamowy, ed., *The Encyclopedia of Libertarianism* (Thousand Oaks, CA: Sage, 2008), 125.

24. Thomas Jefferson, *The Papers of Thomas Jefferson, Volume II, 7 August 1787 to 31 March 1788*, ed. Charles T. Cullen, John Catanzariti, Julian Parks Boyd, and Lyman Henry Butterfield (Princeton: Princeton University Press, 1950), 356.

25. See Os Guinness, *The Magna Carta of Humanity: Sinai's Revolutionary Faith and the Future of Freedom* (Downers Grove, IL: InterVarsity, 2021).

26. Lord Acton's letter to Bishop Mandell Creighton (1887). See John Bartlett, *Familiar Quotations*, 13th and centennial ed. (Boston, MA: Little, Brown, 1955), 335.

27. Lester J. Cappon, ed., *The Adams-Jefferson Letters: The Complete Correspondence between Thomas Jefferson and Abigail and John Adams* (Chapel Hill: University of North Carolina Press, 1987), 339–40.

28. Noah Webster, "Advice to the Young," in *History of the United States* (New Haven: Durrie and Peck, 1832), 339.

29. Quoted in Jonathan Jakubowski, *Bellwether Blues: A Conservative Awakening of the Millennial Soul* (Bremerton, WA: Ballast Books, 2020), 168.

30. Guinness, *Magna Carta of Humanity*, 9.

31. Wilfred M. McClay, *Land of Hope: An Invitation to the Great American Story* (New York: Encounter Books, 2019), 65.

32. Quoted in Thomas Kidd, *Patrick Henry: First among Patriots* (New York: Basic Books, 2011), 232.

33. Mark David Hall, *Did America Have a Christian Founding? Separating Modern Myth from Historical Truth* (Nashville: Thomas Nelson, 2019), 6.

34. Abraham Kuyper, *Lectures on Calvinism* (1898; repr., New York: Cosimo Classics, 2009).

35. Art Swift, "Majority in U.S. Say Federal Government Has Too Much Power," Gallup, October 5, 2017, https://news.gallup.com/poll/220199/majority -say-federal-government-power.aspx.

36. See Augustine, *City of God against the Pagans* or more commonly just *City of God*. A translation I wish had been available when I was a student is that of William Babcock (Hyde Park, NY: New City Press, 2012).

37. *The Fathers of the Church: Saint Augustine, The City of God Books XVII–XXII*, trans. Gerald G. Walsh and Daniel J. Honan (Washington, DC: Catholic University of America Press, 1954), 182.

38. "Poll Reveals 71% of Americans Believe US Is Headed in the Wrong Direction," NBC News Poll, October 31, 2021, https://www.yahoo.com/now /poll-reveals-71-americans-believe-124021203.html.

39. Quoted in George Weigel, *Witness to Hope: The Biography of Pope John Paul II* (New York: Harper Perennial, 2005), 791.

40. Judge Learned Hand, "The 'Spirit of Liberty,'" speech presented during "I Am an American Day," New York City, May 21, 1944.

Chapter 11 How Jesus Followers Have Changed the Pursuit of Justice

1. Quoted and condensed from a several-page account from Corrie ten Boom, with Elizabeth and John Sherrill, *The Hiding Place* (Peabody, MA: Hendrickson, 1971), 142–44.

2. United Nations, "Global Report on Trafficking in Persons, 2012," 16, http://www.unodc.org/documents/data-and-analysis/glotip/Trafficking_in _Persons_2012_web.pdf.

3. United Nations, "Global Report," 10.

4. *Stanford Encyclopedia of Philosophy*, s.v. "William of Ockham," accessed March 22, 2022, https://plato.stanford.edu/entries/ockham/.

5. Gerald P. O'Driscoll Jr. and Lee Hoskins, "Property Rights: The Key to Economic Development," Libertarianism, August 7, 2003, https://www .libertarianism.org/publications/essays/property-rights-key-economic-devel opment. For a deeper dive, I recommend Richard Pipes, *Property and Freedom* (New York: Alfred A. Knopf, 1999).

6. The work of British historian Robert Conquest (1917–2015) is helpful in understanding how Communist leaders created so much bloodshed. See Robert Conquest, *Harvest of Sorrow: Soviet Collectivization and the Terror-Famine* (New York: Oxford University Press, 1986), 6.

7. Alexander Yakovlev, in his important work *A Century of Violence in Soviet Russia* (New Haven: Yale University Press, 2004), estimates that Stalin alone killed over sixty million.

8. The latest figures of seventy million–plus killed under China's Mao Tse-Tung are recorded by Jung Chang and Jon Halliday in their seminal work, *Mao: The Unknown Story* (New York: Anchor, 2006).

9. Quoted in Tara Isabella Burton, *Strange Rites: New Religions for a Godless World* (New York: Public Affairs, 2020), 179.

10. Eckhart Tolle, *A New Earth* (New York: Plume, 2005), 163.

11. Harold Berman, *Law and Revolution: The Formation of the Western Legal Tradition* (Cambridge, MA: Harvard University Press, 1983), 39.

12. Philip Jenkins, "From Justice, Good Lord Deliver Us," Anxious Bench, April 30, 2018, https://www.patheos.com/blogs/anxiousbench/2018/04/from -justice-good-lord-deliver-us/.

13. The Spanish theologians Francisco de Vitoria (1486–1546) and Domingo de Soto (1494–1560) are examples of this. See Ramón Hernández, "The Internationalization of Francisco de Vitoria and Domingo de Soto," *Fordham International Law Journal* 15, no. 4 (1991): 1031–59, http://ir.lawnet .fordham.edu/cgi/viewcontent.cgi?article=1325&context=ilj.

14. See Paul S. Vickery, *Bartolomé de Las Casas: Great Prophet of the Americas* (Mahwah, NJ: Paulist Press, 2006).

15. Robert G. Clouse, ed., *War: Four Christian Views* (Downers Grove, IL: InterVarsity, 1991), 120–21. For further discussion on these criteria and how they developed over time, in addition to many of the sources already cited, see David D. Corey and J. Daryl Charles, *The Just War Tradition: An Introduction* (Wilmington, DE: ISI Books, 2012). Furthermore, the following work is a classic in the field, though less than sanguine about the possibilities of waging a just war: Paul Ramsey, *The Just War: Force and Political Responsibility* (Lanham, MD: Rowman & Littlefield, 2002). Arthur Holmes offers a brief historical overview in his section on "Just War" in Clouse, *War*, 122–30.

16. Clouse, *War*, 119–20. Just war criteria should not be seen as a checklist to be pulled out to justify a war. Rather, they should be employed as an integral part of the discussions when contemplating war. Another fine treatment of just war is Daniel M. Bell Jr., *Just War as Christian Discipleship: Recentering the Tradition in the Church Rather than the State* (Grand Rapids: Brazos, 2009). Paul Ramsey makes a similar point in *The Just War: Force and Political Responsibility* (New York: Scribner, 1968). It is telling that the pacifist Stanley Hauerwas finds this approach compelling, such that he writes a foreword to Ramsey's book and endorses Bell's.

17. Clouse, *War*, 123.

18. Holmes, quoted in Clouse, *War*, 71.

19. For more information on how this happens, see the work of Columbia University law professor Philip Hamburger. If you want to go into detail, Professor Hamburger has written a 646-page book on the subject. If you'd like a brief overview of his argument, start with "Professor Hamburger's Indictment of the Administrative State," Columbia University Law School, July 7, 2017, https://www.law.columbia.edu/news/archive/professor-philip -hamburgers-indictment-administrative-state.

20. L. Gordon Crovitz, "You Commit Three Felonies Every Day," *Wall Street Journal*, September 27, 2009, https://www.wsj.com/articles/SB100014240 52748704471504574438900830760842.

21. See, for example, the work of University of Pennsylvania law professor David A. Skeel Jr. His article "The Unbearable Lightness of Christian Legal Scholarship" can be found at https://www.bc.edu/content/dam/files/centers /boisi/pdf/s08/christian_legal_theory_essay_14_Jan_2008_rev.pdf.

22. John Calvin, *Institutes of the Christian Religion*, ed. John T. McNeill, trans. Ford Lewis Battles (Louisville: Westminster John Knox, 1960), chap. 20, section 6, 1491.

23. Will Durant, *The Story of Civilization, Part 3: Caesar and Christ* (New York: Simon & Schuster, 1944), 598.

24. In a masterful twenty-page paper on politics, religion, and economic development, Professor Timothy Shah quotes 138 sources to demonstrate the connection between the kind of freedom Jesus offered and political, religious, and economic freedom. Timothy Samuel Shah, "In God's Name: Politics, Religion, and Economic Development" (paper prepared for the 9th Annual ALEX Lecture, Lagos State, Nigeria, July 2013).

25. Brian J. Grim and Roger Finke, *The Price of Freedom Denied: Religious Persecution and Conflict in the Twenty-First Century* (New York: Cambridge University Press, 2011), 79, 219.

26. Byron R. Johnson, *More God, Less Crime: Why Faith Matters and How It Could Matter More* (West Conshohocken, PA: Templeton Press, 2011), 122.

27. *The Lord of the Rings: The Two Towers*, directed by Peter Jackson (Burbank, CA: New Line Cinema, 2002), DVD.

Chapter 12 How Jesus Followers Have Changed How We Work

1. Quoted in David Mower, *Antoni Gaudí* (London: Oresko Books Limited, 1977), 6.

2. Quoted in Pat Finn, "'God's Architect': Look Back at the Extraordinary Work of Antoni Gaudí on the Eve of His 164th Birthday," Architizer, accessed February 18, 2022, https://architizer.com/blog/inspiration/industry/a-look -back-at-antoni-gaudi-on-the-eve-of-his-birthday/.

3. Quoted in Cesar Martinell, *Gaudi: His Life, His Theories, His Work* (Cambridge, MA: MIT Press, 1975), 127.

4. Martinell, *Gaudi*, 70.

5. Martinell, *Gaudi*, 188.

6. Gijs Van Hensbergen, *Gaudi: A Biography* (New York: HarperCollins, 2001), 264.

7. Quoted in Martinell, *Gaudi*, 126.

8. Quoted in Martinell, *Gaudi*, 127.

9. Jim Clifton, "The Next Global Pandemic: Mental Health," Gallup, December 3, 2021, https://www.gallup.com/workplace/357710/next-global-pandemic-mental-health.aspx.

10. Jim Clifton, "State of the Global Workplace 2021 Report," Gallup, 2, https://advise.gallup.com/state-of-the-global-workplace-2021.

11. Jim Clifton, "The World's Broken Workplace," Gallup, June 13, 2017, https://news.gallup.com/opinion/chairman/212045/world-broken-workplace.aspx.

12. Jim Harter, "Dismal Employee Engagement Is a Sign of Global Mismanagement," Gallup, https://www.gallup.com/workplace/231668/dismal-employee-engagement-sign-global-mismanagement.aspx.

13. Søren Kierkegaard, "Selections from the Writings of Kierkegaard," trans. L. M. Hollander, *University of Texas Bulletin* 2326, July 8, 1923, https://www.gutenberg.org/files/60333/60333-h/60333-h.htm.

14. Quoted in Dan Heath, *Upstream: The Quest to Solve Problems before They Happen* (New York: Simon & Schuster, 2020), 115.

15. Quoted in William C. Placher, ed., *Callings: Twenty Centuries of Christian Wisdom on Vocation* (Grand Rapids: Eerdmans, 2005), 237.

16. Quoted in Placher, *Callings*, 257.

17. Homi Kharas and Kristofer Hamel, "A Global Tipping Point: Half the World Is Now Middle Class or Wealthier," Brookings Institution, accessed February 18, 2022, https://www.brookings.edu/blog/future-development/2018/09/27/a-global-tipping-point-half-the-world-is-now-middle-class-or-wealthier/.

18. Matt Ridley, "We've Just Had the Best Decade in Human History. Seriously," *Spectator*, December 29, 2019, https://www.spectator.co.uk/article/we-ve-just-had-the-best-decade-in-human-history-seriously-29-december-2019.

19. Titus Lucretius Carus, *On the Nature of Things, Book 2*, trans. William Ellery Leonard, http://classics.mit.edu/Carus/nature_things.mb.txt.

20. Andrew Wilson, "Machines, Power, and the Ancient Economy," *Journal of Roman Studies* 92 (2002): 1–32.

21. "Medieval Inventions," accessed February 18, 2022, http://www.medieval-life-and-times.info/medieval-life/medieval-inventions.htm.

22. John Aberth, *The Black Death: The Great Mortality of 1348–1350: A Brief History with Documents* (New York: Palgrave Macmillan, 2005), 4.

23. Steven Ozment, *The Age of Reform, 1250–1550: An Intellectual and Religious History of Late Medieval and Reformation Europe* (New Haven: Yale University Press, 1980), 193–94.

24. David Routt, "The Economic Impact of the Black Death," EH.net, accessed February 18, 2022, https://eh.net/encyclopedia/the-economic-impact -of-the-black-death/.

25. Ozment, *Age of Reform*, 192.

26. Stephanie Pappas, "It Got Better: Life Improved after Black Death, Study Finds," Live Science, May 7, 2014, https://www.livescience.com/45428 -health-improved-black-death.html.

27. Millard Meiss, *Painting in Florence and Siena after the Black Death: The Arts, Religion and Society in the Mid-Fourteenth Century* (Princeton: Princeton University Press, 1979), 78.

28. John H. A. Munro, "Before and After the Black Death: Money, Prices, and Wages in Fourteenth-Century England," Ideas, 2005, https://ideas.repec .org/p/tor/tecipa/munro-04-04.html.

29. Penelope Carson, "Child Labor: White Slavery," Christian History Institute, accessed February 18, 2022, https://www.christianhistoryinstitute .org/magazine/article/child-labor-white-slavery/.

30. Karl Marx, *Communist Manifesto*, accessed March 22, 2022, www .marxists.org/archive/marx/works/1848/communist-manifesto/.

31. Frederick Engels wrote, "In every historical epoch the prevailing mode of economic production . . . form[s] the basis upon which is built up . . . the political and intellectual history of that epoch." Karl Marx and Frederick Engels, *The Communist Manifesto* (Chicago: Henry Regnery, 1954), 5.

32. In 2015 and 2020, protests supported by the Black Lives Matter organization helped revive the issue of Marxism when BLM cofounder, Patrice Cullors, said, "We are trained Marxists. We are superversed on . . . ideological theories." Some commentators, such as University of Massachusetts professor Richard Wolff, think this is not a cause for concern. "There is really no standard of what Marxism is," he says. But as Stanford professor Russell Berman notes, "If the leadership says it is Marxist, then there's a good chance they are." The Black Lives Matter movement has the strong support of about a third of Americans, and for reasons that may have nothing to do with Marxism. But the *Economist* says that Black Lives Matter–associated causes raised more than $10 billion in 2020. That's almost as much profit as Amazon made in 2020. That kind of money buys a lot of influence for the leaders of such movements. See Mike Gonzalez, "Marxism Underpins Black Lives Matter Agenda," The Heritage Foundation, September 8, 2021, https://www.heritage.org/progressivism /commentary/marxism-underpins-black-lives-matter-agenda.

33. See "Competing Worldviews Significantly Influence Today's Christians," Summit Ministries, accessed March 22, 2022, https://www.secretbattle book.com/research.html.

34. Quoted in Placher, *Callings*, 406.

35. Weber refers to the idea of calling throughout his writings. See, for example, Max Weber, *From Max Weber: Essays in Sociology*, trans. H. H. Gerth and C. Wright Mills (London: Routledge, 2009).

36. Adam Waytz and Malia Mason, "Your Brain at Work," *Harvard Business Review*, July/August 2013, https://hbr.org/2013/07/your-brain-at-work.

37. Karol Wojtyła, "Material," *Frontline*, accessed February 18, 2022, https://www.pbs.org/wgbh/pages/frontline/shows/pope/poems/.

38. Lynne Blumberg, "What Happens to the Brain during Spiritual Experiences?," *Atlantic*, June 5, 2014, https://www.theatlantic.com/health/archive/2014/06/what-happens-to-brains-during-spiritual-experiences/361882/.

39. W. M. Spellman, *A Brief History of Death* (London: Reaktion Books, 2014), 35.

40. Abraham Joshua Heschel, *The Sabbath* (New York: Farrar, Straus & Giroux, 1951), 10.

41. Book of Common Prayer Online, "Compline," accessed March 22, 2022, https://www.bcponline.org/.

42. Quoted in Placher, *Callings*, 266.

43. Placher, *Callings*, 269.

44. Quoted in Placher, *Callings*, 346.

45. Quoted in Placher, *Callings*, 133.

46. Quoted in Placher, *Callings*, 138.

47. Quoted in Placher, *Callings*, 179.

48. Placher, *Callings*, 200.

49. Quoted in Placher, *Callings*, 159.

50. Placher, *Callings*, 211.

51. Gene Edward Veith, "How Vocation Transformed Society," Lignonier Ministries, September 25, 2016, https://www.ligonier.org/learn/articles/how-vocation-transformed-society/.

52. Gerald P. O'Driscoll Jr. and Lee Hoskins, "Property Rights: The Key to Economic Development," Libertarianism, August 7, 2003, https://www.libertarianism.org/publications/essays/property-rights-key-economic-development.

53. Scott David Allen, *Why Social Justice Is Not Biblical Justice* (Grand Rapids: Credo House Publishers, 2020), 110.

54. "Market capitalization" refers to the total value of stock issued in a company. As of this writing, General Motors has a market capitalization of $58 billion, Fiat-Chrysler of $30 billion, Ford of $63 billion, and FedEx of $53 billion.

55. Nancy S. Lee, "Bridging the Wealth Gap: Small Business Growth," Interise, June 2018, https://interise.org/wp-content/uploads/BridgingtheWealthGap.pdf.

56. "Minority Entrepreneurs," U.S. Senate Committee on Small Business and Entrepreneurship, accessed February 18, 2022, https://www.sbc.senate.gov/public/index.cfm/minorityentrepreneurs.

57. Vicki Contie, "Brain Imaging Reveals Joys of Giving," National Institutes of Health, June 22, 2007, https://www.nih.gov/news-events/nih-research-matters/brain-imaging-reveals-joys-giving.

58. Jay Robertson, "9 Positive Effects of Donating Money to Charity," *The Life You Can Save* (blog), July 13, 2015, https://www.thelifeyoucansave .org/blog/9-positive-effects-of-donating-money-to-charity/.

Chapter 13 How to Tell the Truth and Be Nice at the Same Time

1. Herbert Marcuse, "Repressive Tolerance," originally published in Robert Paul Wolff, Barrington Moore Jr., and Herbert Marcuse, *A Critique of Pure Tolerance* (Boston: Beacon Press, 1969), 95–137, online version available at https://www.marcuse.org/herbert/publications/1960s/1965-repressive -tolerance-fulltext.html.

2. "Majority of Americans Want to Scrap First Amendment, Polling Finds," Campaign for Free Speech, October 23, 2019, https://campaignfor freespeech.org/free-speech-under-dire-threat-polling-finds/.

3. Carl R. Trueman, *The Rise and Triumph of the Modern Self: Cultural Amnesia, Expressive Individualism, and the Road to Sexual Revolution* (Wheaton: Crossway, 2020), 55.

4. Victor Sebestyen, *Lenin: The Man, the Dictator, and the Master of Terror* (New York: Pantheon, 2017), 83.

5. Quoted in Sebestyen, *Lenin*, 83.

6. Sebestyen, *Lenin*, 82.

7. Saul Alinsky, *Rules for Radicals: A Practical Primer for Realistic Radicals* (New York: Vintage, 1989), 128.

8. Rod Dreher, *Live Not by Lies: A Manual for Christian Dissidents* (New York: Sentinel, 2020), xiii.

9. Philip Rieff, *The Triumph of the Therapeutic: Uses of Faith after Freud* (Chicago: University of Chicago Press, 1987), 18.

10. Elisabeth Camp, ed., *The Poetry of Emily Dickinson: Philosophical Perspectives* (Oxford: Oxford University Press, 2021), 166.

11. Robert McKee, *Story: Substance, Structure, Style, and the Principles of Screenwriting* (New York: Regan Books, 1997), 13.

12. Brian Godawa, *Hollywood Worldviews: Watching Films with Wisdom and Discernment* (Downers Grove, IL: InterVarsity, 2002), 15.

13. Pew Research Center, "The State of Personal Trust," July 22, 2019, https://www.pewresearch.org/politics/2019/07/22/the-state-of-personal-trust/.

14. Angela Sailor, "Republicans and Democrats Agree on Need to Cancel 'Cancel Culture,'" Heritage Foundation, July 31, 2020, https://www.heritage .org/civil-society/commentary/republicans-and-democrats-agree-need-cancel -cancel-culture.

15. Pew Research Center, "Partisan Conflict and Congressional Outreach," February 23, 2017, https://www.pewresearch.org/politics/2017/02/23/partisan -conflict-and-congressional-outreach/.

16. Quoted in Adam Czerniawski, ed., *The Burning Forest* (Hexham, UK: Bloodaxe Books, 1988), 42.

17. Pew Research Center, "State of Personal Trust."

18. A poll conducted by Summit Ministries and the McLaughlin polling organization in August 2021 asked people how they treat people with whom they strongly disagree: 64.3 percent of people said "listen respectfully"; only 3.1 percent said "cut them out of my life"; and 1.6 percent said "get angry." See "Poll: Country Is Divided and Americans Blame Politicians, Media, and Big Tech," Summit Ministries, August 18, 2021, https://www.summit.org /about/press/poll-country-is-divided-and-americans-blame-politicians-media -and-big-tech/.

19. Albert Mehrabian, "Communication without Words," *Psychology Today Magazine*, 1968, reprinted in C. David Mortensen, ed., *Communication Theory*, 2nd ed. (New Brunswick, NJ: Transaction, 2008), 193.

20. Alan H. Monroe was a professor at Purdue University in the 1930s. This structure is known as "Monroe's Motivated Sequence."

21. "The Division on the Study of American Fears," Chapman University, accessed March 23, 2022, https://www.chapman.edu/wilkinson/research -centers/babbie-center/survey-american-fears.aspx. A PDF of specific fears is available at https://www.chapman.edu/wilkinson/research-centers/babbie -center/_files/Babbie%20center%20fear2021/blogpost-americas-top-fears -2020_-21-final.pdf.

22. Jim Folk, "Feeling of Impending Doom," Anxietycentre.com, May 31, 2021, https://www.anxietycentre.com/anxiety-disorders/symptoms/feeling -of-impending-doom/.

23. Maria Vultaggio, "Gen Z Is Lonely," Statista, February 4, 2020, https:// www.statista.com/chart/20713/lonlieness-america/.

24. R. F. Soames Job, "Effective and Ineffective Use of Fear in Health Promotion Campaigns," *American Journal of Public Health* 78, no. 2 (1988): 163–67.

25. Stanley Milgram, Leonard Bickman, and Lawrence Berkowitz, "Note on the Drawing Power of Crowds of Different Size," *Journal of Personality and Social Psychology* 13, no. 2 (1969): 79–82, https://doi.org/10.1037 /h0028070.

26. Kwame Christian, "How to Become More Influential and Persuasive in Your Negotiations," *Forbes*, May 31, 2021, https://www.forbes.com/sites/ kwamechristian/2021/05/31/how-to-become-more-influential-and-persuasive -in-your-negotiations/?sh=71352d6a7ce9.

27. "Poll: Country Is Divided."

28. Charles Berger, "Influence Motivation and Feedback regarding Influence Outcomes as Determinants of Self-Persuasion Magnitude," *Journal of Personality* 40, no. 1 (1972): 62–74.

29. According to the poll conducted in 2017, 29 percent of churchgoing Christians under forty-five strongly agreed with this statement. Just 8 percent of churchgoing Christians over forty-five agreed. See "Competing Worldviews

Influence Today's Christians," Barna, May 9, 2017, https://www.barna.com /research/competing-worldviews-influence-todays-christians/.

30. Eric B. Dent and Susan Galloway Goldberg, "Challenging 'Resistance to Change,'" *Journal of Applied Behavioral Science* 35, no. 1 (March 1999): 25–41; and Dianne Waddell and Amrik S. Sohal, "Resistance: A Constructive Tool for Change Management," *Management Decision* 36, no. 8 (1998): 543–48.

31. Robert B. Cialdini, Joyce E. Vincent, Stephen K. Lewis, Jose Catalan, Diane Wheeler, and Betty Lee Darby, "Reciprocal Concessions Procedure for Inducing Compliance: The Door-in-the-Face Technique," *Journal of Personality and Social Psychology* 31 (1975): 206–15.

32. Stefanie K. Johnson, "Do You Feel What I Feel? Mood Contagion and Leadership Outcomes," *Leadership Quarterly* 20 (2009): 814–27.

Chapter 14 Truth Really Does Change Everything

1. Alastair McGrath (lecture at Summit Oxford C. S. Lewis Conference, October 7, 2013). McGrath calls the ancient myths Lewis studied "narrated worldviews" to distinguish them from the idea of myth as a thing that is untrue and yet nonetheless believed by many people.

2. Humphrey Carpenter, *The Inklings; C.S. Lewis, J. R. R. Tolkien, Charles Williams and Their Friends* (London: HarperCollins, 1978), 43.

3. Michael Goheen, postscript to Albert Wolters, *Creation Regained: Biblical Basics for a Reformational Worldview* (Grand Rapids: Eerdmans, 2005), 126.

4. Quoted in George Weigel, *Witness to Hope: The Biography of Pope John Paul II* (New York: Harper Perennial, 2005), 801.

5. *Merriam-Webster*, s.v. "wetware," accessed March 18, 2022, https://www.merriam-webster.com/dictionary/wetware.

6. C. S. Lewis, *God in the Dock* (Grand Rapids: Eerdmans, 1970), 110.

7. Dionysius the Areopagite, "The Divine Names IV, 708A-B," in *Pseudo-Dionysius: The Complete Works*, trans. Colm Luibheid (New York: Paulist Press, 1987), 79.

8. George Yancey, "Not White Fragility—Mutual Responsibility," Gospel Coalition, July 27, 2020, https://www.thegospelcoalition.org/article/white -fragility-mutual-responsibility/.

9. See Jason Jimenez, *Challenging Conversations: A Practical Guide to Discuss Controversial Topics in the Church* (Grand Rapids: Baker Books, 2020).

10. Quoted in William C. Placher, ed., *Callings: Twenty Centuries of Christian Wisdom on Vocation* (Grand Rapids: Eerdmans, 2005), 197.

11. Blaise Pascal, *Pensées*, trans. Alban Krailsheimer (New York: Penguin, 1966), 75.

12. Mark Perry, "Fortune 500 Firms 1955 v. 2017: Only 60 Remain, Thanks to the Creative Destruction That Fuels Economic Prosperity," American

Enterprise Institute, October 20, 2017, https://www.aei.org/carpe-diem/fortune -500-firms-1955-v-2017-only-12-remain-thanks-to-the-creative-destruction -that-fuels-economic-prosperity/.

13. Perry, "Fortune 500 Firms."

14. Quoted in Millard J. Erickson, *The Postmodern World: Discerning the Times and the Spirit of Our Age* (Wheaton: Crossway, 2002), 49.

15. Alexis de Tocqueville, *Democracy in America*, trans. George Lawrence (New York: Harper Perennial, 1988), 464–65.

Dr. Jeff Myers is president of Summit Ministries, a Colorado-based nonprofit organization that equips and supports the rising generation to embrace God's Truth and champion a biblical worldview. Summit reaches hundreds of thousands of Christians each year through worldview training, events, books, curriculum, and other online resources. One of America's most respected authorities on Christian worldview, apologetics, and youth leadership development, Myers holds a doctor of philosophy degree from the University of Denver. He lives in Colorado Springs with his family.

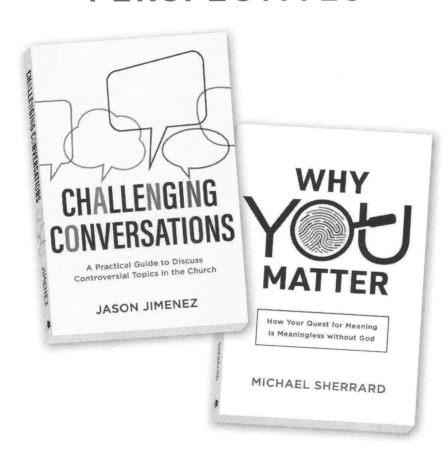

Get your discussion guide to
TRUTH.

> "If we can understand how
> Truth really did change
> everything in the past, then
> we can more clearly see
> what we lose in abandoning
> it and what we could
> gain by reclaiming it.
>
> —— Dr. Jeff Myers ——

Visit
summit.org/truthguide
today!

Made in the USA
Las Vegas, NV
18 October 2022

57635972R00142